Rhys Davies

A Writer's Life

Madame Bovary, c'est moi!
    Gustave Flaubert, *c.* 1857

You complain my characters are gloomy. Alas, this is not my fault! They come out like that without my necessarily wanting them to, and when I am writing I don't feel as though I am writing gloomily. In any case, I'm always in a good mood when I'm writing. It is a well-documented fact that pessimists and melancholics always write in a very upbeat way, whereas cheerful writers generally manage to depress their readers.
    Anton Chekhov, in a letter to Lidia Avilova (1897)

Never trust the artist. Trust the tale. The proper function of a critic is to save the tale from the artist who created it.
    D.H. Lawrence, *Studies in Classic American Literature* (1923)

Short stories are a luxury which only those writers who fall in love with them can afford to cultivate. To such a writer they yield the purest enjoyment: they become a privately elegant craft allowing, within very strict confines, a wealth of idiosyncrasies . . . Another virtue of the short story is that can be allowed to laugh.
    Rhys Davies, in the preface to his *Collected Stories* (1955)

Of all the liars the most arrogant are biographers, those who would have us believe, having surveyed a few boxes full of letters, diaries, bank statements and photographs, that they can play the recording angel and tell the truth about another human life.
    A.N. Wilson, *Incline our Hearts* (1988)

That no personality is amenable to a single interpretation is a caveat which should be carried on the dust-jacket of every biography.
    David Callard, *The Case of Anna Kavan* (1992)

Rhys Davies

A Writer's Life

Meic Stephens

Parthian
The Old Surgery
Napier Street
Cardigan
SA43 1ED

www.parthianbooks.com

First published in 2013
© Meic Stephens 2013
All Rights Reserved

ISBN 978-1-90894-671-3

Cover design by www.theundercard.co.uk
Typeset by typesetter.org.uk
Printed and bound by Gomer Press, Llandysul, Wales

The publisher acknowledges the financial support
of the Welsh Books Council and the Rhys Davies
Trust.

British Library Cataloguing in Publication Data

A cataloguing record for this book is available from
the British Library.

Contents

RHYS DAVIES.
BY WILLIAM ROBERTS.

1927 pencil drawing

One

The elusive hare

Rhys Davies was among the most dedicated, prolific, and accomplished of Welsh prose-writers in English. With unswerving devotion and scant regard for commercial success, he practised the writer's craft for some fifty years, in both the short story and the novel form, publishing in his lifetime a substantial body of work on which his literary reputation now firmly rests. He wrote, in all, more than a hundred stories, twenty novels, three novellas, two topographical books about Wales, two plays, and an autobiography in which he set down, obliquely and in code, the little he wanted the world to know about him.

So prodigious an output was made possible largely because he shared his life with no other person, giving it up entirely to his writing. By temperament a loner, and suspicious of the gregarious instinct in writers – a stance he assiduously cultivated in defiance of prevailing fashions and ideologies – he chose to keep himself apart, especially from other expatriate Welsh writers living in England

1

between the two world wars. Except for a few years as a draper's assistant on first going to London and a short stint of compulsory war-work, he managed to live almost wholly by his pen, his meagre income unsupplemented by any teaching, journalism, broadcasting, or hack-work of any kind. He sat on no committees, signed no manifestos, believed no political nostrums or religious dogma, never read his work in public, attended no foreign conferences, never edited a magazine, engaged in no literary squabbles, spurned all cliques, shunned the company of academics, had no taste or talent for self-promotion, joined no literary societies, never competed for a prize, never sat in judgement on his fellow writers as an adjudicator of literary competitions, and only very rarely as a reviewer of their books. He believed the proper business of a writer was to be writing.

Living in rented or borrowed accommodation from which he invariably soon moved on, he maintained a rigorous work-schedule, writing, eating and sleeping in one small room, and seldom seeking the opinion of other writers. He cultivated detachment as if by not fully belonging to any one place, or by not wholly identifying with any one coterie, he could preserve something of himself, something secret, his inviolable self, which he prized above all else. When immersed in a story, as he often was, he wrote a thousand words a day until it was finished. Domestic comforts, such as a home, a regular partner and some security of income, which make life tolerable for most writers, were not for him. He did not even turn to the anodyne of drink, which has sustained and destroyed so many: it just didn't work for him, he once said, though he was not averse to the occasional glass in one of his favourite pubs. As for drugs, he had seen what they had done to the only woman he cared for, the heroin addict Anna Kavan.

There was a parsimonious, some said a mean streak to his nature. The virtues he extolled were the puritanical ones he had learned in his youth, namely thrift, a horror of debt, and minding one's own business, the last of which he also took, rather surprisingly, to be a specifically Welsh characteristic. Although, after his move to London in 1921, he was sometimes to be seen at the Fitzroy Tavern or the Wheatsheaf, or one of Fitzrovia's other famous pubs, he disliked excessive drinking and always gave the bibulous Dylan Thomas a wide berth. He was, in short, an urbane, mild-mannered, secretive, shy man whose only extravagance was sartorial: he had a taste for fine clothes, almost to the point of dandyism. He owned no furniture and was able to keep all his worldly possessions in a small trunk that went with him with every change of address. Nothing and nobody was allowed to interfere with his writing. This professional single-mindedness, deliberately cultivated, assiduously guarded and reinforced by his equanimity, love of solitude and modest material needs, enabled him to pursue a literary career uninterrupted by any of the emotional or domestic upheavals such as are to be found aplenty in his stories and novels.

There was, moreover, another important fact that needs to be noted at the outset, for it was central both to Davies's life and to his work. Although he maintained complete discretion and 'acted straight', his sexual orientation was expressed as an attraction to other men. Yet most of those who knew him, like his younger brother Lewis, were at a loss to say who his sexual partners were because he never spoke or wrote about them in personal terms. Until the Sexual Offences Act of 1967, homosexuality in Britain was illegal and those who practised it were liable to prosecution and imprisonment. Nonetheless, Davies regularly sought fleeting encounters with strangers, often penurious Guardsmen, about whom he had a homoerotic fixation. He also had romantic crushes on younger, heterosexual men that were not reciprocated and so made him unhappy. But he enjoyed no lasting sexual relationship with another person, and with the women who found him kind, gentle, charming and excellent company, like Anna Kavan, the very type of difficult woman to whom he was drawn, he maintained strictly platonic friendships. Above all, he protected his privacy and independence, fearing intrusion into his inner life by anyone who came too close, man or woman.

Nevertheless, the reader will find many clues in Davies's books that reveal him as a writer concerned with proclivities he dared not describe directly. Writing about growing up in Glasgow in the 1920s and 1930s, the distinguished poet and critic Edwin Morgan put his predicament as a homosexual like this:

> To anyone of my generation, the inhibitions were enormous, and habits of disguise and secrecy, inculcated at an early age, are hard to break... I wanted both to conceal, and not to conceal.[1]

Every stage of Davies's life and every aspect of his work was deeply implicated in his sexual identity, so that it is not difficult to read his books from this perspective alone.

But reader, beware. The enigmatic title of his 'autobiographical beginning', *Print of a Hare's Foot*, a most unreliable book from start to finish in that it often fails to tally with the known facts and disguises people and events with adroit use of smoke and mirrors, is in fact a reference to its author's own ambiguous sexual nature. It conceals much more than it reveals.[2]

The book's title was well chosen: the image of the hare, a lunar, richly secretive creature in folklore, said to change its shape while always remaining resolutely itself, sexually active, living by its wits and giving out misleading signals, a symbol of paradox, contradiction and transitoriness, both lucky and unlucky, damned in Deuteronomy and Leviticus as unclean and forbidden, an endangered species, lying low and leaving only the lightest of prints before disappearing into its form in its own mysterious way – this image was central to both Davies's writing and his life. As M. Wynn Thomas puts it in his chapter in *Rhys Davies: Decoding the Hare*, the fullest study of the writer so far published:

> What better image could be found of Davies's own situation relative to a homophobic culture? He could not just run free; he had to accommodate his movements, as man and writer, to the temper and tempo of his times. As a homosexual – however discreet, and however inactive – he found his identity was inexorably defined, and negatively constructed, by the dominant heterosexual culture.[3]

This need, and instinct, to dissemble, also explains to some extent the detached, almost clinical way in which

Davies observed other people without becoming
emotionally involved with them, except in so far as he was
fascinated by the play of human emotion and made it the
mainstay of his fiction. 'A creative writer can't afford to
wave a flag', he wrote in a BBC script in 1950. 'He
mustn't write social propaganda or political speeches, his
task is to look into the secrets of the eternal private heart.'
His detachment also accounted for the evasiveness with
which he habitually responded to enquiries about himself.
Asked by a publisher in 1954 whether he would write an
autobiography, he told friends, 'It would be too gloomy
and the truth (what use is a book without truth?) wouldn't
bear telling.'[4] A brief autobiographical note he wrote in
1958 made it clear how reluctant he was to say anything
that would reveal his true self:

> The blankness of a page waiting for notes about
> myself is much more dismaying than page 1 of a
> projected new book. Temptations for Exhibitionism!
> So much to conceal, evade, touch-up![5]

Such a man, such a writer, the quintessential misfit and
outsider, again in Wynn Thomas's phrase, 'a lifelong
cryptographer', presents challenges for the biographer
who has to know when the false trails deliberately laid
down by Davies are leading nowhere and how to decipher
the code in which he habitually wrote about the things
that mattered to him. It is, of course, possible to read his
work solely for the literary pleasure it affords, but for a
fuller appreciation we have to know something about the
writer's personality and career that, thirty-five years after
his death, are still recognisably contemporary and

relevant. Although Davies was a man very much of his place and time, his achievement as a writer was that, by the mysterious process we call art, he left work that is timeless and universal, and that still speaks to the human condition.

At a time when so much English literary criticism seems to be the fruit of academic theoretical discourse, this book is a biography first and foremost, free of the methodology of fashionable exegesis. But for every biographer a writer's life is soon inseparable from his or her art, the two going hand in hand, and so an attempt has to be made to throw light on the places, people and events that went to the making of Rhys Davies the man and writer, and to show how his life was indeed writ large in his books. It is left to others to examine his books from critical perspectives that shed more light on his literary achievement.

Notes

1   Edwin Morgan, introduction to the anthology *And Thus Will I Freely Sing* (ed. Toni Davidson, Polygon, 1989)

2   *Print of a Hare's Foot: An Autobiographical Beginning* (Heinemann, 1969; Seren, 1998); all subsequent quotations from the work of RD are from this book, unless otherwise noted.

3   M. Wynn Thomas, '"Never Seek to Tell thy Love": Rhys Davies's Fiction', in *Rhys Davies:Decoding the Hare: critical essays to mark the centenary of the writer's birth* (ed. Meic Stephens, University of Wales Press, 2001); from now on this symposium will be noted as *Decoding the Hare*.

4   Letter to Redvers and Louise Taylor (22 May 1954)

5   *Wales* (ed. Keidrych Rhys, September 1958)

Clydach Road, Blaenclydach, c.1900

Thomas (1872-1955) and Sarah Davies née Lewis (1877-1956),
the writer's parents, 1895

Two

The Blaenclydach
grocer's boy

For all his later dissembling and evasion, the plain facts of Rhys Davies's early life are clear enough. He was born at 6 Clydach Road in Blaenclydach, about a mile from Tonypandy in the Rhondda Valley, on the 9th of November 1901 – not 1903 as he sometimes claimed. He was delivered by a midwife known in the village as Mrs Bowen Small Bag and his parents named him Rees Vivian.

Blaenclydach, with contiguous Cwm Clydach, makes up the continuous Clydach Vale, also named by the writer as his birthplace, and lies in the valley of the Clydach, a tributary of the Rhondda Fawr, which it joins downstream at Tonypandy. For local government purposes, the villages today form what Rhondda Cynon Taf Council designates as Cwm Clydach, and the two are sometimes jointly called Clydach, despite the existence of at least two other places of that name in South Wales. The demarcation between Blaenclydach and Cwm Clydach is not apparent to the visitor's eye but clear enough to those who live there, one of the many micro-geographies in the Rhondda that are stoutly defended by their proud inhabitants.

As the historian Dai Smith, a native of Tonypandy, makes clear:

> The boundaries of somewhere like Tonypandy are indefinable. Those who have lived there will tell you, within a street's length or span where Tonypandy 'proper' began and Llwynypia ended, or where Clydach Vale swoops down to end in the 'grander precincts' of De Winton and Dunraven Street or when you have left Tonypandy and entered Penygraig. This intense delineation of territory is nothing to do with council boundaries, political wards or ancient land grants. It is certainly not to do with a separating, physical sense of place since all of mid-Rhondda, and, by extension, large tracts of the coal mining valleys in South Wales blur indistinguishably the one into the other.[1]

In other words, the Rhondda Fawr (the greater Rhondda) is a built-up area extending from Blaenrhondda at the top of the Cwm, down via Porth, where the river meets the Rhondda Fach (the lesser Rhondda), as far as Trehafod, near Pontypridd, at which point the waters of the Taf (*ang.* Taff) receive the Rhondda's tribute before proceeding downstream to Cardiff.

For a description of Tonypandy in 1910 through an outsider's eyes, this by a reporter sent to the Rhondda in the wake of the Riots of that year conveys something of the topography and living conditions in which the Valley's people lived:

[Tonypandy lies] in a narrow winding valley confined by squat denuded hills upon whose bleak sides tower huge mounds of rock and rubbish excavated from the numerous coal tips. The river, sometimes almost dry, sometimes rushing down in tempestuous flood, but always pestilential with all manner of garbage and offal, is crossed and recrossed by the railway over which, all day and night, roll the never-ending coal trains on their way to the distant sea-port. The high road, where it may, runs its course alongside the odorous river, but for the greater part of its length it has to hug the steep slopes of the cheerless hills... long rows of steep gardens rise sheer from the roadside to a line of small stone-built four-roomed cottages. A paved alleyway at the rear, the length of the terrace, gives access to the houses, and from this narrow alleyway, another series of gardens continue the ascent to a similar row of cots, and so the terraces rear themselves until the topmost is reached from which the roadway, the pits, the railway and the river are seen in panoramic array. Each alley has one waterspout, common to all the homes in that row. The two tiny back rows are darkened by the overhanging gardens of the higher terrace, and the houses are so low that a man must stoop before entering.[2]

Rhys Davies, as a child and youth, was absorbed in the life of this place and, 'born into it', conveys in his writing like no other writer of his generation the very essence of its teeming life, what Dai Smith calls 'the synaesthesia of the private': 'You do not, either in the end or in the beginning, go to Rhys Davies for the fact-of-the-matter, you go to him for the matter-of-the-thing.' He is, too, 'an incomparable guide' to such sensations as:

> its packed spaces of noise, its sudden spilling of light onto darkness when cinemas or variety theatres disgorge their audiences, or the sour mash smell of smoke-fugged saloon bars and the sticky sweetness beneath eiderdown covers as pink face-powder is washed off by the ravenous kisses of the young.[3]

The community in which Davies grew up suffered its share of fatal accidents caused by the mining industry. Most took place underground and were therefore not witnessed by the boy but, on the 11th of March 1910, there occurred an event, prefiguring the Aber-fan tragedy of 1966, which he saw with his own eyes:

> Nobody had taken notice of the old sealed level piercing far into the lower slope of a mountain above rows of houses and a chapel and another school in that high part of the vale. It had been one of the pioneering coal-yielding levels, abandoned after the Cambrian colliery opened, and the thread of water always trickling from a low chink in its walled-up entrance went disregarded. One afternoon a roar was heard from this evil throat of the mountain. The sealed entrance had burst and a gigantic spout of black water hurled out, gathered impetus down the slope, demolished three terraced houses, bombarded the chapel, swept across the main road, flooded the

full school, and found partial outlet in a steep gulley leading to the river. It poured for half an hour. Colliers going home from a shift heard the roar and reached the school in time for rescue. A baby, carried down from the smashed terrace houses, was snatched dead out of the swirl, and there were other dead. We were kept back in our school until the waters abated… We saw a stream of acid water coming from the floor of the jagged hole, quietly enough now. In the gaping middle of the terrace below, a brass bedstead hung from a broken room. There was an acrid smell of the mountain's inside. The nine [*sic*] who lost life were buried in a great ceremonious funeral, there were benefit concerts for a fund, and for a long time afterwards, memories were dated from before or after The Flood.[4]

Davies's parents kept a small grocer's shop, known 'for some far-fetched reason' as Royal Stores, which stood with a few others just across the road from the imposing redbrick Central Hotel, a large public house, one of seven in the village, that features in his books as The Jubilee. The three-bedroomed house at 6 Clydach Road, where the family lived behind and above the shop, is distinguished from others in the row by a commemorative plaque put up by the Rhys Davies Trust in 1995.

Vivian, as he was known in the family, was the fourth child of Thomas Rees Davies and Sarah Ann Davies, *née* Lewis. His mother, before her marriage, had briefly been an uncertificated pupil-teacher (that is, one who taught younger children and was herself taught) in Ynys-y-bŵl, near Pontypridd. At the time of the 1891 Census the

Lewis family were living at 17 Thompson Street in the village and in 1895, at the time of Sarah Ann's marriage, at 10 High Street. John Lewis, her father, is described as an underground timberman; there were two other daughters, and a son, who was a collier, that is, one who worked at the coal-face. The address given for Thomas Rees Davies on his marriage certificate was 84 Court Street, Tonypandy.

As so often in early twentieth-century industrial South Wales, when people were, at most, only two or three generations removed from working on the land, the writer subscribed to the mythology found, for example, in some of the poems and stories of Dylan Thomas, and widely disseminated, that presents the people of the coalfield as having lived in a rural paradise before they were plunged into the hell of industrialism. Davies claimed his forefathers 'had lived in the deeper nooks of the restrainedly beautiful shire [of Carmarthen]; it was "the country" of my childhood ears, everlastingly green in my eyes, sweet-smelling in my broken nose', though he had no personal experience of living in this lost Arcadia, visited only once or twice, and saw it through rose-tinted spectacles.

There was, it seems, little or no contact between the Davieses of Blaenclydach and their relatives in West Wales. There were no childhood visits and whatever conception the writer had of life there must have come from the lips of his Rhondda-reared mother. That his connection with what he called 'my West Wales' was mythic rather than actual accounts to a large extent for the fanciful element some of his critics have detected in his dealing with rural themes, in contrast with his much more authentic depiction of life in the Rhondda; one critic, Stephen Knight, has gone so far as to describe him as 'a rural fantasist'.[5]

Rhys Davies once told a student who was writing a dissertation on him at the University of Brest that his father had been raised in an orphanage in Neath.[6] This may have been designed to put any future enquirer off the scent, something he was apt to do whenever he thought his privacy was being invaded. However, in the 1891 and 1911 Census reports his father's place of birth was indeed given as Glynneath, although no evidence has come to light to show he was brought up in an orphanage. In fact, Davies's grandfather, James Davies, a coal haulier in Tonypandy, had been raised in Merthyr Tydfil where his illiterate father, John Davies, born in 1842, had been killed in a pit accident. On the certificate showing details of James Davies's marriage to Margaret Rees, the daughter of a lampsman, also of Merthyr Tydfil, in 1863, both bride and groom signed with the cross of illiteracy. A generation earlier, the writer's great grandfather had been a metal wheeler in the Dowlais ironworks and his great great grandfather a carpenter in the same town. In the generation prior to that the Davieses had moved to Merthyr from Boncath in Pembrokeshire and it was this fact which had been preserved in family tradition.

On both the spear and distaff sides Davies's people had been, for generations, of the labouring poor. But his mother came from a slightly better-off background and had more definite connections with west Wales, though she had been born in Aberdare and brought up in Maerdy in the Rhondda Fach, where she owned a number of houses on which she collected rent. Her father, John Lewis, was a native of Cilrhedyn, a village near the upper reaches of the Cych in Pembrokeshire. She would say three centuries of Lewises were buried in the churchyard at Cilgerran, the parish in which Cilrhedyn is situated. She also claimed they were related to a preacher who had made his name ministering to the spiritual needs of the London Welsh, namely Howell Elvet Lewis,[7] better known as the hymn-writer Elfed, though it has not been possible to determine precisely what the kinship may have been. Even in the writer's day, a John Thomas, belonging to a branch of the Lewis family, farmed Fuallt near the village of Cilrhedyn; other Lewises had once been at Blaenpibydd, Ffynnon Las and Cwm Morgan in the same neighbourhood. Thomas and Sarah Davies, the writer's parents, gave the name Lewis to their youngest son in fond remembrance of this connection.

Thomas Davies had been apprenticed, at the age of 12, to a grocer and was working as a shop manager in Tonypandy when he met his future wife. He was 21 and she was 18 when they married on the 19th of February 1895 at the Registry Office in Pontypridd. The reasons for this are unclear but it was not because she was pregnant; both were Congregationalist in religious affiliation and it would have been more usual had they married in a chapel. Almost immediately, and in the last decade of Queen Victoria's reign, they opened a shop in Clydach Vale, higher up the Cwm and opposite the Bush Inn, but soon moved down to Blaenclydach, nearer Tonypandy, where they spent the rest of their lives and where their three youngest children would be born.

Whatever the facts of his lineage may have been, and beyond the evidence of the Census there is some uncertainty, particularly on his father's side, it is clear the writer's male antecedents in the more immediate past had been labourers and craftsmen, first in Merthyr Tydfil and then the Rhondda. They had been brought to South Wales in the middle years of the nineteenth century by the prospect of much higher wages than could be earned on the land. This was the time when South Wales was rapidly being established as one of the great engines of the Industrial Revolution. The earliest extraction of bituminous coal in the Rhondda had been undertaken at Dinas by the lugubriously-named Walter Coffin in 1809. A similar enterprise had been opened at Blaenclydach in 1847 and the first deep pit in the village had been sunk in 1863.

The economic historian Brinley Thomas gave a succinct description of the process by which South Wales had been industrialised to such dynamic effect:

For half-a-century, the keynote in South Wales was growth and expansion. In spite of temporary set-backs in the coal trade and iron industry, the curve of production rose rapidly; and in less than twenty or thirty years remote valleys which used to be inhabited only by a few farmers and shepherds were transformed into congested towns and villages pulsating with life. Coal pits were being sunk in quick succession by enterprising businessmen, and around them arose, almost like mushrooms, houses and institutes, shops and chapels, railways and roads and tramways. Every valley was the scene of bustling activity. Young men from the countryside made their homes in these villages where they earned far more than agriculture could offer them; and they all quickly got used to their new life and gave up all intention of ever moving out.[8]

The economy, society and topography of the Rhondda were all transformed as the population grew apace from 1,363 in 1841 to 113,735 in 1901, the year of Rhys Davies's birth. Some two-thirds were Welsh-speaking. The sylvan parish of Ystradyfodwg, in the words of Rhondda's historian E.D. Lewis, was changed 'from a secluded pastoral area of sheep walks and small farms into an immense mining conurbation inhabited by a new industrial class, with problems and a character of its own'[9]; in 1901 the Rhondda Urban District Council, founded in 1897, was the second largest in Wales. By the time Davies was 20 the population had increased again, to 167,000.

The great majority of the Rhondda's male population were employed in the mining industry and these men, 'alert, courageous and democratic', became leaders of British mining unionism in the first three decades of the twentieth century. In 1901 a total of 150,412 men worked in the Valley's mines, which produced more than 39.2 million tons of coal; by 1923, these figures had increased to 252,617 men and 54.25 million tons, the peak of production. The Davieses and Lewises were among the many thousands of immigrants from the counties of West and North Wales, as well as from the West Country and Ireland, and even further afield, who had flocked to the Klondyke of upland Glamorgan. Rhys Davies was born and brought up at a propitious moment for the Rhondda because, in the first decades of the twentieth century, its steam coal fired not only the boilers

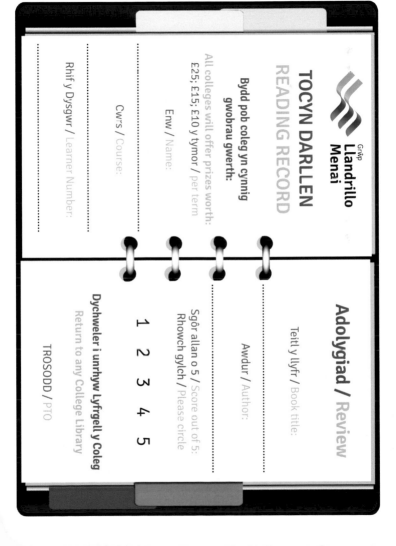

TOCYN DARLLEN
READING RECORD

Bydd pob coleg yn cynnig gwobrau gwerth:

All colleges will offer prizes worth:
£25, £15, £10 y tymor / per term

Enw / Name:

Cwrs / Course:

Rhif y Dysgwr / Learner Number:

Grŵp
**Llandrillo
Menai**

Adolygiad / Review

Teitl y llyfr / Book title:

Awdur / Author:

Sgôr allan o 5 / Score out of 5:
Rhowch gylch / Please circle

1 2 3 4 5

Dychweler i unrhyw Lyfrgell y Coleg
Return to any College Library

TROSODD / PTO

Cynnwys y llyfr / Book content: ....

Hoffi fwyaf a hoffi leiaf / Likes & dislikes: ....

of the British Navy but many of the manufacturing industries on which the Empire depended, and so it was in great demand.

In a review of *Print of a Hare's Foot*, when it appeared in 1969, Goronwy Rees described South Wales in the 1920s:

> It was in many ways a savage and violent society, marked by the scars of some of the harshest industrial conflicts this country has ever known. Yet its harshness was tempered by the dignity and warmth, a sense of shared humanity, which the South Wales miner never lost in good times as in bad. Yet it was also, in one of its aspects, an almost claustrophobically closed society; the strange landscape of the South Wales mining valleys, in which the rural and the industrial combine so dramatically, was the background to a peculiarly close and intimate social life in which religion, beer, song, rugby football, socialism and whippets all had their part to play. Yet, in another aspect, it was a society which was open to all the world; the valleys, the grimy streams that ran down them, the coal that came out of their bowels, the tramline following the course of the single village street of the Rhondda, all made their way down to the docks and ships of Cardiff, and through them made their presence felt at the end of the world. The Rhondda was a major factor in the industrialisation of the planet; and in the same way the miner's struggle for a life which recognised his human dignity made him a participant, and a leader, in a world-wide conflict.[10]

Into this society Tom and Sal Davies brought five other children, besides Vivian: Gertrude Elizabeth (known as Gertie), born in 1898; her sister Gladys May, born in 1899; John Haydn (known as Jack), born in 1900; Sarah Margaret Lilian (known as Peggie), born in 1910; and Arthur Lewis (known as Arthur and later as Peter), born in 1913. Jack, extrovert and sports-loving, studied to be a mining engineer at the School of Mines in Trefforest but joined the Royal Flying Corps, the precursor of the RAF, shortly after his eighteenth birthday and was killed in action over France during the last months of the First World War; his observer's log-book, lovingly preserved by his family, shows that in the days before he was shot down he had been dropping bombs on 'the Hun' positions along the Somme; his body was never found. Two of his sisters, Gertie and Peggie, became teachers and the other, Gladys, a nurse, while Lewis, who died in December 2011 at the age of 98, read History at the University College of Wales, Aberystwyth, and worked as a librarian at Odhams Press in London. Only Peggie married and none of the siblings had children of their own.

The Davies household was strongly matriarchal. Tom left all domestic and commercial responsibilities to Sal, his capable wife, preferring to spend his free time at the local Liberal Club, which he had helped establish, or at the Penrhys Golf Club or in the local Chamber of Commerce, where he was able to keep up the business contacts on which his social aspirations depended; he was also active with the Freemasons. 'We hardly ever saw him, except on Sundays,' Lewis Davies told the present writer.

Rhys Davies was to create many a female character as shrewd, not to say hard-headed, and as dignified, as his mother, while his menfolk tend to be much weaker creatures, bemused, hapless victims of misfortune. From his mother he inherited a strength of will and a knack of cutting his cloth to suit his often straitened circumstances, as well as her puritanical streak, but not her business acumen. His father gave him a calm, unruffled temperament and a phlegmatic acceptance of whatever life would throw at him, as well as an impractical streak in matters financial and administrative. He was also loquacious: 'My father was such a talker that I stopped listening. His verbosity filled my mother with foot-tapping impatience; she had a constant cry of anguish – "come to the *point*!" It had no lasting effect.'

The Davieses' status as members of a small shopocracy set them apart from a working-class community on which they relied for custom and which, in turn, was almost wholly dependent on the coal industry. There was a huge gap between the lifestyle of a man in a white apron who cut butter for a living and one in moleskin trousers who, stripped to the waist, hewed coal in the bowels of the earth. The gulf may not have been reflected entirely in terms of income and, when the Rhondda was stricken by industrial strife, Royal Stores was expected to extend credit to its customers while still having to pay its wholesalers, a fact often pointed out by the writer. But even so, the Davieses were altogether better-off. They kept a pony and trap for jaunts into the country and a horse and cart with a part-time driver, for deliveries, and they employed a maid, took holidays in Porthcawl on the South Wales coast, and had their own pew at Gosen, where young Vivian was decked out for chapel attendance like Little Lord Fauntleroy. During the Cambrian Lock-out, when miners' children were fed from soup kitchens because their parents were struggling to live on strike pay, he was not eligible for the free food handed out at school: 'We had enough food at home and did not lack cake throughout the strike.'

In short, the Davieses were in the wider community but not quite of it. Some of Rhys Davies's attitudes in later life, such as the parsimony already noted, were distinctly *petit bourgeois* and in this he was unlike most of his Welsh literary contemporaries, writers like Jack Jones, Gwyn Thomas and Lewis Jones (another Blaenclydach boy), who were variously but staunchly proletarian in upbringing, sympathies and lifestyles. Davies's portrait of shop-keepers is generally more sympathetic than that of other Welsh writers of his generation because he sees in them an embattled group who are resented by the people they serve: clearly, Davies felt both part of his community and yet excluded from it by his status as the grocer's son. His sense of alienation, of a divided self, his bewildered sense of 'difference', of being at a tangent to the world, may be traced to this fact. It was to be compounded by sensibilities that slowly grew from his awareness of his own sexual nature.

The settlements of Blaenclydach and Cwm Clydach were dominated by the presence of two collieries, the double-shafted Cambrian (pronounced locally with the stress on the second syllable) and a drift-mine known as the Gorki that was located in Blaenclydach itself, not far from Royal Stores. Both were the focus of bitter and violent industrial strife, most notably during the Cambrian Lock-out that led to the Tonypandy Riots of November 1910, the most famous civil disturbance in the history of

South Wales after the Merthyr Rising of 1831.[11] The boy watched the clashes between miners and police on Clydach Road from the safety of his bedroom window, thus assuming the observer's position he was to adopt so often in later life.

Davies was well informed about the history of 'the turbulent valley', as he called it, reading all he could find about its industrial past and clipping stories from newspapers about the disasters, strikes, lock-outs, economic depression and social deprivation that were such prominent features of Rhondda life. Among the books he later owned were several copies of Idris Davies's *The Angry Summer* (1943), 'a poem of 1926', the year of the General Strike when the miners held out against Stanley Baldwin's government for seven months before bankrupting their communities and being starved back to work. There is no evidence the two Davieses were acquainted but they may very well have met during the 1940s at Foyles bookshop in London, where expatriate Welsh writers gathered, or later at Griff's Welsh Bookshop in Cecil Court.

The coal mines in Blaenclydach and Cwm Clydach, barely a mile apart, were part of the Cambrian Combine, a group of pits amalgamated and owned by D.A. Thomas, a former Liberal M.P. who was to be raised to the peerage as Viscount Rhondda in 1918 for wartime service as Minister for Food. He was a ruthlessly efficient but relatively progressive owner in that he was prepared to recognize and negotiate with the South Wales Miners' Federation, which had been founded in 1898. Thomas's enormous wealth derived from coal mining and his global interests in shipping, patent fuels and newspapers.

The events of 1910-11 were caused by the men's grievances over payment for work in abnormally difficult conditions at the Ely colliery, one of the pits owned by the Cambrian Combine: they refused to work a new seam at the price per ton offered by management. This dispute led to the dismissal not only of the eighty men directly affected but also the locking out of all 800 men from the Ely. The Cambrian mines were managed for D.A.Thomas by the autocratic Leonard Llewellyn, whose immediate use of blackleg labour at the Glamorgan colliery in Llwynypia, a quarter of a mile to the north of Tonypandy, was a major factor in precipitating in early November 1910 a fierce, close-quarter clash between about seven thousand miners and a hundred policemen brought in to protect the mine. Bands of men went from colliery to colliery preventing officials, engine-men and stokers from working. At the Cambrian Colliery in Clydach Vale officials were stoned out of the electric power-house. Soon about 12,000 mid-Rhondda men were out on strike and the South Wales coalfield had become the arena for a classic clash between labour and capital.

The workers' anger over the provocative use of blackleg labour in the Engine House at the Glamorgan colliery spilt over into an attack on about sixty of Tonypandy's shops. The strikers thus registered their disapproval of the links between the coalowners and the town's shopocracy. Royal Stores was spared, or so Rhys Davies averred, only because his father was known to give credit to unemployed miners, to have helped less literate customers with such matters as correspondence and, during the Riots, had sheltered one of the strikers in his stable. The rioters certainly discriminated in the damage

24

they caused, passing by the chemist's shop of Willie Llewellyn, a former rugby-player who had played a prominent part in the famous defeat of the All Blacks by the Welsh Rugby XV in 1905.

This was social rebellion as well as industrial strife. The controversial decision by Winston Churchill, then Home Secretary, to despatch detachments of the Lancashire Fusiliers and 18th Hussars, as well as mounted Metropolitan Police, to the townships of mid-Rhondda, where they remained for almost a year, ensured that the name of Tonypandy would become a byword for industrial militancy and that Churchill's name and image would be booed in the cinemas of South Wales for generations to come.

Rhys Davies was only nine years old at the time of the Tonypandy Riots but the social disturbance they caused is vividly evoked, if not always clearly explained, in several of his books. This much is crystal-clear: the Riots caused intense and widespread suffering among the people of Rhondda and ended in ignominy when the miners were forced to return to work on the owners' terms. Davies's account is a mixture of moralizing and annoyance at the violence perpetrated by the 'slavering and barbaric eyed' workers on the innocent shop-keepers of Tonypandy. Dai Smith describes it as:

> essentially a diorama rather than an analysis. This sense of the relationship of these visceral moments to the longer time sequence which connected them to the successful national strike of 1912 for a minimum wage is as attenuated as his grasp of the progressive movements being incubated, then and

there in the Rhondda, for both pragmatic Labourism and quasi-revolutionary forms of syndicalism… But, then, Rhys's politics, conditioned perhaps by his Liberal father or just withering on the vine of a greater indifference, were never typical of his native ground.[12]

It is indeed true that, although he claimed his sympathies were broadly with the workers, Davies was never to take their side wholeheartedly, and in the clash between miners and police acting on the owners' behalf the lad found himself betwixt and between. Above all, and his father's Liberalism notwithstanding, Davies was careful not to take a party-political stance. He may, as a 20-year-old, have looked in on the local Marxian Club (founded in the 1890s), out of curiosity about the militant Communism beginning to take root during the 1920s in places like Maerdy, a village in the Rhondda Fach known after the General Strike of 1926 as 'Little Moscow', but that was largely for the purposes of self-education. He must, too, have been personally acquainted with many members of the Independent Labour Party, with the Syndicalist philosophy of workers' control and direct action as set out in *The Miners' Next Step*, written in Tonypandy in 1912, which was categorically opposed to the conciliatory 'Lib-Lab' attitudes of the older miners' leaders such as William Abraham (Mabon), Rhondda's M.P. from 1885 to his death in 1920. As for the Tories, in the Rhondda they were as rare as butterflies on an iceberg.

But largely unconcerned in his writing with political or social questions, and certainly not with abstract ideas or philosophical theories, Davies kept his views pretty much to himself, and never allowed his characters to become mere mouthpieces for propaganda. He was temperamentally detached from the miners' cause. His commitment was not to the social but the individual, to the imaginative, emotional and sexual liberation of the self. Always the wryly-amused onlooker rather than the involved participant, he was unlike the single-eyed Gwyn Thomas in that he was, in Roland Mathias's words, 'a writer of many eyes, most of them bland, a few penetrating, all non-committal'. He witnessed the catastrophic collapse of the coal industry in the inter-war years and the social deprivation it caused but it never seemed to raise his hackles. The only instances on which he clearly expressed a political opinion was when, in 1929, he admitted to Charles Lahr, his first publisher, that he prayed every night for a Labour victory and when, in 1943, he expressed himself in favour of self-government for Wales.[13] Even so, he had a lifelong horror of 'engaged' writing. At times, the callow youth even seemed blissfully, or heartlessly, unaware of the plight of the unemployed, as when he wrote: 'Groups of Rhondda colliers idling all day on street corners had looked contented enough to me.' At his worst, he could be quite supercilious, and not only about the working class. He had, moreover, the same inscrutable quality that Alec Guinness had as an actor, so that his opinions are often masked by language that is cold, objective and shorn of personal commitment.

As for his religious beliefs, they were just as muted. The Rhondda, like most of South Wales, had been swept by the Revival of 1904-05 led by Evan Roberts, and hot gospellers had come into Blaenclydach in search of souls to save. But this was an episode of heightened fervour, less vital in reality than the day-to-day influence of the Nonconformist faith on social life. The chapels gave the Welsh people an identity and a moral code for living as well as a focus for their cultural life – choirs, drama groups, debating societies, singing festivals, eisteddfodau and so on – and they served as a cohesive force of deep significance. But after the Cambrian Strike of 1910, some ministers grew wary of the Rhondda workers' new radicalism and disowned the younger militants, thus sometimes bringing about a schism between those who sang about the bread of heaven and those who wanted bread on earth today: the most progessive elements were driven out of the fold for ever. Even so, it took a great deal to challenge what Davies called 'the tyranny of the chapels', so pervasive was the influence of Nonconformity, even in places like 'red Rhondda', on the everyday lives of the people for a generation or more after 1910.

Although the fervour and sectarianism of evangelical Nonconformity – pulpit oratory, emotional public conversions, rivalry between the chapels and street processions of the 'saved' – excited Davies as a boy and were to exercise him as a writer, he did not allow them to touch him deeply as a young man: 'Sitting flannel-shirted in Gosen chapel, the expert choir-singing crashed disregarded over my head; such heavenly noises were not a taste of mine, perhaps because I couldn't sing a note.' A Revivalist preacher, the handsome, Welsh-speaking collier Reuben Daniels, who has the same initials as the author, was to be the hero of his first novel, *The Withered Root*, but he is portrayed as a sick and disillusioned man destroyed by the conflict between spirit, mind and flesh.[14]

Religious belief and practice get short shrift in Davies's work. He was not going to be trapped by allegiance to shibboleth and dogma any more than he was willing to settle down, take a job or commit himself to any one person.

His abhorrence of puritanism had its corollary in his joy in the natural world untrammelled by any sense of original sin. 'There is a primitive shine on Wales,' he wrote in his travelogue *My Wales*.[15] 'One can smell the old world there still, and it is not a dead aroma.' He detected the virtues he admired most in the person of his great hero, Dr William Price of Llantrisant – quack, druid, Chartist rebel, exponent of free love, nudism and moon-worship, and pioneer of cremation – whom he described as 'the seer who sought to bring back to his people the spirit of an ancient, half-forgotten poetry.' In 'A Drop of Dew', his chapter on Dr Price in *Print of a Hare's Foot*, he wrote of him:

> The bee in his fox-skin bonnet hummed from a need
> to give people liberty beyond the prosaic advantages
> of better wages and pit conditions. He did not lose
> faith in the old druidic gods.

The free-thinking Dr Price, a man singularly unafraid to live according to his own lights, was for Davies a cipher for the freedom that the future might hold for people like him.

The Davies family, largely as a matter of form and without much conviction, attended Gosen chapel, a short distance from their shop, where Welsh was in regular use as the language of worship. But the parents, both of whom were Welsh-speaking, had made only half-hearted efforts to pass the language on to their children, believing like so many in their day that getting on in the world meant it was best to speak English, or, in the words of the industrialist David Davies of Llandinam, owner of the Ocean Coal Company and Liberal M.P. for Cardigan Boroughs, they thought English was the language to make money in. Yet in the Census report of 1911 Tom and Sal Davies were enumerated as being Welsh-speaking, as were their children, Gertie, Gladys, Jack, Vivian and Peggie. What this means, almost certainly, is that Welsh was the language of the home when the children were small but that the family had turned to English – the *lingua franca* of the village, its bustling streets, the works, the shops, the schools, the newspapers and the wider world – by the time they were adolescents. Lewis Davies told the present writer he had never once heard Rhys speak a word of Welsh and that their parents used the language only when they wished not to be understood by their children.

As a result, young Vivian grew up with only a few Welsh phrases at his command – and sometimes got the spelling wrong when attempting to put 'the old language' into the mouths of his characters. In his copy of *Welsh in a Week* (a popular booklet published in Tonypandy *c.* 1930) he ticked the phrases he knew, and they were pitifully few. It was not long before the tedium of sitting through services in a language he did not understand would propel the rebellious youth from the austere Congregationalism of Gosen into the High Anglican rites – 'bells and smells' — of St Thomas's church, just up Clydach Road from Royal Stores, where worship was in English. There he encountered the Reverend Meredith

Morris, the remarkably eccentric but gifted vicar, an authority on traditional Welsh music, who caught Davies's imagination one Sunday with, in lieu of a sermon, a talk on Maeterlink's *The Blue Bird*. On another occasion, after roundly attacking the vindictive God of the Old Testament, he flung the Bible to the pulpit floor and riveted his congregation's attention with the question, 'Are we to believe that a loving God would want to smear *shit* on people's faces?' The following Sunday, there was not enough room for everyone who wanted to attend the service.

Davies's motives for attendance at St Thomas's may have been more aesthetic than spiritual because the dramatic utterances of the Welsh pulpit and the *hwyl*, or rhetorical frenzy, to which many Nonconformist preachers whipped themselves, was not to his liking; the more impersonal aesthetics and restrained ritual of the Anglican Church were more to his taste. But he was soon followed to church, first by his father, who undoubtedly saw the move as enhancing his social standing, and then by the rest of the family. Davies's younger brother Lewis told the present writer that he was confirmed by the Bishop of Llandaf and was an acolyte for the Anglican priesthood but changed his mind at the age of 17 on realizing that he too was homosexual.

In later life Rhys Davies was to turn against all forms of religious observance and declare himself an atheist. One of the characters in *The Withered Root* is made to say:

> You Welsh! A race of mystical poets who have gone
> awry... To me there seems to be a darkness over
> your land and futility in your struggles to assert your

ancient nationality. Your brilliant children leave you
because of the hopeless stagnation of your miserable
Nonconformist towns: the religion of your chapels
is a blight on the flowering souls of your young...

As for the Welsh language:

To me it is a lovely tongue to be cultivated in the
same way as some people cultivate orchids, or keep
Persian cats: a hobby yielding much private delight
and sometimes a prize at an exhibition.[16]

In his first novel, he saw Wales as 'an old woman become
lean and sour through worrying over trivialities, though
there are the remnants of a tragic beauty about her
nevertheless'. This may not have the animus of Joyce's
reference to Ireland as 'the old sow that eats her farrow'
but it is uncommonly plain speaking. Not even Caradoc
Evans, once castigated as 'the most hated man in Wales'
because of the venom with which he had satirised the
countryfolk of West Wales, went quite as far.[17] These
views inevitably proved an impediment to an appreciation
of Rhys Davies in some parts of Nonconformist Wales.
Only the Welsh-language critic Aneirin Talfan Davies,
always a good friend to Welsh writers in English, and a
Churchman who knew Davies in London, was willing to
put in a good word for him.[18]

Blaenclydach, a microcosm of the Rhondda and of
industrial South Wales in general, racked as it was by
political and religious turmoil, was a vital place in which
to grow up during the early years of the twentieth century.
The detachment with which Rhys Davies observed the life

around him seems to have been ingrained in him from an early age and remained the most characteristic trait in his personality. As the knickerbockered lad who helped serve customers from behind the counter of Royal Stores, where there was always some drama unfolding, and who accompanied his father on a daily round up and down the Cwm, he was in a good position to get to know the Valley's people. But this is the thing: the men of Blaenclydach seldom came into the shop; it was the womenfolk who were the Davieses' customers and they always had a story to tell or some gossip to impart. Young Viv listened attentively and sympathetically to every tale of woe. It was thus he learnt the courtesy, patience and wry tolerance of other people's peccadilloes that are among the hallmarks of the grocer's trade, and of his fiction.

Among the people who bought their groceries at Royal Stores was a man whom Davies called The Gentleman Collier. An Englishman, or perhaps an American, but certainly not a local man, he is described thus:

There was no other like him. His landlady said he owned nine pairs of shoes which he polished as no shoes had ever been polished. He wore smart jackets of maroon or green velvet, fanciful neckwear, kid gloves, and no hat or cap on his long, carefully arranged Botticelli hair... He always chose his own groceries, his landlady cooking for him.

It is clear from the admiring way in which this man was regarded that The Gentleman Collier fascinated young Vivian and was something of a role-model for the growing boy: not for him the ubiquitous cloth cap, or Dai-cap as it was known in the Rhondda, but the stylish trilby or boater in which he was invariably photographed. The grown man paid almost obsessive attention to people's clothes in what Katie Gramich has called 'a complex system of vestimentary codes' that disguise an uneasy gender position such as he had felt since his youth.[19]

Davies had fond memories of Royal Stores, where he spent a few hours every day:

The shop smelled of wholesome things. Golden sawdust, thrown fresh every morning on the swept floor between two long parallel counters, retained its breath of sawn trees. There was one chair, for stout old women panting on arrival from up or down hilly Clydach in our wonderful bad weather. There were lettered canisters of black and gold, an odorous coffee-machine, mounds of yellow Canadian and pallid Caerphilly cheeses, rosy cuts of ham and bacon, wide slabs of butter cut by wire for the scales, and bladders of lard. Behind the counter over which my mother presided stretched wall-fixtures stacked with crimson packets of tea, blue satchels of sugar, vari-coloured bags of rice, dried fruits and peas, weighed and packaged by hand out of chests and canvas sacks on quiet Monday. Soaps gave their own clean smell, especially the favoured kind which arrived in long bars and, cut into segments, was used both for scrubbing houses and washing pit-dirt from colliers' backs and fronts. Slabs of rich cake lay in a glass case on an intersecting counter stacked with biscuit tins. Packets of Ringer's tobacco, black chewing shag, spices, almonds and dried herbs occupied a row of drawers under a counter, though not in the one always chosen by our cat for her frequent *accouchements*...

The shop, open all hours and stocking foodstuffs of all kinds, was a focal point for Blaenclydach in ways that can no longer be fully appreciated by people who do their shopping in supermarkets or over the internet.

Life in the village was not all wholesome. The fascination with the rituals of death that is a feature of Davies's stories and novels had its origin in a macabre habit he took up with a schoolfriend, one of the 'rough boys' whom he chose as street-companions.

We would go in search of front windows draped all over with white bedsheets or tablecloths. That winter we roved through the streets as far as Llwynypia and Penygraig. It was his idea. He was the one who knocked at the door and, his face very polite and humble under his shining blond fringe, ask if we could pay our respects. It was normal in colliers' families to allow any grown-ups to view the laid-out. We were denied only once, and then it was because the body wasn't ready – 'Come back tomorrow', an old man told us. People were impressed by this tribute from boys in knickerbockers and school caps. Sometimes the body lay neat in a coffin on trestles in the front parlour; more often in a bed upstairs, which it was a triumph to penetrate. We viewed a dozen or more corpses that winter. On one occasion it was a candle-lit baby, from whose white, white face a silent woman drew away a piece of black-edged notepaper.

The same pastime is described in Davies's short story, 'The Dark World', in which the more sensitive of the boys (doubtless the writer himself) realizes, on being shown the corpse of a young woman who had once been in service at Royal Stores and, cradled in her arms, 'a pale waxen doll swathed in white', her dead baby, that he is witnessing raw human tragedy and not just participating in a schoolboy's prank.[20] His companion in this real-life pastime, Jim Reilly, was killed in an accident underground at the age of 20, or died of silicosis in his thirties – Davies typically gave both versions of his best friend's fate in different drafts of *Print of a Hare's Foot*.

Death by misadventure was no stranger to the people of Blaenclydach and it was often, in the words of Gwenallt's great poem *'Y Meirwon'* ('The Dead'), 'the industrial leopard that leaps sudden and sly out of fire and water upon men at their work, the hootering death, death dusty and smoky and drunk…' There are more fatal accidents, widows' weeds, murders, corpses, coffins, undertakers, wreaths, legacies, funerals, cold ham and mournful hymns in Davies's books than in the work of any other Welsh writer. 'Myself, I favour a dark, funereal tale,' he wrote laconically in the preface to his *Collected Stories* (1955), and, always one step ahead of those who expected consistency from him, adding, 'but not always'.[21] There are, too, frequent references to chrysanthemums, a flower that seemed to have some special significance for Davies, perhaps for no other reason than that he admired the great story by D.H.

Lawrence, 'Odour of Chrysanthemums', in which the wife
of a collier killed in a pit accident prepares his body for
burial: the flowers' cold, deathly smell has unhappy
associations for her and so, too, for Davies.

Fortunately for Davies's readers, his treatment of this
theme is not at all morbid or lachrymose; indeed, some of
the funniest scenes in his stories take place during the
rituals of death and bereavement. In his story
'Resurrection', for example, a woman whose body has
been laid out in a front parlour ready for burial
inconveniently revives and faintly asks for a glass of
water, only to be coaxed to lie down again so that her
avaricious sisters can get their hands on her money.[22] At
such moments Davies found his countrymen at their most
primaeval, their greed and hypocrisy the very stuff of
satire. 'Another virtue of the short story,' he added in the
preface, 'is that it can be allowed to laugh'. Short stories,
to borrow the title of a collection by B.S. Johnson and
Zulfikar Ghose, could be 'statements against corpses', an
affirmation of living, in Davies's estimation.[23]

It was about his thirteenth year that Davies had his
first erotic, heterosexual experiences. After chapel on
Sunday evenings he would walk with a friend up and
down Dunraven Street, Tonypandy's main thoroughfare,
the traditional place for young men to 'chat up' or, if
lucky, 'get off' with girls, though this never happened in
Davies's case. More to the point, he described how he had
taken part in a mock-marriage ceremony held in a disused
coke oven, with Vanna, the tomboy daughter of an Italian
who kept an ice-cream parlour. In mid-ceremony, however,
the youngsters were discovered by the village bobby,
though not before the bride had 'whipped up the front of

her frock. She wore no drawers. I saw the forbidden mystery. It was like a dusky apricot'. That sex was closely linked in his mind with theft, illicit behaviour and trespass is illustrated by the scrumping incident in which Davies is caught in the branches of a pear-tree with the soft, round fruit fondled lusciously and lasciviously in his hands, only to have his pleasure interrupted by the tree's irate owner.

He also gave an account of how, at about the same age, he had had to share a bed with a servant girl he calls Esther[24] because his maternal grandparents from Ynys-y-bŵl had come, unexpectedly, to stay at Royal Stores.[25] The boy is placed to sleep in the servant's small back bedroom:

> Unaccustomed to sharing a bed with anyone, I did not sleep for a long time. Hard-working Esther went into slumber with a healthy lack of worry. Flat on her back, she lay breathing unfussily as a locomotive taking rest. The depths of night must have been reached when I put my hand up her nightdress. I received an eerie shock. I had touched an electrically tingling bush. It was like putting my fingers in a prickly nest still warm from a thrush's sitting. Esther gave a grunt and heaved over onto her side. Her back was an enormous negative which of course I accepted. Curiosity had been satisfied.

The portrait of the domestic servant, who hailed from Cardigan, or so he tells us, and was paid a pound a week, is one of the most percipient and sympathetic in *Print of a Hare's Foot*. When she goes to the aid of her brother,

caught up in a street skirmish at the time of the
Tonypandy Riots, the boy watches from his bedroom
window, petrified not by the man's plight but by 'my first
glimpse of a woman demolished by emotional excess'.
Years later, having left Royal Stores, Esther calls on the
Davieses as a respectable, dressily well-off, married
woman.

> My adolescent embarrassment lasted throughout
> tea. I ate and drank in an agony of uncertainty.
> Formerly it was her eyelids that were nearly always
> lowered, and mine up; mine kept down now, and her
> eyes shone on me without stint. My fingering of her
> bush had returned. Again I heard her grunt as she
> turned over. Had she *known?* I could scarcely accept
> that I had done such a thing to this well-spoken lady
> whose corset made a tiny noise of creaking as she
> leaned forward to take a piece of sponge cake... I
> gladly escaped into the shop when my father came
> in for a quick cup of tea, and when he returned I
> went out for a walk. Esther had left by the time I
> returned. In the manner of visitors coming from the
> country, she had brought us a present. It was a
> plucked duck, and, since the weather was warm, she
> had stuffed it discriminately with sage leaves and a
> quartered onion.

Although there are passages in *Print of a Hare's Foot*
relating to family life at Royal Stores, the book should be
read with caution because many of the anecdotes,
enjoyable though they are, do not tally with the known
facts and the chronology is sometimes askew. A more

reliable portrait of the Davieses is to be found, lightly fictionalised, in the novel *To-morrow to Fresh Woods*, published in 1941, by which time Davies had more than a score of other books to his name.[26] Indeed, the novel can be read as a third-person, thinly-disguised account of his childhood and youth once the characters have been identified as members of his family. The book, it comes much nearer to autobiography than the charming but deliberately misleading 'autobiographical beginning' with which the hare chose to put his pursuers off the scent.

In the novel Davies gives us a portrait of his parents that was drawn from life:

Hannah was a well-made, definite-looking woman, handsome and steadily blue-eyed, and outwardly confronting the world, for all her inner distrust, with a natural right to her place in it. For a year or two before marrying she had been a pupil-teacher at one of the new national schools. He, though sturdy and abundantly in the world, had more mystery in his agate eyes; his views of things were romantic, even poetic, and he could not describe a footballer making a goal or a politician a speech without rhetorical exaggerations. Also he was emotionally moved to charity and he listened to any sad whining. While she, standing direct-eyed and judicious, wanted accurate versions of everything, her scepticism pruning away any decorations, tearful or otherwise. Since the trade in their busy shop was run on credit, her curbings of his generosities were needed, for later on, in a bad week or a strike, many a collier's wife saw no reason to economise if things could be obtained and pay in the future.

The most fully-rounded characters in the novel are Hannah and Dilys, the first a portrait of Davies's mother and the second of his eldest sister, Gertie. In the absence of the good-natured, easy-going father, called Roderick in the novel, each vies for control of the household and, in particular, of young Penry, a self-portrait of Vivian, whose faltering progress towards becoming a writer is the book's main theme. It must be concluded that the clash of personalities between his mother and sister left an indelible mark on the writer's psyche, particularly his view of power, rather than love, as the prime determinant in human relations. It was also one of the reasons why he could not abide bickering and disputation. Wynn Thomas has suggested that Davies had a lifelong love-hate relationship with his mother, but this view was rejected out of hand by his brother Lewis in discussion with the present writer. It is nevertheless true that if there is any veracity in the depiction of mother and son in *To-morrow to Fresh Woods*, the Lawrentian relationship was uncommonly intense and formative. When Penry refuses to study for a career in banking and announces his intention of going to London:

> She saw in his eyes the steely glint of a being that had formed itself beyond her jurisdiction at last. He saw, with a far-away quiver of pain, the broad clear face that he had never known to whimper or crouch from life, familiar and yet not now familiar: he felt separate from her... Yet all the time, having seen

that hot steely pin-point in his eyes, she recognized
that he had to go. Perhaps she would have despised
him had he submitted to her.

As for Gertie, Davies's eldest sister, she is portrayed thus:

> Dilys, in the full flush of her womanhood, was apt
> to try to wrest dominion of the house from Hannah.
> She would like – indeed she expected – everything
> to be referred to her for judgement. Also she
> expected the best chair to be kept vacant for her, and
> the lion's share of the hearthrug. She required
> constant acknowledgement of her use on earth – and
> that she was useful was undeniable. Possessed of
> high moral principles according to her energetic
> lights, her physical movements were didactic and
> much too firm. She had never learned the subtle
> victory of yielding nor could she understand the
> power that yielding can give. Her mother, vigorous
> in expressing her opinions of Roderick's little
> failings, yet allowed him to indulge in them – hence
> she kept the extravagance of his nature nicely
> curbed. Dilys, so like Hannah in many things, lacked
> this wisdom, and her need to dominate with such
> stridency irritated her mother.

Davies seems to have been able to shrug off both women's
demands on his affections by not taking sides with either.
From an early age, he was an observer, rather than a
participant in the tensions of family life brought on by
their rivalry and stratagems. Only the death of his brother
Jack in 1918 proved traumatic. Lewis Davies told the

present writer that Vivian may have had his first
homoerotic experiences while sharing a bed with Jack. Be
that as it may, he kept the scroll that was presented to the
families of all who had 'passed out of the sight of men' in
the service of king and country during the Great War,
though, according to Lewis, he would always clam up
when Jack's name was mentioned. In *To-morrow to Fresh
Woods* he is unable to bring himself to describe the scene
in which his father brings the fateful telegram informing
them of his son's death, and it is all the more moving for
being left unsaid:

> Then one day, early in 1918, Roderick, grey-faced
> and trembling, went into the living-room with a
> piece of paper and a coloured envelope in his hand.
> Hannah was sitting at the table stoning raisins.
> Madoc loved a fruit cake: she sent a parcel to him
> every week... She looked up. Her eyes caught the
> coloured envelope first. A nerve writhed in her
> temple. Slowly her eyes, gone a naked blue, lifted
> themselves to him in beseeching. He went towards
> her humbly.

It was the mother who played the most vital role in
forming Davies's character. The tension between the
personalities of mother and son makes for an electric
atmosphere in which sparks might fly at any moment.
According to his brother, Vivian had inherited a great
deal of his mother's personality and bore a strong facial
resemblance to her. Nevertheless, it must be noted here
that Lewis believed he was neither mother-dominated
nor mother-fixated. 'He respected her as a fighter and

thinker,' he recalled towards the end of his life. 'But he could stand up to her, too. He was nothing like D.H. Lawrence: there was none of that sickly Paul Morel stuff in Viv.' This is borne out in *To-morrow to Fresh Woods* in the portrait of Madoc, a version of the author's eldest brother Jack: 'Madoc, sterling at heart and with the proper sensuality of a young man, feared his mother; an elementary fear of her puritanism. But Penry, instinctively more aware of her, did not. For him, she was not monumental.'

The first major challenge to Mrs Davies's authority had to do with Vivian's education. Ambitious for all her children, she entertained great hopes for him in particular, seeing in his passing of 'the scholarship', the examination that gave admission to Porth County School, rather than the school at Tonypandy, a way of preparing him for a professional career in the wider world. The school, of which the motto was *Gwell dysg na golud* ('Better learning than riches'), itself a variation of Rhondda's motto, *Hwy clod na golud* ('Praise lasts longer than riches'), was generally considered to be the best in the Rhondda of its day and, unlike Tonypandy, where Lewis Davies was later a pupil, prepared its pupils for university entrance. Its catchment area was the whole of the Rhondda Fawr. Davies was the only Blaenclydach boy among the sixty to pass the entrance examination in his year; what is more, he may have been the only one whose parents could afford the sovereign a term it cost to send boys to the school, and to pay for textbooks and uniform to boot.

But his schooldays were to prove mute and inglorious. Having dropped Welsh in favour of French – the old execrable option in the grammar schools of those days –

if he excelled at any subject other than English, his school
reports do not mention it, and under 'Successes' and
'Remarks' the record is conspicuously blank, except to say
that he left at the end of the summer term 1915 to
become 'a grocer's assistant'. Only in his English class had
he been moved to wonder, particularly by the
headmaster's inspired reading of excerpts from *The
Odyssey* and by his discovery of John Webster's play *The
Duchess of Malfi* which 'whisked the Rhondda world
away' and gave him a taste for murder stories. He also
saw his first dramatic performance, playing gooseberry
with Esther and her young man at the Empire Theatre in
Tonypandy, where one of his own plays would later be
performed. At about this time, too, he began smoking, a
lifelong habit that was to bring on bouts of bronchitis: 'I
had good pocket money, took to cigarettes, chose my own
shirts, and developed an impatience of the County
School.' He also bought a pair of spats and a silver-topped
malacca cane, to be sported not in Blaenclydach (that
would have been asking for trouble) but on his solitary
trips to Cardiff and Porthcawl.

For a while he was known among his schoolmates by
the nickname Cashbox Davies on account of the tin box
he carried everywhere:

> The black-and-gold tin box, its handle on the lid's
> centre, had been discarded in our shop; I kept
> crayons, foreign stamps and marbles in its
> beautifully-fitting trays. Early anxiety, rooted in
> guilt, had manifested itself in fear of loss of my
> beloved box. It went with me in the streets, to bed,
> and, once, to chapel.

Just what he felt guilty about at this stage of his young life Davies does not say but clearly the box served as a talisman of some sort in his adolescent mind.

He was a pupil at Porth County for barely two years, and was able to leave in July 1915 because the statutory minimum leaving age of 14 would not come into force until three years later. He was not expelled but left of his own volition, much to the chagrin of his parents who did their utmost to dissuade him. Questioned by his brother Lewis, Davies would sometimes reply that the journey to school was too tiring, a rather ingenuous explanation given that he also admitted to walking the seven miles to Porth in order to save the train fare and supplement his pocket money. On another occasion he said, with a touch of youthful arrogance, that he thought the teachers were stupid. He left school in the middle of comparatively prosperous times for the coal industry and likewise for his family's business. Had he been faced with the economic collapse of the Depression years of the 1920s, his decision might have been different.

In *To-morrow to Fresh Woods* a recalcitrant Penry is thrashed by his father in an attempt to encourage him to return to school but his will remains unshaken, and so it was in real life. Davies's parents thought he was throwing away a promising career, never specified but vaguely sensed by people who had no experience of higher education or the professions themselves, and that his only prospect appeared to be to work in their family business and, in due course, to take it over. It is doubtful this was a future he would have chosen for himself and, as for family responsibilities, they did not count for much with him. Quite what would become of Viv could hardly have been clear to his parents, and yet it seems he was possessed of an almost preternatural sense of his own destiny: he was going to be a writer, or perhaps a painter. And so he dug in his heels and, by what he called 'passive resistance', had his way.

In the official history of Porth County School, published years later, Rhys Davies has a whole section devoted to him. A fulsome tribute, it employs the time-honoured language of the school magazine:

> The Rhys Davies Story is untypical of Porth County and Rhondda. It has, in the sober Rhondda judgement of his day, elements of the ne'er do well, the drifter and gambler, an irresponsibility of behaviour which we are unlikely to find in the careers of our most successful. This is the pedagogic view of those who follow paths other than the well-trodden and the direct, for Rhys Davies was dedicated to the exercise of his talent regardless of convention, fame or fortune. There is, in his story, a feeling of emancipation, of freedom from the obsession with security which has burdened, restrained and restricted our talent. He was a freer spirit; not for him the limits imposed by formal education, a recognised profession, a job for life... His life style and behaviour must have stunned his contemporaries here with incredulity, in their unwillingness to accept that there was anything rational or natural in them. This kind of thing might be all very well for the less responsible scions of the aristocracy, and for those of independent means, but for a boy from Blaenclydach it was unheard of.[27]

Generous though it was meant to be, the ex-headmaster's circumlocution avoided the issue of Davies's homosexuality by meeting code with code.

The six years between Davies's leaving school and his departure for London in 1921 were the formative ones in the development of his character and writing. 'I always think of this period as a burial, with myself lying somnolent in a coffin, but visually aware of the life going on above me, and content to wait until the time came for me to rise and be myself,' he told R.L. Mégroz, who published a small critical sketch of him in 1932.[28] This image of confinement, or entrapment, was to recur in various forms in many of Davies's stories and novels, whether as a prison, or hospital, or even a settled address, and certainly as a permanent relationship from which there was 'no escape'.

Even so, Davies spent the time working for his parents in Royal Stores, an experience that was to develop his powers of observation and understanding of character, particularly of women, for whom he felt a real affection and whose gossip he relished. One of the recurring references in his stories is to the Ledger of Old Accounts, 'durable as a lichened tombstone', in which his mother, more stringent than his soft-hearted father, kept a record of the customers' debts and around which more than one story unfolds. Tom Davies, through his golfing and Liberal Club friends, was well-connected and, despite the lad's lack of formal qualifications, there were attempts to get him a job in a local branch of Barclays Bank or in some clerical capacity at the Cambrian Colliery. But Davies's way of failing the interviews was to remain monosyllabic throughout and deliberately to botch the arithmetic tests.

A Sunday afternoon visit underground, when no work was done at the Cambrian, filled him with even greater horror:

> There was nothing but the gigantic silence of unshifting death. It was not a hostile silence. Only the forgetfulness of death lay in this silver-ored beyond. It was not a place for me.

Typically, the young aesthete's attention was caught by a fossilized oak-leaf rather than by the machinery and dreadful conditions underground. But even what might have proved more congenial employment as a junior reporter with *The Rhondda Leader* or in the offices of the Rhondda Urban Council was deftly evaded; unsurprisingly, his parents complained that he was without motivation. 'You're an enigma,' said his father, exasperated. 'You must make up your mind,' his mother nagged. 'I had, interiorly. I wanted to live in London.'

Throughout his teens Davies's writing was a secret, solitary act, of which his parents and siblings remained unaware – like so many budding poets he used to stuff his poems under the bed mattress – and his reading was similarly surreptitious and unsupervised. But guided by some unknown hand, probably that of a disabled collier who ran the Library and Institute of the South Wales Miners' Federation in Blaenclydach, and who was called 'Moses One Leg' in *The Withered Root*, he moved on from comic papers like *The Magnet* and *The Gem*, his father's copy of *John Bull* and his mother's *Home Companion*, towards the world of books, especially the literature and art of the 1890s.

In Cardiff, some twenty miles and an hour's train
journey down the Cwm, where he ventured almost
immediately after leaving school, he bought a copy of
Oscar Wilde's *Salome*, with illustrations by Aubrey
Beardsley, and immediately fell under the spell of 'these
sensuous drawings of perverse yet truthful human beings'.
The drawings and Wilde's text reinforced in him a growing
sense of the trap that women represented. He had read it
in bed and, we are given to understand, used it as an aid
to masturbation. The book served an even more important
purpose:

> Beardsley taught me that I couldn't draw. I gave up my
> dream of becoming a painter and stopped chalking
> heads on the coloured sheets of thick paper in which
> our raisins, currants and sultanas were packaged on
> Mondays. Poems were my compensation.

At the end of the same solitary week, on holiday in
Porthcawl, where he had at last had a chance to sport his
spats and malacca cane, he claimed to have had sex in the
dunes with a woman of about thirty. He had met her,
prosaically enough, in a bar at the Esplanade Hotel, but
was not at all perturbed when she told him afterwards
that she was a reincarnated Egyptian. There is, as ever,
some doubt as to the veracity of this anecdote: the
impression is given that the mysterious stranger might just
as easily have been a man, since there is no mention of
contraceptive precautions and the incident has all the
hallmarks of a homosexual pick-up. If true, and whether
his partner was a man or a woman, Davies must have
been a quite remarkable fourteen-year-old or else a writer

who did not let the truth get in the way of a good story. In any case, the whole incident, it seems, was soon over. Rapid and anonymous couplings are a feature of several of Davies's novels: Edith Stevens in *Rings on her Fingers* (1930) and Cassie Prosser in *Jubilee Blues* (1938) both manage them and they were also a feature of his own mode of homosexuality.[29] [30] There were almost certainly other adolescent sexual encounters but Davies did not write about them, except in some of his stories such as 'The Public-House', clearly the Central Hotel in Blaenclydach, in which a middle-aged spinster makes a young boy feel uncomfortable:

> Generous and lively, she spoke to him in a jokingly rancorous way as if he were a grown-up, and gave him pieces of mint-toffee and often a penny. But sometimes she lifted him and stood him on the bar counter, oblivious of the men in the saloon, and, clasping his bare knees with her big moist hands, she would ask him laughingly if he loved her and would he love her always, for ever and for ever. She would make him grin, and because her manner was raucous, he was not offended or humiliated. Yet she made him feel cautious too and he experienced a vague, unformulated feeling when she gripped his knees and, lifting him down from the bar counter, her hand lingered about him. She was a strong woman.[31]

Later the boy falls into the river and, lest his mother scold him, allows the woman to take him up into her living quarters above the pub where she bathes and appears to fondle him:

He stood very still but once, as if trapped, he gazed round wildly at the door. Miss Sanders's well-known arms, hard and brisk with power, encircled him. They dexterously peeled off his clothes. He was clammy and shivering, and he was overcome with some strange new feeling that presently solidified into a knot of resentment in his mind. Too late! She had got him into the bath. She rolled up her sleeves and, telling him that presently they would have some nice hot tea and pineapple together, she soaped him. There was no denying her. Busily, talking all the while with a bright, hard gallop of words, she kneaded and rubbed his flesh. The resentment swelled into anger. At home he washed himself without help now. But he could not bring his tongue to protest. She had the large, high power of the adult, and before this she had always behaved as a friend.

Having dried him, Miss Sanders gives the boy two pennies and enjoins him not to say anything to his mother. He never goes near the pub again.

In *To-morrow to Fresh Woods* the character Shan says to Penry, 'Well, you *are* a bit feminine.' Davies's inchoate sexuality at this time was crystallizing into a homosexual orientation which, if it allowed for close emotional relationships with women, was erotically confined to men. Though by necessity extremely circumspect and cryptic about his homosexuality, the writer never concealed its importance. In 1977, about eighteen months before he died, he admitted in an interview that he had a strongly feminine sensibility which was expressed through his writing from a woman's perspective, adding that he thought most writers and artists did, too; very few, he pointed out are 'rugby playing types'.[32] That said, the writer's feminine side never expressed itself in either dress or manner, both of which were overtly masculine. Even so, it seems more than likely that a growing awareness of his sexuality was a contributory factor in his rejection of educational opportunity and his precipitate flight from the macho culture of the Rhondda where a very clear sense of gender roles and a distinct construction of masculinity based on physical strength and heterosexual potency were the norm.

Davies, having spurned conventional education, now set out on a course of self-education in the autodidactic tradition of industrial South Wales. He had already encountered the Greek myths in translation and been enthralled by the vengeful, destructive female figures who appear in them, and *The Odyssey* had been the first book to awaken the boy's imagination at Porth County School: 'I could not be parted from my *Odyssey*. It was always in my satchel on my way home, to be read in bed by candlelight.'

There was, however, a lighter side to his reading. He was to learn a great deal from the French and Russian masters, whose books he borrowed from the well-stocked Fed library in the village, especially the *Contes* of Maupassant, slivers of experience set down for no other reason than to tell a good story. A precocious and voracious reader, before his sixteenth birthday Davies had read English translations of Anatole France, Flaubert, Zola's *Germinal*, Baudelaire, and Voltaire's *Candide* – 'surely one of the most nourishing books for wholesome boys ever written,' he remarked wryly.

But the writer who meant most to him, then as in later life, was Russian:

> My God was Chekhov. I had bought with my spare cash the small green volumes of Constance Garnett's translations and seldom went anywhere without one in my pocket.[33]

Happily, these books by 'the beloved Russian sorcerer', the son of another provincial grocer living over the shop at Taganrog on the Sea of Azov, survived Davies's peripatetic lifestyle, albeit in dark blue bindings, and are now in the possession of the present writer.

The attraction Chekhov held for Davies, not just as a youth but throughout his life, is easy to see. Two of the Russian outsider's recurrent themes are romantic disillusionment and the search for intimacy, nearly always thwarted. He was uneasy in the world but unsentimental about it, with a hatred of compromise and confrontation alike, and his sexual nature constantly eludes us by being understated and concealed. He liked women but was incapable of loving them, his marriage to the actress Olga Knipper three years before he died notwithstanding. Tolstoy saw in him 'the woman under the skin'. His art was profoundly humane, yet in his own life he held back, coldly and perhaps fearfully, from any real commitment, and his stubborn reserve was lifelong. In short, he stood, as E.M. Forster remarked of Cavafy, 'at a slight angle to the universe'.

As for the French masters, it was Flaubert whom Davies most admired, and especially his tragic heroine, Emma Bovary.[34] In the novel, first published in the *Revue de Paris* in 1856, Emma Rouault, a farmer's daughter, is educated in a convent which she leaves with her head stuffed with sentimental religiosity and dreaming of a life full of luxury and Byronic lovers. She marries Charles Bovary, a country doctor, but finds small-town life in Normandy with a dull, if adoring, husband very unlike the one depicted in the novels she has read. She takes lovers, falls into debt and is blackmailed by her creditor. In despair, she persuades an infatuated chemist's assistant to provide her with a quantity of arsenic, with which she poisons herself.

What Davies admired about Emma (who was modelled on a former mistress of Flaubert's) was the power of her imagination, what later critics came to call the Bovaric angle, because it could outstrip reality. He saw how her early religious enthusiasm turned so easily into sensuality, and how she yearned to escape her constrained existence in the backwater that Flaubert called Yonville. Davies, too, wanted to escape his native patch and would not begin to be happy until he had done so; for him, there was no difference between Yonville and Blaenclydach. The novel is not only a tale of adultery but also a satire on the French provincial middle class of the day, especially its stupidity, its narrowness and its hypocrisy: the point was not lost on Davies.

The other influence was D.H. Lawrence.[35] The women in Davies's stories usually achieve their victories by dint of personal revolt against convention, a favourite theme of his, and by embracing the Lawrentian values inherent in a passionate response to life. The plots of Lawrence's stories and novels often revolve around three sisters, or a young headstrong woman, or a middle-aged spinster, or else a wife fretting against the restrictions of an unhappy marriage, who eventually rise above their circumstances and achieve a kind of liberation. Women, in Davies's fiction, are locked into a dignified respectability which they endeavour to maintain in the face of poverty and in defiance of drunken, loutish or feckless husbands. The writer's feminine nature meant that, throughout his life, he was to feel a great empathy with females and their struggle against both domestic and sexual oppression. He developed a platonic closeness with certain women, notably the novelist Anna Kavan, his friends Louise Taylor and Greta Quinain, that far exceeded anything he enjoyed with men.

Apart from his reading of 'the Decadents', Davies had little knowledge of contemporary English writing at this time and no access to the leading literary periodicals of the day. Yet he persisted in writing, derivatively and without hope of publication, and made his first adolescent attempts at stories and poems that showed, according to his brother Lewis, a remarkable command of English idiom and imagery. For a youth who had never been much further than Porthcawl it must have seemed the true stuff of literature lay beyond the confines of his narrow Cwm. But in this he was mistaken: the material with which he was to make his name lay all around him as he served in his father's shop or roamed the streets of Blaenclydach.

Even so, as he grew more aware of the first stirrings of his sexual nature, one for which he had as yet no name, which he could not discuss with anyone, and which in the male-dominated culture of the Rhondda would have made him, at least in some quarters, a figure of fun, he made up his mind to leave home. He was, too, daunted by the endemic grime and coarseness of workaday life in the Valley's townships, the banausic character of its built environment and what he saw as the joylessness of its chapel culture. There was no way he could express his undisclosed sexuality except in reading books and looking at pictures that seemed to speak to him of his secret self.

He had now set his sights on London. It was not that he was unhappy at home in Royal Stores, but that he found home life stifling and inimical to his artistic temperament.[36] When his sister suggests he should go to sea if he wants 'adventures and to see the world', Penry in *To-morrow to Fresh Woods* says to himself:

> No, he did not want it that way, adventures outside himself. Nothing spectacular. Not now. No climbing of Everests or skipping like a monkey up ships' masts on Caribbean seas; no crossing of deserts and no heroics on ice-fields. Such adventures were fly-blown. Already they seemed trivial compared to the adventures that went on inside a man. He did not want to drive tin-tacks home with a sledge-hammer. No pomp and no oratory. But he wanted to trace the stream of being to its source. Tap the unending treasure in man. That's what he wanted.

In an unpublished biographical note dated May 1946 he wrote, 'At this time I had only the vaguest idea of becoming a writer and was really only concerned with flight and the need to escape family domination.' As a first step, to slacken the bonds keeping him at home, he took a job at a men's outfitters in the railway and docks town of Barry and then another filling sacks in a potato and corn merchant's warehouse in Cardiff, after which he drifted from job to menial job. Sometimes he found ways of leaving his workplace to spend hours in the free Central Library, but Cardiff in those days was not the cultural capital it is today: there were few good bookshops, no publishers, no writers, no magazines, no literary societies and no arts centres to welcome a youth with literary yearnings. London was the only place for such as him.

At last, in 1921, and with no apparent misgivings, he was ready to leave. His mother, as mothers do, opposed his going right up to the last moment but, with the strength of will he had inherited from her and with which he had defied her in leaving school, he went nonetheless, to face the destiny for which, albeit obscurely, he seemed to have been preparing all along.

Notes

1   Dai Smith, *Wales: A Question for History* (Seren, 1999)
2   Anonymous article in *The Times* (23 November 1910); quoted in Dai Smith, *Wales: A Question for History* (Seren, 1999)
3   Dai Smith, 'Rhys Davies and his "Turbulent Valley"', in *Decoding the Hare*
4   The five children and one adult who lost their lives in The Flood are commemorated by a plaque in the village. In the Aber-fan Disaster (21 October 1966), near Merthyr Tydfil, part of a coal-tip slid into the valley, crushing houses and burying a school; 116 children and 28 adults were killed. RD gives another, much exaggerated, account of The Flood in *To-morrow to Fresh Woods* (William Heinemann, 1941).
5   Stephen Knight, '"Not a Place for Me": Rhys Davies's Fiction and the Coal Industry', in *Decoding the Hare*
6   Jean Pol Le Lay, *Rhys Davies as an Anglo-Welsh Story-teller*

(Faculté des Lettres et Sciences Humaines, Brest, 1968-1969)

7   Howell Elvet Lewis (Elfed; 1860-1953), poet and hymn-writer, was born near Blaen-y-coed, Carms.; he was Archdruid of Wales (1924-28) and minister at Tabernacl chapel, King's Cross (1904-40).

8   Brinley Thomas, 'The Changing Face of South Wales', *The Listener* (23 March 1938)

9   E.D. Lewis, *The Rhondda Valleys: A Study in Industrial Development, 1800 to the Present Day* (Phoenix House, 1958)

10   Goronwy Rees, *Encounter* (August 1969)

11   A popular rebellion that grew into an armed insurrection, the Merthyr Rising was caused by workers' grievances over wages, municipal administration and parliamentary reform. One of their number, Richard Lewis, known as Dic Penderyn, was hanged on a trumped-up charge of wounding a soldier, for which he is regarded as the first martyr of the Welsh working class. See Gwyn A. Williams, *The Merthyr Rising* (2nd edn., University of Wales Press, 1988)

12   Dai Smith, 'Rhys Davies and his "Turbulent Valley"', in *Decoding the Hare*

13   'From my Notebook,' *Wales* (2, October 1943)

14   *The Withered Root* (Robert Holden, 1927)

15   *My Wales* (Jarrolds, 1937)

16   *My Wales* (Jarrolds, 1937)

17   Caradoc Evans (1878-1945) was a prose-writer who inflamed public opinion in Wales with his short stories and novels, notably his first collection of short stories *My People* (1915). Gwyn Jones, introducing his anthology *Welsh Short Stories* (Oxford University Press, 1956), wrote of Evans, whom he greatly admired, 'Not even his best friends would call him a saint. Many local authorities in Wales banned him from their libraries; and to one fell the distinction of burning his books in the public incinerator... Upon all the

fires of controversy that blazed about them [his books] he was prompt to splash petrol – for a more sardonic exhibitionist and mischief-maker would be hard to find.'

18 See, for example, Aneirin Talfan Davies, *'Pencampwr y Stori Fer'* ('A master of the short story'), in *The Western Mail* (28 June 1969).

19 Katie Gramich, 'The Masquerade of Gender in the Stories of Rhys Davies', in *Decoding the Hare*

20 'The Dark World', in *A Finger in Every Pie* (William Heinemann, 1942); *Collected Stories* (ed. Meic Stephens, Gomer, vol.1, 1996); the Gomer volume should not be confused with the one in the next footnote.

21 *The Collected Stories of Rhys Davies* (William Heinemann, 1955)

22 'Resurrection', in *The Things Men Do* (William Heinemann, 1936); *Collected Stories* (ed. Meic Stephens, Gomer, vol.1, 1996)

23 B.S. Johnson and Zulfikar Ghose, *Statement against Corpses* (Constable, 1964)

24 In the 1911 Census the domestic servant enumerated as living at 6 Clydach Road was named Rebecca Evans and her place of birth given as Bethesda, 'near Carnarvon' [*sic*].

25 RD disliked his maternal grandfather, John Lewis, whom he saw as a stern, unsmiling chapel deacon; within a few weeks of losing his first wife this man scandalised the Davieses by marrying again.

26 *To-morrow to Fresh Woods* (1941); the novel's title, which is a quotation from the last line of Milton's *Lycidas* (1646), preserved the hyphen of the usage current at the time.

27 Owen Vernon Jones, *Porth County: the School and its Boys* (Prefix, 1991). The school records show that Rees Vivian Davies was a pupil there from 9 September 1913 to 23 July 1915.

28 Rodolphe L. Mégroz, *Rhys Davies: A Critical Sketch* (W. & G. Foyle, 1932)

29 *Rings on her Fingers* (Harold Shaylor, 1930)

30 *Jubilee Blues* (William Heinemann, 1938)

31 'The Public-House', in *The Trip to London* (William Heinemann, 1946), *Collected Stories* (ed. Meic Stephens, vol. 2, 1996). In their essay '"Unspeakable Rites": Writing the Unspeakable in Rhys Davies', in *Decoding the Hare*, Simon Baker and Joanna Furber write: 'Although this passage certainly reads as a woman/boy sexual initiation, it surely works more effectively as a man/boy encounter.'

32 Delyth Davies, 'Remembering Rhys Davies' (BBC Radio Wales), was recorded in February 1977 and broadcast posthumously on 28 September 1978.

33 Among the best recent biographies of Anton Chekhov (1860-1904) are those by Donald Rayfield, *Anton Chekhov: a Life* (Faber, 1997) and Philip Callow, *Chekhov: The Hidden Ground* (Constable, 1998); see also Louis S. Friedland (ed.), *Chekhov: Letters on the Short Story, The Drama and Other Literary Topics* (Vision, 1965) and Rosamund Bartlett (ed.), *Anton Chekhov: A Life in Letters* (Penguin, 2004).

34 Among more recent books about Gustave Flaubert (1821-80), see Frederick Brown, *Flaubert: a Biography* (Little, Brown, 2006); see also Richard Rumbold, *Gustave Flaubert: Letters* (Weidenfeld & Nicolson, 1950). The best recent English translation of the novel is the one by Adam Thorpe, *Madame Bovary* (Vintage, Random House, 2012).

35 See John Worthen's three-volume biography of D.H. Lawrence (Cambridge University Press, 1991-98) and the same author's *D.H. Lawrence: The Life of an Outsider* (Allen Lane, 2005)

36 In the interview with Delyth Davies, RD said, 'I didn't want parents telling me to do this, that or the other. I wanted to be myself, alone.' The interview was broadcast by BBC Wales shortly after the writer's death; a transcript is included in Sarah Leigh Mabbett's unpublished MA dissertation (University of Wales College of Swansea, 1996).

Rhys Davies 1928

Three

London legs

Contrary to the impression given in *Print of a Hare's Foot*, Rhys Davies did not alight from the Cardiff train at Paddington in March 1921 fully equipped as a writer or with any clear idea as to how he was going to make his way in the literary life of London. He knew no one in the capital and had only his determination, and a few pounds from his parents, to see him through the first months of living in what was, for him, as for many a young person arriving from the provinces, a metropolis larger and more bewildering than anything he had experienced hitherto: Pontypridd, 'Gateway to the Valleys', was for all its bustle only a sleepy market town in comparison and even Cardiff, the largest coal-exporting port in the world, paled in comparison. Nor did he have any way of knowing how to make contact with the bohemian world and artistic life he craved; several years were to pass before he found his milieu.

What he did have was a remarkable degree of self-sufficiency: 'I wished for no possessions, and, since taking my leap over the mountains, I had learned in my initial year or two how to be alone.' This wish for solitude, for liking his own company best, was typical of the man and was to be a major factor in shaping his career as a writer. After living in the close community of Blaenclydach, where everyone knew everyone, especially the grocer's son from Royal Stores, he revelled in the anonymity of the city, an ideal place in which to feel alone and be himself.

Like Caradoc Evans before him, Davies took various menial jobs in the drapery business, including one in a men's wear shop in Ilford. The 'slim, bowler-hatted youth', as he described himself, lived in lodgings with a Miss Davies at 43 Third Avenue in Manor Park, a dreary no-man's-land not far from Kensal Green Cemetery and between the dormitory town and the West End proper. It was at this address his brother Lewis visited him at the time of the British Empire Exhibition of 1924. His fellow-lodger was a young man called John Pope, who also worked as an assistant at a gentleman's outfitters, with whom Davies kept in contact for years after Pope moved back to his native Luton to set up in business on his own. Although Pope had no literary interests, Davies would invariably send him signed copies of his books. The manager of the draper's shop, 'a ferociously bad-tempered and drunken Welshman', would read passages from Gibbon's *History of the Decline and Fall of the Roman Empire* to the staff during their lunch-hour. It might not have been to everyone's taste but it found a ready listener in the literary-minded Davies.

His brother Lewis believed it was an identification with H.G. Wells's Mr Kipps that lay behind Davies's choice of gentleman's outfitter as an occupation; a secondary factor may well have been that it was a favourite form of employment among homosexuals, who tended to congregate in 'service' jobs. Although he worked in the shop for nearly seven years, Davies never wrote about it, either fictionally or in the various sketches that purported to be autobiographical, and he made no friends there. But good clothes meant a lot to him and he was always well turned out, even in the days when he had little or no money and during the war when clothing was rationed. Never without a collar and tie, he favoured smart tweed jackets, silk ties and well-pressed grey flannel trousers.

As soon as he found his London legs he took to life in the city with gusto. It was the sense of unimpaired personal liberty that most animated him:

> I was my own interior master now. My feet trod the London streets without anxiety. The Twenties, in hindsight the sunset close of an era, were not a conclusion then. They coruscated with intimations of complete personal liberty. The animated metropolis thrived in a sociable attempt at demolition of class attitudes, the Labour Party was intellectually and morally acceptable, and Freud a newly canonized redeemer. It was a time to be young in; and also industrious. God had lost his formal terrors, and the Communists of the Thirties were in bud. Bounty, especially from the enfranchised women, was rife. Necessities were dirt cheap, and death at a halt. I never seemed to hear of anyone I knew dying. I was the right age for rose-tinted spectacles.

Living on a staple diet of poached eggs on toast, gorgonzola cheese, biscuits and gas-ring coffee, he used the 'eggcup wealth' his parents sent him to pay his rent. If there was anything left over from his meagre wages, he spent it on the occasional visit to the theatre, where he saw the legendary Eleonora Duse playing Ibsen shortly before her death: 'the old woman went into a chink of my mind and stayed there for ever'. He also went to see Diaghilev's *Ballets Russes*: 'after life in the Rhondda Valley the heap of ballets I saw was a rainbow wash of the mind. They assisted in liberation'.

It was precisely for this reason that he avoided the society of the London Welsh:

Here and there in London were close alcoves of the Welsh, highly exclusive and more obdurately Welsh than those at home. I was not one to cultivate them; I wanted educating in different spheres.

A copy of *The London Magazine*, in which Dylan Thomas later roundly castigated the expatriate Welsh –'"Ecktually", they say, "I was born in Cwmbwrla, but Soho's better for my gouaches"' – was found among the contents of Davies's flat after his death, with that caustic sentence scored in pencil. Davies would also have concurred with Thomas when he wrote in the same piece:

On the other hand, too many of the artists of Wales stay in Wales too long, giants in the dark behind the parish pump, pygmies in the nationless sun, enviously sniping at the artists of other countries rather than attempting to raise the standard of art of their own country by working fervently at their own words, paint, or music. And too many of the artists of Wales spend too much time talking about the position of the artists of Wales. There is only one position for an artist anywhere: and that is, upright.[1]

Davies preferred the ambience of what came to be known as Fitzrovia.[2] This was a neighbourhood in central London near the West End and a little to the north of Soho. It was bounded on the south by Oxford Street, on the west by Regent Street and Portland Place, on the north by Euston Road, and on the east by Gower Street and part of Tottenham Court Road as far as Charing Cross Road. It took its name from the Fitzroy Tavern on the corner of Charlotte Street and Windmill Street, where artists and writers had congregated since the eighteenth century. Although only Tottenham Court Road divided Fitzrovia from Bloomsbury, the two were worlds apart: Bloomsbury was regarded by bohemians as dilettante and effete, while Fitzrovians saw themselves as down-to-earth and sturdily professional. Davies had arrived in London just in time to see Fitzrovia starting to become the English equivalent of the Left Bank in Paris or New York's Greenwich Village, and this was the district where he would find the artistic milieu that suited him best.

His first contact with the literary life of London came when he happened upon Harold Monro's Poetry Book Shop in a dingy street off Theobalds Road. There he heard Edith Sitwell 'tinkling out her early verse' and the 'spectral' T.S. Eliot in a tightly-fitting dark overcoat, 'as if buttoned up against the damp souls of this world', reading 'The Lovesong of Alfred J. Prufrock'. He also bought a rhymesheet at the shop, a poem by Blake with decorations by Lovat Fraser, 'Never seek to tell thy love / Love that never told can be...', which hung for years on the walls of his various bed-sits and became something of a talisman for him. Among the women he met at this time were the the left-wing, Negro-obsessed, exhibitionist and alcoholic heiress Nancy Cunard, the poet Anna Wickham, and Nina Hamnett, the painter from Tenby who harked back to the golden age of Montparnasse. Hamnett had known Modigliani, Stravinsky, Cocteau, Picasso and Erik Satie, and been one of Gaudier-Brzeska's mistresses. Davies was to remain on friendly terms with her until the artist's mysterious death in 1956.

The hub of bohemian London in the 1920s was the Café Royal and Davies, as yet with no published work to his name, was quickly accepted as one of the crowd who sat nightly at its marble-topped tables. Although he soon became aware of 'that dread thing in English life, class-consciousness', he now found himself, for the first time in his life, mixing with middle-class intellectuals. It was about this time he began to modify his accent to conform to Received Pronunciation as favoured by the BBC, though in conversation with compatriots he still spoke with the mid-Rhondda accent that was his true register. He had already decided to call himself Rhys as a badge of his nationality, a name that some of his non-Welsh acquaintances persisted in pronouncing 'Rice' or, unable to reproduce the aspirated 'rh', 'Reeze'; his surname they sometimes pronounced in the English manner as 'Daveys'.

All the while he was writing. He was soon, however, to give up verse because he found it as 'unsatisfactory as self-abuse' and very few of his poems appeared in little magazines. One, 'The City', a pastiche of T.S. Eliot, was published in *transition* and later in *Wales*, and two others survived to appear in Keidrych Rhys's capacious anthology *Modern Welsh Poetry* (1944).[3] But he soon discovered his true forte was the writing of short prose. Creatively, he was still under the spell of Chekhov rather than Maupassant: 'The perfect machinery of Maupassant is well-hidden, but its grinding can be heard. There is no machinery in Chekhov, only natural leaves, an opening bud.' And he resolved to write short stories:

> Short story writers are saints. Their revenue is not much of this earth. They work largely for love. While great poets continue to be born, all fiction-writing is unnecessary, but if the prosy activity cannot be dropped, then the short story approximates closer to poetry than the noisy and dense novel.

It was during a trip to the West End in November 1925 that he bought a copy of the first number of a magazine, *The New Coterie*, attracted by a striking drawing by William Roberts on the front cover. Roberts (who, despite his name, was not Welsh but a Londoner) was a leading member of the Vorticist Group, one of the most important British art movements in the first half of the twentieth century. He was to become firm friends with Davies, drawing his portrait for *The New Coterie* and illustrating the dust-jacket of his first novel.[4] The magazine which brought them together was edited by Paul Selver, a Czech emigré who was the first translator into English of Jaroslav Hašek's *The Good Soldier Švejk,* and devoted to contemporary 'advanced' writing and illustration. Among the writers whose work appeared in his magazine were Liam O'Flaherty, H.E. Bates, T.F. Powys, Hugh MacDiarmid, C.L.R. James, Rupert Croft-Cooke, Aldous Huxley and D.H. Lawrence, as well as Malachi Whitaker and H.A. Manhood, the two last-named now known only to students of the period.

According to Davies, his own arrival on the literary scene was next to effortless. One wet Sunday in December 1926, he sat down in his Ilford lodgings and three brief stories had flowed down his arm: 'Now that I was quite freed of the dour Valley of my upbringing I must subsconciously have seen it in a new rich light, and the stories came with the greatest ease.' He immediately sent them off to *The Transatlantic Review* in Paris, but they were returned with a note from Ford Madox Ford, the editor, explaining that they would have been accepted had not the magazine been about to close down. Nothing daunted, he then sent them to *The New Coterie* and they were duly accepted for publication: 'A Gift of Death' in the magazine's second number, 'The Sisters' in the third, and 'Mrs Evans Number Six' in the fourth; a further story, 'Aaron', appeared in the sixth issue, a double number, which was to be the last of the magazine's brief but distinguished run before it too folded in 1927. Davies was paid two guineas for each of his stories, and was given a complete set of Maupassant.

Shortly after the first of the stories had appeared, their author was asked to call at the Progressive Bookshop at 68-69 Red Lion Street, High Holborn, where the magazine's publisher had an office. The magic door was about to open for Davies and, although he was to go on living in Manor Park until 1929, and was still employed as a shop assistant, he was now to be delivered from the darkness of the outer suburbs into the bright heartland of London's literary life: '"There's wonders!" an old collier I knew in the Rhondda used to exclaim at any event. A sense of youthful wonder remained, I think, untarnished in me.' The man who opened the door for him was Charles Lahr.

Karl Lahr (to give him the original German form of his name) had been born in Bad Nauheim, a few miles to the north of Frankfurt in the Rhineland Palatinate, in 1885, and spent his boyhood in nearby Stein-Bockenheim. Apprenticed to a chemist uncle at the age of 13, he became an anarchist while still in his teens and, in 1905, escaped to England to avoid conscription in the Kaiser's army. In London, where he found work as a baker, he became active in anarchist circles and a key figure in the British section of the Industrial Workers of the World (the Wobblies),[5] an international union founded in 1905 which, in 1923, had more than a hundred thousand members.

Shortly after the outbreak of the First World War Lahr was interned in Alexandra Palace as an enemy alien; there he pulled off the remarkable feat of seducing the caretaker's wife while her husband was away at the war, an episode fictionalised by two of his protégés, namely H.E. Bates and James Hanley. Released in 1919, he married Esther Argeband, whose surname was anglicized as Archer, a Jewish cigarette-maker from the East End; with her he joined and then promptly left the British Communist Party after the shooting of mutinous sailors at Kronstadt in 1921. According to his daughter, Sheila Leslie, Charlie Lahr was about to be expelled, anyway, for 'levity', after being heard cracking a joke at the Party's expense; the Bolsheviks had no truck with persiflage and he was an inveterate joker. During the Second World War Lahr and his wife were to be interned again, this time on the Isle of Man.

The Lahrs had taken over the Progressive Bookshop in 1921 from Harold Edwards, having bought the business for £25. The premises, according to Kenneth Hopkins in his nicely sardonic memoir *The Corruption of a Poet* (1954), measured some eight feet by twelve and the walls were piled high with unsold stock. Among the periodicals on sale were *Moscow News, Tribune, Labour Monthly, Socialist Vanguard* and the *Daily Worker*. Habitués of the place were allowed to borrow whichever books they pleased, but no record was ever kept. There was an office at the rear where the Lahrs published an array of books and pamphlets, now collectors' items, by some of the leading lights of London's literary and artistic avant-garde. Lahr's own translations from the German included works by Bakunin and Kropotkin, the leading anarchists of their day; he also, between 1911 and 1914, published articles in *The Herald of Revolt*, the anarchist newspaper.

Kenneth Hopkins, quoting from the manuscript of his own unpublished novel, *Poor Heretic*, described the Bookshop's proprietor, whom he calls Charles Lear, as:

> a man of about fifty, with greying hair and brushed straight back. His moustache and goatee beard were of a faded ginger hue. His rather gaunt face appeared to have met all weathers, and now it had taken the colour and almost the texture of old leather. Mr Lear found it convenient to wear a shirt

of bright orange, and as his trousers were grey and his coat blue Christopher [the narrator] thought himself justified in supposing the socks would be green; but there were no socks. Mr Lear's feet were contained in sandals. They were large and clean, and funnily enough they didn't look cold.

Generous to a fault, Lahr was also described by H.E. Bates in his memoir *The Blossoming World* (1971):

Of slightly more than average height he was, when I first met him, possessed of a singular, almost maniacal energy which enabled him to cycle, run or walk about London in a passionate and tireless search for books. His devotion to writers, and indeed to painters, was phenomenal; and his shop, never capable seemingly of holding more than six people, always seemed to be populated by a couple of dozen, with more chatting and lounging away in the passage outside.[6]

The habitués of the Progressive Bookshop were described by Rupert Croft-Cooke in his book *The Numbers Came* (1963) as 'threadbare, ill-shod and unshaven, not in the abominably affected manner of today but because they had not the money to buy clothes and shoes, or, very often, razor blades.' Liam O'Flaherty called the bookseller 'a rare boyo of a character' and R.M. Fox in *Smokcy Crusade* (1937) remembered the shop as 'a rendez-vous for rebels and world-shakers with an interest in books and ideas'.

Lahr knew everyone in literary London.[7] But he seemed to be a lover of books for themselves rather than for their contents. His brief attention span meant that he rarely read even the books he published, and sometimes he appeared to be more interested in politics than in literature. Though always styling himself an anarchist, he belonged during the course of his lifetime to nearly every extra-parliamentary grouping of the British Left, eventually ending up in the ranks of the Independent Labour Party, to whose headquarters in King's Cross Road he eventually moved after his own premises had been bombed by the Luftwaffe, for the second time, in 1941. Several Nationalist leaders frequented his shop, among them Jomo Kenyatta, Krishna Menon, and Maud Gonne, the Irish revolutionary with whom W.B. Yeats was infatuated. Lahr's funeral in 1971 would be attended by a representative of the Trotskyist Workers' Revolutionary Party.

The Lahr household was nothing if not louche. A subscriber to the fashionable doctrine of free love, Charlie kept a mistress, Phyllis Marshall (formerly Margaret Bressler), the wife of a Swansea solicitor who had left home and four children for the delights of London. One of the many women who found Rhys Davies sympathetic, she became his confidante, initially because he was privy to what was going on between her and Lahr. Even so, the freedom Lahr claimed for himself was not extended to his wife and when Esther had a brief fling with James Hanley, who had been given free lodgings under their roof, there was friction and, in the end, fisticuffs, after which Davies, ever loyal to his first patron and disliking confrontation, had no more to do with Hanley.

It seems likely that Davies saw in the unworldliness of Charlie Lahr – the payment of royalties was a haphazard affair – and in Esther's commercial acumen, a reflection of his own impractical father and more businesslike mother. Be that as it may, as a result of the mismanagement of the Bookshop's finances, exacerbated by Lahr's largesse to writers, things got so bad that, in 1933, a group of them came together in an attempt to raise some money for him. Eighteen of his protégés, including Rhys Davies, H.E. Bates, Seán Ó Faoláin, Liam O'Flaherty and T.F. Powys, each contributed to a miscellany of short stories to which the title *Charles' Wain* was given. The story by Davies, 'Emily', about two former lovers meeting by chance in a graveyard off the Gray's Inn Road complete with chrysanthemums, remains uncollected. However, due to patchy distribution, the book hardly sold, the publisher went bankrupt and Lahr's financial situation remained much as before. Even worse was to follow: he was arrested on a charge of handling stolen books and threatened with deportation to Nazi Germany if he did not plead guilty. He promptly did so and was given a six-month sentence in Wormwood Scrubs. The incident is described in the story 'No Country' by H.E. Bates. The books in question were by L.A.G. Strong, then a prominent critic and reviewer, and Davies went to see the author to plead his friend's case, but to no avail. He visited Lahr in prison and remained on friendly terms with him until the latter's death, paying him a last tribute in the obituary he wrote for *The Times*.[8]

Lahr promoted the careers of many young writers but if he can be said to have 'discovered' any it was doubtless Rhys Davies. He was the means by which the Welshman achieved the status of a writer with books to his name. Gathering the four stories that had appeared in *The New Coterie,* and adding three more – 'History', 'The Lily' and

'The Song of Songs' – Davies brought out his first collection, *The Song of Songs and Other Stories*, in 1927.[9] On the title-page the publisher is identified as E. Archer, Lahr's wife's maiden name; this to counter anti-German prejudice and for tax purposes. The drawing of Davies by William Roberts that had first appeared in *The New Coterie* was reproduced as a frontispiece.

> My carnal little stories were long-trousered productions, a Welsh mining valley their background, family avarice and brutal sex their themes. For some reason I knew how to arrive at a full stop; and now that I lived two hundred miles distant from the Rhondda the valley took on a form as restrictive as an urn's. I also gave some flesh tints to Anglo-Welsh writing, of which there was none except that of the savagely bleak Caradoc Evans.

These last remarks are percipient. As J. Lawrence Mitchell has pointed out,'Wales would be the clay with which he shaped creation; but to write about her, he needed the kind of perspective that only distance can bring.'[10]

It is known, moreover, that Davies had read *My People* (1915), the collection of stories with which Caradoc Evans had, in the words of Gwyn Jones in his lecture *The First Forty Years* (1957), 'flung a bucket of dung through the Welsh parlour-window, and in case anyone was genteel or well-meaning enough not to notice anything amiss, had flung the bucket in after, with a long-reverberating clangor', for a copy with his mother's name on the fly-leaf was kept among the books he treasured. The book is described in the *Companion to the Literature of Wales* (1998) as presenting an unsparing picture of a brutish peasantry, a debased religion and a grudging soil, in which the mainsprings of action are greed, hypocrisy and lust, and their consequences pain, misery and death... the book is probably the most powerful and unforgettable, as it was certainly the most notorious, collection of stories so far written by an Anglo-Welsh author.[11]

This, then, was the only model Davies had if he was going to be a Welsh writer, for he spurned the romances of Allen Raine and her imitators, and henceforth it was inevitable that he would be compared with Caradoc Evans.

Although there are significant differences between them, Evans was undoubtedly the Welsh writer to whom Davies was psychologically closest at this point in his writing life. He may not have had Evans's vitriolic turn of phrase, and wrote about the proletarians of South Wales rather than the agrarians of West Wales, but he possessed the same *saeva indignatio*, strove for the same economy of style and emulated his attempts at rendering the peculiarities of Welsh speech in English, at least in his early stories – as in this, a mild example, from the first page of 'A Gift of Death':

'A strict man was my father, Aunt Ann. Stricter than a preacher was he, and every day was a Sunday for him. Like a Sunday-school too he made life in this house. There's hated him I have sometimes. Mam was as bad also. A horrible life have I had between both of them.' And as Aunt Ann made sucking noises of distress in her teeth, she continued, 'The truth it is. Now that they are dead, judge them I can. An old maid they have made me, and no pleasures have I had. The Bible for breakfast, dinner and supper it's been. There's awful religion makes some people.' [12]

However picturesque, not to say outlandish, the effect may have seemed to English readers charmed by the Irish-inflected dialogue of J.M. Synge, with its inverted syntax, literally translated idioms, singsong rhythms, and so forth, this local colour can seem exaggerated and tedious now, especially to readers in Wales, who are understandably hyper-sensitive to what strikes them as attempts to present them as poetic simpletons. One of the most apoplectic of Welsh commentators, D. Tecwyn Lloyd, always a stern critic of Welsh writers in English, denounced this 'Welshified' English as an idiom not spoken anywhere on earth: *'Tu yma i'r sêr nid oes neb byw yn siarad fel yna'* ('From here to the stars no one alive talks like that').[13] Yet this way of speaking is no more grotesque than, say, the Nottinghamshire dialect of D.H. Lawrence. All the same, the clangor of Caradoc Evans's bucket was to reverberate in Welsh ears for a while yet.

Even as early as 1927 the comparison between Davies and Evans, and the question of whether either wrote about the Welsh 'as they really are', was troubling readers in Wales, many of whom expected absolute realism in the depiction of their countrymen. English readers, on the other hand, were oblivious to such considerations. While *The Times Literary Supplement* called *The Song of Songs* 'fresh and talented... marked by deep and controlled feeling', the *Western Mail*, which had been the prime mover in the denunciation of Caradoc Evans twelve years before, was rather more gentle, if guarded, in its response:

> Though the stories of Welsh life contained in this book are distinctly of the Caradoc Evans variety, showing to some extent the influence of that writer, they are yet the expression of a very different personality. Mr Caradoc Evans might easily have written some of the uglier tales had he been born in one of the industrial valleys of South Wales instead of rural Cardiganshire, but lacking Mr Davies's detachment, sense of humour, and broader sympathy, he (as we know him) could never have woven the story we have here of the woman who sickened for 'a big organ with a mirror in the middle and a little row of pipes each side, like the one I did see in a shop in Pontypridd last summer', or the yarn purporting to give the history of consumption of tripe in South Wales. Mr Davies, though merciless, is just. Those who have lived in the peopled valleys and have known the life intimately will have to admit that his pictures and suggestions of jealousy, avarice, and vanity are, unfortunately, founded on fact to a certain extent.[14]

Nevertheless, one of the stories, 'The Lily', was singled out for opprobrium in the Welsh press. It is, certainly, a savage tale about an innocent, simple-minded girl who is seduced by a Pentecostal minister; by the end the girl has gone mad, her child is dead, and the preacher has hanged himself.[15] The verdict on Rhys Davies delivered by the *South Wales News* was: 'It is a pity that such a fine craftsman should sometimes dabble with mud when his true material is marble.'

As for the charge that he wrote for the amusement of the English, one often levelled by Welsh-speakers against those of their countrymen whose work is done in *yr iaith fain* ('the thin language'), Davies responded:

> At first I felt myself a foreigner in London, more *en rapport* with European exiles there than with English people. I found among the English an indulgent dismissal of Wales. It was a country where visitors climbed the Northern mountains or, getting wet, stood admiring those impressive arrangements of earth's furniture. The native language was a joke. Among the middle-class Socialists I met there was a degree of interest in the crusades of the South Wales miners, and no knowledge of their domestic life. But nobody dreamt of taking a trip to those bitter and sweet parts... Otherwise, the Welsh, like the Scottish and Irish, were expected to be idiosyncratic and, better still, amusing.

So at least Davies was aware of what he called 'the ancient recoil' of many English people from things Welsh and of the dangers inherent in trying to depict his compatriots in fiction. Even so, it is a moot point whether his stories and novels encouraged what amounted to racial prejudice on the part of English readers.

With his first book of short stories now in print, Davies was ready to take his next big step as a writer by attempting a novel. It was through Charlie Lahr that he was introduced to 'a trio of idealistic young men down from Cambridge' who called their publishing imprint Robert Holden and Co. On production of a 10,000-word synopsis he was given a contract and an advance of fifty pounds for a novel to be entitled *The Withered Root,*[16] about the Evangelist Reuben Daniels, in which many of Davies's themes – the struggle between flesh and spirit in particular, with spirit always the heavy loser – were first adumbrated. The novel was soon completed and typed up by Lahr, to whom it was dedicated. In the same year, 1927, a veritable *annus mirabilis* for Davies, Lahr published his short story 'Aaron' in a limited edition aimed at the book collector's market.[17] The story received no notices but the novel, when it appeared in 1928, though not widely reviewed, was well received, most critics agreeing it was flawed only in the ways most first novels are flawed.

Its main character, based on Evan Roberts, leader of the Revival of 1904-05, is Reuben Daniels, a former miner, who strives to draw the Valleys' folk to God.[18] But disillusioned by the rootless, spiritless people to whom he ministers, he loses faith in himself and goes off with a sympathetic prostitute, only to collapse and die after struggling through mid-winter snow to his drunken mother's home. The emphasis throughout is on personal tragedy, not on the religious or political aspects of the story. Among the memorable minor characters are the educated, tubercular and highly literate Philip and his beautiful cousin Eirene Vaughan, the first of Davies's Flaubertian heroines. Stephen Knight detects early interest in D.H. Lawrence in this novel, but also, perhaps inevitably, the influence of Allen Raine, who also wrote about the Revival in *Queen of the Rushes* (1906). James

A. Davies says of the novel, 'Essentially, this is an anti-religious book, expressing the anger of the disappointed supplicant.'[19]

Flushed with the *succès d'estime* of his first novel, but remaining in his Manor Park lodgings, Davies decided now was the moment to give up gentlemen's outfitting and become a full-time writer. He had high hopes for an American edition of his novel and, while waiting for news from his agent Curtis Brown, found he had time on his hands. He was, in any case, tired and in a state of post-creative depression that he found hard to shake off. Deciding he needed a change of air, and with a little money in his pocket, he agreed to accompany Lahr, William Roberts, H.E. Bates and a few other associates on a trip to Germany, more specifically to visit Stein-bockenheim, the village near Bad Kreuznach in the Rhineland, where Karl had grown up. In the haphazard chronology of *Print of a Hare's Foot*, the trip is described as having taken place in the 1930s – the streets are swarming with Brownshirts and Hitler Youth – but in fact it was in August 1927.

The month they spent in Germany was uneventful except for a visit to a brothel sketched in unrevealing detail in *Print of a Hare's Foot*. After going upstairs with a woman of about forty whom he had selected at random, Davies records:

I knew almost no German. Everything went wrong. The substantial corset and frilly drawers, although fresh-laundered, upset me. Soon after their wearer had come into the room she asked for her pay. It was a very reasonable sum. I remained on a straight-backed chair at a table covered with a plush cloth. The bed looked spick-and-span. After tucking her money inside her corset-top, the woman opened an album of photographs on the table. There were staid family groups; she pointed to a photograph of a baby, then to between her thighs, and I understood the child was hers and she was obliged to support it. I lost all interest and remained at the table. Nonplussed, she fetched a short black whip from the back of an enormous picture hanging on the wall and made an inquiring gesture towards her behind. I shook my head... I tried to convey as gallantly as I could that I wanted nothing. She was not a whit put out.

Needless to say, the version of this episode recounted by Lahr to his daughter Oonagh years later was somewhat different: while the others were upstairs with the women of their choice, Davies had spent an hour drinking beer with the brothel's proprietor. Even this detail is suspect. Lahr, German peasant and womaniser that he was, did not like homosexuals, even though there were many among his associates, so Davies's account may be true after all. On the other hand, his sexuality may not have been apparent at this point and, even if it were, he was not letting on. In a letter he wrote to Lahr in 1929 he ended with congratulations on the birth of his second daughter Sheila, adding, 'My word, you'll be quite a family man now. I'm sure I'll be imitating you soon.' It was thus he kept up his pretence even with his closest associates.

Davies makes no mention of Lahr's claim that H.E. Bates, who at the time was in love with the woman he would later marry, declined the invitation to join the others in visiting the brothel, thus incurring Lahr's scorn and the soubriquet Master Bates. Nor is there any mention of the brothel visit in H.E. Bates's memoir *The Blossoming World* (1971), although he does give a full account of the lavish hospitality the visitors to Stein-Bockenheim were given by their hosts: 'For all the singing and rejoicing and dancing, I finally reached a point where I never wanted to see, let alone drink, a glass of hock again'. The bacchanalian scene is also the background for H.E. Bates's story 'A German Idyll', in which the narrator's eye is caught by a young woman called Anna who kisses him surreptitiously but whom he knows he will never see again.

On his return from Germany, Davies, reinvigorated by a change of scenery but once again with empty pockets, went back to Blaenclydach and 'the truly democratic Valley', as he always did when he was short of money. His attitude to his native patch was always a mixture of love and hatred and certainly his motivation in going back was as much economic as a return to the source of his material. On this occasion he was to stay for nearly a year in 'this mangy hole', as he described it to a friend in 1928, writing every day and building up a body of work that he would send to editors and publishers over the next decade. But as he waited for news from Curtis Brown his depression returned. Writing to Esther Lahr, he reported:

As you see, I'm in Wales trying to persuade myself that the country is doing me good... it's raining persistently now, the coal-dusty hills are all sopped with wet, the people are quite blank with poverty

...in the nights one seems to be sucked into a
cylinder of unutterable gloom. I shan't stay long
after my American advance arrives... but my people
are as chirpy as ever – fat, red-cheeked, always
eating and bickering with each other – it keeps
them alive.

Clearly, the well-fed Davieses were better off than their
neighbours in Blaenclydach. But there is no mention in
his correspondence of any friends, neighbours or other
shopkeepers in the village.

South Wales had changed during Davies's absence in
London. In the aftermath of the General Strike of 1926,
the miners had stayed out for another seven months until
their communities were bankrupted and they had been
virtually starved back to work in conditions worse than
before. The coal industry had suffered a sharp decline
from which it would not recover until the beginning of the
Second World War and 'the wreck of Rhondda', as Auden
described it in *New Year Letter* (1940), had become a
severely depressed area. These were the years when, in
the poet's words, 'Glamorgan hid a life / Grim as a tidal
rock-pool's in its glove-shaped valleys'.[20] At home things
were almost as bad. The Davieses, whose livelihood
depended on the miners, were on the verge of bankruptcy
and there seemed no prospect of their surviving as
shopkeepers. Davies had no social life and, apparently, no
friends with whom to while away the time, and very little
money of his own, the advance on his novel having gone
to pay for his trip to Germany. The only consolation was
that there was no distraction from his writing. He would
write in the morning, walk the dog in the afternoon, then

return to his desk in the evening. His sister typed up several of his stories – Davies never mastered the typewriter – and he persevered with that dogged determination that stood him in such good stead throughout his career.

Wales, he now thought, contained 'a fresh, abundant life of its own which needed expressing. But also I felt that Wales lived rather too much in her own past, an interior life which, though attractive up to a point, had the danger of stagnancy.' The primaeval tug Davies felt for Blaenclydach was beginning to slacken. After his parents and sister Gertie had visited him in London in 1928, he saw them off from Paddington with a feeling of relief. Writing to Charlie Lahr, he informed him:

> They've all gone back to Wales at last. I was glad to see the retreating back of my sister [Gertie]. She is particularly irritating. The worst of it is she's not like my other sister [Gladys], who obviously has no use for me and thus leaves me in peace – the one professes affection which she ferociously manifests as a sort of duty. Irritating! But they are all filled with horror at my intention to abandon all jobs except writing. Platitudes have been trotted out with ruthless zeal.

It may very well be that Davies, in his use of hyperbole to describe his family, was merely showing off to an English friend and making clear that he was no longer part of their culture. The truth is, he had been too much affected by London and the wider world he had entered to feel completely at home in the village or among his family ever again, even though, like Maupassant in Normandy, he was bound to the place as if by some umbilical cord. But whereas the Rhondda was economically depressed, the London of the 1920s was comparatively well-off and the capital's cultural life, particularly in theatreland, was as flourishing as ever. The metropolis held an attraction that he was unable to withstand. He now resumed the bohemian life in which, as a published author, he had found his place, and it had a liberating effect on him.

Even so, the small group of writers gathered around the Progressive Bookshop had begun to disperse and all were soon to go their own ways. Davies fell out with Liam O'Flaherty on account of a less-than-enthusiastic introduction he had written for one of the Irishman's collection of stories. Louis Golding, after the success of his novel *Magnolia Street* (1932), an immensely popular depiction of Jewish life, detached himself from the group. The friendship with Bates, not a metropolitan by nature, ended after an unfavourable review he wrote of one of Davies's books in 1932.

Only with Rupert Croft-Cooke, prolific novelist and friend and biographer of Lord Alfred Douglas, did Davies maintain anything like a steady relationship during the inter-war years. Though the Englishman was later to turn against the Welshman, describing him as 'cold and remote', they attended homosexual parties together in the late 1920s. In an uncharacteristic display of sentiment Davies wrote to Croft-Cooke in 1926: 'I stayed in yesterday and wrote a few pages of my new story, slept a little, ate, listened-in, thought of you, and went to bed early.' According to his brother Lewis, Davies – who although by his own admission did not know the term 'homosexual' until he went to London – was very promiscuous during his early years in the capital, after his discovery of its homosexual milieux. He was known to other men as Rhoda, an alias near enough to the name of the Valley about which he wrote so prolifically. If he was promiscuous, as his brother claimed, the names of his partners have not been recorded, because none lasted beyond the one-night stands and furtive encounters that were his preferred options.

Lewis Davies told the present writer that his brother may have been one of Croft-Cooke's many sexual partners – they had adjacent rooms at 90 High Holborn – but, if so, there is only one reference to him in the volume of Croft-Cooke's elegantly-written memoirs dealing with the 1930s:

> Rhys Davies was another [writer], known for his rather gloomy tales about people in South Wales who, as soon as they had come out of chapel behaved with a surprising lack of inhibition... He had already published two novels, *The Withered Root* and *Rings on her Fingers*, and had no time for exuberant anticipations. He was a dedicated writer, quite without panache, in his life as in his prose, quiet and fastidious. We had been friends since 1925 but though I was five months older than Rhys and had been abroad and ranged far in a number of directions while he had brought himself only from South Wales to London, he made me feel painfully adolescent, over-enthusiastic, talkative and egotistic. He was a splendid companion with a gentle cynicism and an innocent-seeming ribald sense of humour

which I found engaging. He was also generously ready to reveal trade secrets he had discovered, who was starting a new review for short stories, which publisher was looking for young writers and so on. Instead of working, all too often we would chatter the morning away, then if we could raise a shilling or two each, walk to the Nanking restaurant in Denmark Street for lunch. After that we would call to see Charles Lahr a few yards from Roy Hardy's flat and meet some of the strange literary jetsam to be found there and I would reflect that the little circle had grown seedier since its *New Coterie* days. We would make tea on a gas-ring and before either of us had done much work it would be time to go our separate ways for the evening. All very well for Rhys who could pick up a writing pad and sitting in an armchair do the next thousand words of a story without fuss.[21]

Two very close friends of Davies's in the early 1920s were a brother and sister, Geoffrey and Eve Kirk, to whom his second novel was dedicated. Eve, a painter and Junoesque beauty who sat for Augustus John, kept a studio in Fitzroy Square. Davies was a frequent visitor, and often stayed there during Eve's absences from London, thus starting a habit of living in rooms temporarily vacated by his friends as a way of saving on rent. Her brother is the figure disguised as Anthony in *Print of a Hare's Foot*. He and Davies went on a walking holiday in northern Italy, a trip fictionalised by Davies in the novel *Two Loves I Have* (1933), published under the pseudonym Owen Pitman.[22]

It was at one of Eve Kirk's parties that Davies first met Nina Hamnett, painter and 'Queen of Bohemia', described by Michael Bakewell as 'Fitzrovia's most notorious inhabitant'.[23] Sickert called her England's finest draughtsman but she preferred to squander her gifts socially rather than employ them artistically and drink was to be her undoing. In the autumn of 1928, learning that Davies was about to go to France on the American proceeds of *The Withered Root*, Hamnett gave him several useful addresses and sundry bits of advice. Thus equipped, with the trunk that held everything he owned and 'disciplined against pleasure', he set off for the South of France. It was there he was to meet the English writer he admired most.

Notes

1   *The London Magazine* (vol.1, no. 7, August 1954)

2   It was the poet Tambimuttu who claimed to have coined the name Fitzrovia, though it first appeared in print in the William Hickey gossip column written by Tom Driberg in *The Daily Express*.

3   'The City' was published in the magazines *transition* (June 1927) and *Wales* (21, December 1945). RD presented the collector Sir Louis Sterling with a holograph copy of 'The City', together with copies of four other poems: 'Hymn', 'Tea Party', 'Sigh' and 'Nocturne' (all four unpublished). Among Davies's manuscripts acquired by the Sterling Library, University of London, is an unpublished play in four acts, 'Eagle and Lamb'; see *A Catalogue of the Printed Books and Literary Manuscripts collected by Sir Louis Sterling and presented by him to the University of London* (privately printed, 1954).

4   The drawing by William Roberts is now owned by the Rhys Davies Trust.

5   Among the utopian aims of the Wobblies was the abolition
     of the wage-system and the introduction of a form of
     workplace democracy which would allow workers to elect
     their own managers.

6   See H.E. Bates, *An Autobiography* (Methuen, 2006), which
     includes *The Vanished World* (1969), *The Blossoming World*
     (1971) and *The World in Ripeness* (1972). For an account
     of Lahr's career see David Goodway, 'Charles Lahr:
     Anarchist, bookseller, publisher' in *The London Magazine*
     (June-July 1977) and Chris Gostick, *T. F. Powys's Favourite
     Bookseller: the Story of Charles Lahr* (Cecil Woolf, 2009).
     One of the best fictitious accounts of Lahr is to be found in
     the story 'Vicarage Party' by John Lindsey, a pseudonym of
     John St Clair Muriel.

7   In 1934 Lahr was a witness to Hugh MacDiarmid's second
     marriage to Valda Trevlyn Rowlands.

8   *The Times* (18 August 1971)

9   *The Song of Songs and other Stories* (E. Archer, 1927).
     Contents: 'A Gift of Death', 'The Sisters', 'Mrs Evans
     Number Six', 'History', 'The Lily', 'The Song of Songs'.
     Frontipiece portrait by William Roberts. An edition limited
     to 900 copies with a further 100 in a special binding and
     signed by the author.

10   J. Lawrence Mitchell, 'Home and Abroad: the Dilemma of
     Rhys Davies', in *Planet* (70, August/September 1988)

11   *The Oxford Companion to the Literature of Wales* (ed. Meic
     Stephens, Oxford University Press, 1986); up-dated edn.,
     The New Companion to the Literature of Wales (University
     of Wales Press, 1998); both were also published in Welsh-
     language editions as *Cydymaith i Lenyddiaeth Cymru*.

12   'A Gift of Death', in *The Song of Songs* (1927) and *Collected
     Stories of Rhys Davies* (ed. Meic Stephens, vol. 3, Gomer,
     1998)

13   *Barn* (December 1962). See also the *Western Mail*: 'A Novel
     of Wales: strange people and bad dialogue' (24 November

1927); T. Gwynn Jones, 'English as spoken in Wales: the dialogue of *The Withered Root* (3 December 1927); J.W., 'Welsh dialect and *The Withered Root*. Testing the literal translation' (8 December 1927); T. Gwynn Jones, '*The Withered Root* controversy. Cymricized English picturesque' (10 December 1927).

14 Undated clippings from the *Western Mail* found among the author's papers and now in the National Library of Wales.

15 It was this kind of writing that the poet Harri Webb, forty years on, would satirise in his poem 'Synopsis of the Great Welsh Novel', in which Blodwen is expecting Dai K's baby – 'there's been a Revival' – and the mad preacher Davies the Doom burns the chapel down: 'One is not quite sure / Whether it is fiction or not'.

16 *The Withered Root* (Robert Holden, 1927)

17 *Aaron* (E. Archer, 1927); privately printed in an edn. of 100 copies.

18 Evan Roberts (1878-1951), a native of Loughor in Glamorgan, evangelist and leader of a religious revival that swept through Wales in 1904 and 1905; the enthusiasm died away after he suffered a mental breakdown.

19 James A. Davies, '"Love... and the Need of it": three novels by Rhys Davies', in *Decoding the Hare*

20 W.H. Auden, poem 10 in 'Look, Stranger!' (Faber, 1936)

21 Rupert Croft-Cooke, *The Last of Spring* (Putnam, 1964). The author was a prolific writer of autobiography. In his memoir, *The Verdict of You All* (1955), he describes how he was gaoled for 'gross indecency'. He dedicated his collection of short stories, *A Football for the Brigadier* (1950), to RD.

22 Owen Pitman, *Two Loves I Have* (Jonathan Cape, 1933)

23 Nina Hamnett (1890-1956), painter and bohemian, a native of Tenby in Pembrokeshire, was one of the most colourful characters in Fitzrovia; see Denise Hooker, *Nina Hamnett: queen of bohemia* (Constable, 1986) and Michael

Bakewell, *Fitzrovia: London's Bohemia* (National Portrait Gallery, 1999). Hamnett wrote two volumes of memoirs: *Laughing Torso* (1932) and *Is She a Lady?* (1955).

Tom Davies, the writer's father, c. 1936

Jack Davies, the writer's brother, killed in action, 1918

Four

A visit to Lorenzo and Frieda

After spending two days in Paris, during which he picked up a young Swede and saw a performance of *Andromaque* at the *Comédie Française*, Rhys Davies left the Gare de Lyon for Nice, the eight-hour journey costing him the equivalent of about a pound. Unlike the consumptive Chekhov, who had made the journey south in 1891 in order to convalesce, Davies found the Mediterranean conducive to work, despite the temptations of culinary delights and blue-sky weather, for both of which he had a lifelong fondness. 'Novelists should be imprisoned, fairly comfortably, until their grind is completed,' he wrote in *Print of a Hare's Foot*:

> The azure and blond coast, with its beckoning drones, was a kingdom of Circe; there was an all-night bar near the railway station, rooms for short-term hire above it, which her swine would have recognized. But I worked; I had been reared in the hard Rhondda.

With the help of another pick-up, a monocled, wealthy, Goethe-reading flâneur of masochistic tendencies whom he called Ernst, Davies found a room for a pound a week in the centre of Nice at 16 rue Alberti, a *pension* kept by a Madame Franceschini, an Englishwoman addicted to heroin whom he disguised as Madame S in his book. The only distraction from the Stakhanovite's schedule was when, once a week, for exactly an hour, he heard the landlady, a married woman, in noisy congress with her lover in the next room: 'except to fiddle with commas, it was impossible for me to continue working during the performance'. But he was able to learn even from this unsettling experience:

> I began to see amost everybody and everything as a potential subject for a story... I tried not to be cold-blooded about this, however: the problem was to find the right seat for a detached view – not too far away, not too close.

Another irritant was an infestation of the crabs, a common name for the condition *phthiriasis pubis*, a parasitic invasion of the pubic hair that is usually spread by sexual intercourse, in this case after 'a lyrical night' with an unnamed partner. The ailment was treated by the ever-attentive Ernst with the flame of a match and jar of ointment, and after a few days the itching stopped. Shortly afterwards Davies was able to describe himself as 'physically on top of the world, and also rather sullied morally, for both of which I was grateful to the indulgent gods'.

No sooner had he settled in with Madame Franceschini

than he received an invitation to join Liam O'Flaherty and his wife at the Hôtel Beau Séjour in the village of La Colle-sur-Loup, in the Alpes Maritimes.[1] At first, things went well with the old friends, but the Irish writer was in the throes of writing a novel and increasingly oblivious to the presence of others. Finding herself at a loose end, the novelist's wife now turned her attentions to Davies, much to his alarm. Utterly masculine in demeanour and capable of forming close rapports with the opposite sex far more easily than with men, he was often to be troubled by women who perceived his friendliness as a prelude to something more. As he wrote to Lahr:

> Residence in La Colle, beautiful though the district is, taught me one or two things. First, I am not meant for village life; secondly, matrimonial squabbles are apt to become monotonous; thirdly, though I was never a very intense admirer of Liam O'Flaherty, I thought I liked him, but have now come to other conclusions; fourthly, I can't allow myself to be used as an iron from which to strike the spark of jealousy.

It was to be thirty years before Davies quarried a story from the interlude in La Colle: in his collection *The Darling of her Heart* (1958) the story 'Tears, Idle Tears' gives a thinly fictionalised version of the episode.[2] 'Women,' Davies confessed wearily to his brother Lewis in old age, 'have been the main problem in my life', a richly ambiguous remark if ever there was one.

After two months or so, the novels he was working on in Nice, namely *Rings on her* Fingers[3] and *The Red Hills*,[4] were beginning to drag. Then, out of the Mediterranean blue, there came a letter that was to fill him with wonder and excitement. The address was given as Hôtel Beau Rivage in Bandol, and it said:

> Dear Rhys Davies,
> Mr Lahr sent me your address. Would you care to come here and be my guest in this small and inexpensive hotel for a few days? Bandol is about 20 minutes on the Marseilles side of Toulon: 20 minutes from Toulon. My wife and I would be pleased if you came. I'm not sure quite how long we shall stay here – but anyhow ten days.
> Sincerely,
> D.H. Lawrence

The idea that Lawrence, the pre-eminent English novelist of his day, and idolized by the young, should want to meet a Welsh writer who had only just started out, was astonishing. Lawrence and Lahr had never met but they had been in contact ever since *The New Coterie* published Lawrence's story 'Sun' in its fourth number in 1926, and Lahr had told him of Davies's proximity. The Welshman had bought and read *The Rainbow* and *Women in Love*, and been overwhelmed by them; he wrote to Lahr to thank him for making the introduction.

A week later, Davies took the train along the coast to join Lawrence in Bandol:

> Besides this exciting opportunity to meet the great man I longed, after two months among the flotsam of Nice, to talk to someone authentically English.

Such work of Lawrence's as I knew glowed with the true puritanism of England... He had become a legendary figure bathed in messianic thunder-light and crying aloud, sometimes incoherently, of the deceit, falseness and dangers of the apparently victorious after-war years. He was a kind of John the Baptist in a wilderness. And there he was fifty miles away in quiet Bandol.

It is clear that Davies showed more enthusiasm about the prospect of meeting Lawrence than he did for any other writer among his acquaintances. In fact, he rarely expressed much enthusiasm for the work of any of his contemporaries, except for James Joyce – not as the author of *Ulysses*, for he deplored experiment in the novel, but for Joyce's masterpiece, the story 'The Dead', which Davies claimed to have read every winter. As for *Finnegans Wake*, it was 'beyond my simple, Bible-educated mind,' he told Charlie Lahr. Davies also mocked the work of Gertrude Stein: 'The one advantage of Gertie's stuff is that it can be read backwards just as well.'

He was to make the journey from Nice to Bandol three times that summer, staying in the room at the Beau Rivage that Katherine Mansfield had been given in 1918. There he built a relationship with Lawrence founded on a genuine but guarded liking for the man and a professional admiration for him as a writer. At the same time he was wary of the English novelist's incandescent rage and warmly appreciative of the common sense and aristocratic hauteur that his wife Frieda brought to the often fraught atmosphere at the Beau Rivage.[5]

The portrait of Lawrence in the chapter entitled 'The Bandol Phoenix' in *Print of a Hare's Foot* is a finely drawn and moving record of a writer at the height of his fame but soon to die from tuberculosis. At first the meeting was placid enough. The two had a good deal in common. Both had been raised in a pit village and both had attended a Congregational chapel. Both their mothers had been uncertificated pupil-teachers; what is more, Lawrence's mother had kept a shop in the front room of his birthplace, 8a Victoria Street, Eastwood, just like the Davieses at 6 Clydach Road, Blaenclydach. Both mothers had been major influences on their adolescent sons and had ambitions for them beyond the confines of their class. Both writers had grown up in households dominated by women, with their fathers taking a secondary place in their affections. Both had been marked out as 'different' and had kept themselves to themselves. Both had grown up as outsiders. Both had lost beloved brothers. Both had discovered that their loneliness could be assuaged by art and literature and their mastery of the English language. Both had borrowed books to feed their imaginations, Davies from the Miners' Institute Library in Blaenclydach, Lawrence from the Mechanics' Institute in Eastwood. Both men, moreover, had taken flight through art and the intellect from the communities that had bred them but which they needed as material for their books. Both felt out of place in the literary world of London. Both made the exercise of power the key component in sexual relations. For both, writing was their life and their life, writing. The description of Lawrence by his biographer John Worthen is equally true of Davies:

Becoming a writer would eventually be Lawrence's way of leaving the past and its attachments behind; of breaking out, understanding and being independent while still constantly recreating in his writing the mining village, his family, its tensions and concerns. He would, so to speak, come home repeatedly in his writing, acknowledging how intimately he belonged to his family and its quarrels and its loving mother, even as he wrote his way out of it (declaring that he rejected any idea of home, or love, and hated Eastwood and the past).[6]

Davies was aware of Lawrence's background and it must have made it easier for him to establish a rapport almost immediately.

But two hours into their meeting the paranoid Lawrence began, as was his wont, to rail against the young, who in his view were not doing enough to smash the old world, and their elders, whom he accused of shutting their minds to the voice of the spirit: 'All you young writers have *me* to thank for what freedom you enjoy, even as things are – for being able to say much that you couldn't even hint at before I appeared. It was *I* who set about smashing down the barriers'. The unbridled fury of the man would have made many tremble but Davies took it in his usual calm, unruffled way. Nor was he put out when Lawrence would not believe him on hearing the younger man say how much Lawrence was respected by his generation.

Then, the rant over, they settled down to talk business, specifically about *Lady Chatterley's Lover*, which was probably the real reason why Lawrence had invited Davies to Bandol. The novel was available at that time only in an expensive edition of a thousand copies published by Pino Orioli in Florence. It was being widely pirated in Paris, and Lawrence was anxious to see a popular edition, both to staunch the piracy and to give the book a wider circulation. The novelist asked Davies whether he thought Charlie Lahr would bring out a cheap edition in London. Lahr, when approached, replied that his legal status in England was too precarious to make *Lady Chatterley's Lover* a possibility for him. Because his German citizenship had lapsed and he had not taken British citizenship, he was a stateless person: he would therefore be in danger of deportation in the event of an obscenity trial. He did, however, agree to distribute copies of the novel and he published an unexpurgated edition of Lawrence's poems, *Pansies*, in 1929. Although the poet was in due course disappointed by its typography, he appreciated Lahr's pluck and energy. He thought him 'very good and absolutely honest' and if 'a wee bit of a muddler, and careless in details, he is a man in ten thousand'. It was Davies who agreed to carry a complete manuscript of *Pansies* to London, running the gauntlet of Customs and the risk of prosecution. An incomplete set of the poems had previously been seized by the postal authorities on grounds of indecency:

There was nothing in this incomplete set of the poems, or in later additional ones, that could be construed as indecent by a normal person; there were merely some bits of plain speaking in good household English.

Despite getting on well with Lawrence, Davies at first found him puritanical, 'chapel-English', irritable and malicious about other writers, and reproachful when the Welshman told a risqué story. He was disappointed, too, when Lawrence referred to Chekhov as 'a second-rate writer and a willy wet-leg', which was blasphemous in Davies's view. But with his unfailing powers of observation, he saw the Englishman clearly enough: 'Within the charm and vitality lay a seductive despotism.' Nor did he take him seriously as a socialist:

> Lawrence, a collier's son, seemed to be no socialist – at least, not in a political sense. His old dream of a community of choice spirits living in some untarnished place (with, of course, himself as ordained leader) surely held the world's welfare at heart from a safe distance?

He was not even sure Lawrence liked him at first: 'I think he judged me prosaic and too rational.' More serious was the incident that took place one morning after Davies had met Frieda Lawrence by chance and gone with her to a café for apéritifs, returning late for lunch at the Beau Rivage. Lawrence threw a tantrum, the only occasion on which Davies was caught in the crossfire of the stormy marriage; it subsided, however, almost as quickly as it had begun.

Frieda, too, had not taken to Davies immediately. 'We have a friend here, a young writer, quite nice and faithful,' Lawrence wrote to his mother-in-law. 'First Frieda did not like him because he's not beautiful, but now she thinks him quite good-looking and she likes him.' At dinner in the

Beau Rivage restaurant one evening, Lawrence used the word 'fuck' in conversation with Frieda, which made Davies look around to see whether any of the English people among the diners had heard. It was not long before Davies found himself on the friendliest of terms with Frieda, as he often did with women. The incident that had made Lawrence so angry occurred soon after Frieda's infidelity with Angelo Ravalgi, who would become her third husband, and it is possible that Lawrence felt his wife was up to something with their visitor, but was not quite certain what. As usual, the fact of Davies's homosexuality was being kept from those who thought they knew him.

Some critics, such as Richard Aldington and Middleton Murry, doubtless influenced by the Freudianism that hung in the air of the 1920s, saw Lawrence's rages as evidence of repressed homosexuality. Ever since his youth in Eastwood some had discerned a 'girlish' streak in him. Rhys Davies was at once a more intimate and less crass witness, neither a disciple nor a detractor of Lawrence, and his impressions are perhaps the closest we can ever come to an objective assessment of a man who, after Freud, was probably the greatest influence on ideas about sexuality in the twentieth century. It may very well be, too, that Davies's less than macho manner was found attractive by Lawrence.

The worst Davies would say of Lawrence was, 'Crotchety in a schoolmasterish way though he was at times, he seldom irritated me,' although he did admit this much:

One idiosyncrasy of his became tedious: an insistence on a belligerent kind of masculinity was a foible apt to display itself gratuitously at any moment. Surely, I thought, one took a hairy-chest quality in a man for granted – or not, if it just wasn't there. A forced he-manship was tiresome. Was Lawrence over-aware of the element of feminine sensibility he possessed so definitely (and which was so valuable to him as a novelist)?... It was his depiction of masculinity in his novels and stories, especially those with a coal mining background, that had led me to expect, naively, a tough, louring person waiting for me on Bandol station; instead I found someone fine-grained, a light-footed man of high-bred quality, a man clear of class-consciousness and other preposterous blockages to esteem and understanding. Patience was needed for his foible. The same schoolyard insistence on masculinity mars some of the work of Ernest Hemingway. Men novelists cannot afford to be 100 per cent male.

There is a curious coda to Davies's visit to Lorenzo and Frieda. When, during the 1960s, there began to be widespread speculation as to whether and to what extent Lawrence was homosexual, Davies became very agitated in the presence of a young Welsh friend, Graham Samuel.[7] He told him he had been in close proximity to Lawrence and had on one occasion, in Paris and in the absence of Frieda, shared a bed with him and that, in his estimation, Lawrence had no homosexual inclinations whatsoever, a view confirmed by all the novelist's biographers. John Worthen, the most reliable of them, concluded that despite his liking for the company of men with whom he could talk as intellectual equals, he was definitely not homosexual. Brenda Maddox suggests that, in inviting Davies to visit him in Bandol, he may simply have wanted a young protégé and a new buffer against the formidable Frieda, or that he may have been indulging in a bit of flirtation that he knew would irritate his wife.[8] Either way, as a successful novelist, he could now summon people when he wanted their company and he liked especially looking after the young. Clearly, he had taken a shine to young Davies in whom he recognized so much of his younger self.[9]

After six months in the South of France, Lawrence and Davies took a trip to Paris in May 1929. Frieda had gone to see her mother in Germany and Lawrence was still hankering after finding a publisher who would bring out a popular edition of *Lady Chatterley's Lover*. Davies willingly agreed to accompany him to Paris, his expenses paid by Lawrence. Writing to Aldous Huxley, then living on the city's outskirts, to inform him of their imminent arrival, Lawrence described the Welshman as 'by no means thrilling or dazzling. I expect you and Maria will think him unspeakably pedestrian – but he's no fool really, and one can be quiet with him – he's not nervy or nerve-racking.' This last comment may be taken as a guarded reference to the tiffs Lawrence regularly had with his wife. 'It was ugly sometimes this awful quarrelling,' she wrote in her foreword to *The First Lady Chatterley*:

We might have spared ourselves and used a little common sense, but we did not. We took it all so very seriously. Sometimes I meant to say something spiteful and he did not notice it. Then, I would say something I thought harmless and he flew into a rage. But I could always be completely myself with him. He had no preconceived, fixed idea of what a wife should be. I was I and if I was at times perplexing, then that was that.[10]

Davies, in any case, knew better than to take sides between husband and wife, and his presence seemed to have had a calming influence on the bickering couple. But his powers of observation enabled him to make some telling points. A number of them were ostensibly about the Lawrences but a few harked back to his own experience at Royal Stores:

> Frieda did not impose on her husband, ill though he was, that female bossiness, that stealthy overpowering need to subjugate, which women, crying to themselves that they are doing a man good, can wind round him in oppressive folds.[11]

Lawrence and Davies took adjoining rooms at the Grand Hôtel de Versailles, 60 Boulevard Montparnasse, for nearly a month. They visited Sylvia Beach at Shakespeare and Co, the famous bookshop at 12 rue de l'Odéon, where she had published the first edition of Joyce's *Ulysses*, but she could not be persuaded to risk prosecution by bringing out *Lady Chatterley's Lover*. By now Lawrence was seriously ill and needed constant attention. During the hours he was free from looking after him, Davies strolled among the *bouquinistes* on the banks of the Seine and, his French still 'very vague', did some sightseeing. He was disapponted by the Mona Lisa and wrote a poem entitled 'Louvre', one of the last he was ever to write.[12]

All the while, as Lawrence's health deteriorated, Davies served as his companion and nurse.

> But his nights became restless; often I woke to his coughing and writhing in the next room. One night, instinctively, but half asleep, I hurried through the communicating door and found him as though in mortal combat with some terrible invisible opponent who had arrived in those mysterious dead hours that follow midnight. The dark tormented face and haggard body was like some stormy El Greco figure writhing on the bed... Alarmed, I suggested a doctor and went towards the telephone. But at once he flew into anger. No, he would not have a doctor. But if I would sit quietly by the bed for a while... I think he needed the aid of some human presence. Soon he was calmer, lay back exhausted, unspeaking but triumphant. The opponent had gone.

Davies kept Frieda appraised of her Lorenzo's health and she thanked him for his solicitude: 'Lawrence says you are so nice with him. I can't remember that he ever said it of anybody else!'

During his stay at the Hôtel de Versailles, Davies's mother and eldest sister Gertie came to see him – their first trip abroad. His mother had refused to read any of his work since the appearance of 'The Sisters', his second published story, and was highly censorious of Lawrence who had been pilloried in the popular press as a sex-fiend.[13] But both women soon succumbed to his charm and they hit it off immediately.

Lawrence also gave encouragement to the younger man,

offering advice and contacts with a view to furthering his career, even volunteering to review his books. In return, Davies introduced Lawrence to P.R. Stephensen, an Australian who ran the Mandrake Press, which would publish an edition of *Pansies* in 1929.[14] Stephensen, later one of the leaders of the proto-fascist Australia First movement, was to write a book about Jorgen Jorgensen, *The Viking of Van Diemen's Land* (1954), which owed something to Davies's *Sea Urchin* (1940). In the same year, 1929, the Mandrake Press, as a *quid pro quo*, also published Davies's novella *A Bed of Feathers*.[15] The reviewer in *The New Age*, after accusing Davies of having read too much Lawrence, dismissed him as 'the highbrow's Elinor Glyn', which made him smart. Elinor Glyn, the Jackie Collins of her day, was the pioneer of erotic women's fiction for the mass-market whose sensational romances had a tremendous influence on popular culture in the early twentieth century; she it was who coined the word 'IT', meaning sex appeal. The jibe struck at the heart of Davies's view of himself as one who aspired to be a serious writer whose work had literary merit.[16]

It is as well to note that Lawrence was not entirely approving of Davies's work. He had read *The Withered Root* and thought it 'weird', though he did not elaborate on what he meant. His advice to the impressionable young Welshman was:

What the Celts have to learn and cherish in themselves is that sense of mysterious magic that is born within them, the sense of mystery, the dark mystery that comes with the night especially, when the moon is due, so that they start and quiver, seeing her rise over the hills, and get her magic in their blood. They want to keep that sense of the magic mystery of the world, a moony magic. That will shove all their nonconformity out of them.

This moonshine, typical of a certain English view of the Welsh ever since Matthew Arnold's emphasis on 'Celtic magic', chimed in the impressionable young Welshman's mind with his admiration for Dr William Price of Llantrisant.[17] At the same time, he knew that Lawrence had been to Wales just once, and only to Llangollen at that.

By the end of his six months in France, Davies longed for Wales and London: 'One can suddenly get one's fill of a foreign country, its alien chatter and food, its bad habits and shortcomings, and I did not care for Parisians as much as for the southerners.' After a last meal with the Lawrences, at which neither he nor the Englishman made any fond farewell, he was glad to be going home to Blaenclydach: 'I could never settle "abroad" myself.' Lawrence's suggestion that Davies edit a new satirical magazine to be called *The Squib* was deftly set aside.

The draw which Blaenclydach had on Davies at this time was expressed by Penry, his *alter ego* in the autobiographical novel *To-morrow to Fresh Woods*:

He was glad to be back. Glad not to have yielded to the Mediterranean temptation again, with its sunny drag. Glad to be away from the studio chatter, the café conferences over the world's problems, the midnight parties, the Parisian terrace talk of art, art, art and the unanchored decorative women and the rootless men. Glad to have cut away from the cerebral love affairs, the communism, and the restless search for a security which could not exist in these years. The old defeatist pain was defeated here [in Blaenclydach]. Here was tough homespun. If its pattern was plain, it was also real. He felt that a period had closed for him. The 'wild oats' period, he supposed. But he did not feel a prodigal son. And there had been some glory, for himself at least if not for others.

Even so, Davies's admiration for Lawrence remained undimmed and they continued to write to each other like old friends. In the autumn of 1929 Davies told him he would soon be going with Lahr on their annual visit to the home in West Chaldon of the reclusive T.F. Powys, whose novel *Mr Weston's Good Wine* (1927) he admired greatly. The trip ended in a car-crash that left Davies with two broken ribs, prompting a letter from Lawrence in which he wrote, 'I believe ribs aren't important – witness Eve.' To convalesce, Davies spent a few weeks on the coast near Genoa, the setting of his pseudonymous novel, *Two Loves I Have* (1933).

It was at a newspaper stand outside the British Museum that Davies read of Lawrence's death in a sanatorium near Vence on the 3rd of March 1930. Poignantly, only a few days previously he had written to Frieda telling her Lawrence must greet the spring triumphantly as before and reminding her of the day they had taken a trip into the countryside and found the first anemones. She replied:

No, you won't make him a chaplet of anenomes any more, but anenomes crown his grave now. His death was so simple and somehow great, his courage in facing death and fighting inch by inch and then at the end asking for morphia. He looked so proud, so beyond all these silly ugly dogs barking, so unconquered when he was dead. I know you grieve too.

It was to be many years before Davies would write Lawrence out of his system and he resolved to do so with his usual steely determination. A complete set of the English writer's novels, stories and essays remained among the books he left at his death.

On his return to Britain in 1929, Davies was again penniless. He had published little in the previous two years and had a huge backlog of unpublished work. Even so, it seems a whiff of his literary reputation had blown as far as Blaenclydach. Writing to Charlie Lahr, he reported:

The *Western Mail* published a paragraph about me the other day and mentioned I was home. That day three reporters called here for interviews, and one of the evening papers here had a column or so with photo and containing a lot of inaccuracies... I had a letter from some religious bloke who is organizing a bazaar for his church in a place near here – asking could I give him a signed copy of my novel for the Royal Stall (for which Queen Mary has given something or other)! 'As one of our great Welshmen I appeal to you,' he continues oilily and concludes that he hopes I'll have good health to continue my 'great work'. What a joke! Especially after the evening paper [the *South Wales Echo*] printing what I said about 'horrible Welsh religious hysteria'.

While Davies was uncomfortable with the label 'working-class writer', and any other label for that matter, he had a natural sympathy with the conditions of the workers' lives. In a feature published in the *Western Mail* he was quoted as saying:

> I have been brought to task for my apparent 'cruelty' to the working classes, but that is the last thing I would wish to be, for my sympathy with the Welsh proletariat is very real and very deep. I do feel, however, that there are in Wales phases of life and types of humanity so raw and crude that if one writes of them with sincerity, one might easily appear cruel.[18]

Davies's use of the word 'proletariat', which was not in widespread use in 1927, shows that he must have been aware of Marxist terminology. But the charge that he was not a writer of the working class lingered for many years thereafter. B.L. Coombes, for example, himself a miner and author of *These Poor Hands* (1939), must have had him in mind when, in a BBC broadcast in 1947, he said:

> If you, a working-class writer, leave the valleys and live for one year away from them... their lives and their thoughts will fade from among your closest memories, and in that interval many fresh problems

will have arisen, which you know nothing about.
Many a working-class writer has been ruined by
going away from the only life he knows anything
about, and trying to live on his mental capital. You
won't catch me leaving my valley.

Once again wintering in Blaenclydach, Davies now set
about making approaches to London publishers. The
1930s were to be a busy time for him, for he published
twenty-two books during the decade. The reader for Victor
Gollancz had turned down *Rings on her Fingers* but
reporting to Davies's agent Curtis Brown on his next
novel, *The Red Hills,* he wrote:

> I feel the man has a future; but I don't find in these
> two the touch of genius which would tempt me to
> publish a good deal which, though perfectly bona
> fide, would certainly make an appeal to the sort of
> public I don't want to cultivate.

The reader was almost certainly referring to the erotic
content of these books, the elements that had prompted
The New Age to call Davies 'the highbrow's Elinor Glyn'.
Davies's rejection by Gollancz drew from him the
comment that it was

> a nasty smack in the mouth of the small but select
> public that seems to get pleasure out of my books!
> Snubbed by Mr Gollancz, the publisher of Sarah Salt
> and Isadora Duncan. Dear, Dear! This is what comes
> of being the Elinor Glyn of the highbrows.

There were times when Davies wanted to be seen as a writer of literary merit, and others when he longed to write best-sellers.

His second novel *Rings on her Fingers* appeared in both a British and an American edition in June 1930. It was the first fully-drawn portrait of the headstrong woman who would henceforth be predominant in his fiction. Essentially a study of marriage, it deals mainly with the vicious effect a monotonous existence in a mining community closely resembling Pontypridd has on a young woman of romantic inclinations. Davies's sojourn in France had no doubt helped steer his imagination along Flaubertian lines, for like Emma Bovary, Edith Stevens seeks relief in her intense and violent way, only to be further disillusioned. The daughter of a large, impoverished family living in squalid circumstances, Edith determines at all costs to escape, but it is left to her husband, an effete little man with the occupation of a draper and the soul of a very minor poet, to effect it. The novel is partly set in a seaside town on the coast of South Wales called Cawl, that was doubtless meant to stand for Porthcawl, Davies's favourite resort – though '*cawl*', a word for sea-kale, also means 'soup' or, more colloquially, 'a mess', in modern Welsh. The novel is a description of the conflict that goes on in her mind between the desire for comfort and security, which her husband satisfies, and the desire for a life of stormy sensuality, symbolized for her in the person of a passionate, high-principled Socialist who spurns her advances. Although Edith, with her 'horrible calculating anguish', is a woman who might well do anything, she is led inexorably to a climax that is, to say the least of it, implausible. Although far from pleasant, the book was saved from the tragic gloom suggested by its setting and theme by a vein of humour and more than a pinch of delicious malice. Those who know Pontypridd may find the novel's setting somewhat odd, but Davies carries off the incongruity with panache.

Before 1930 was out, Davies's *Tale*[19] was published by Charlie Lahr as a Blue Moon booklet and his novella, *The Stars, the World, and the Women,*[20] also appeared. The main character in the latter is Bryn Watts, a bookish collier who is bullied into a middle-class way of life which eventually kills him after he revolts against his wife's tyranny. The novella is a good example of Davies's critique of the Wales he had recently left, in that gender and class are seen as integral parts of a working-class Nonconformist respectability that aspires to middle-class mores. Liam O'Flaherty, who introduced the book, gave high praise to Davies:

> He is a poet, with passion and a fine judgement. I believe that his story *A Bed of Feathers* is one of the finest things written since the war. He has now been writing a number of years, yet the general public has taken no particular notice of him... What I fear is this. If Rhys Davies does not get the appreciation he deserves soon, he may be driven by gross bodily needs to becoming a literary critic, a reviewer, or an essayist, or a publisher's reader.

This was meant to be encouraging, but when a selection of the Irishman's stories, under the title *The Wild Swan and Other Stories,* came to be included in the series two years later, Davies, who was never a back-scratcher, called one of them, 'unclean', 'sour and sordid… too bald and definite in its squalor to become literature'. These remarks did nothing to heal the rift between the two writers. In later life Davies remembered O'Flaherty as 'a rather grand figure', who was already well known as the author of *The Informer*, but he nevertheless thought him to be 'like many Irishmen, witty but without humour'. Their friendship, already strained by events in the South of France, abruptly ended.

Several of Davies's early books were published in limited, signed editions, a fashion that lasted throughout the 1930s and seemed to be coterminous with the vogue for little literary magazines. Davies commented:

> There was a period craze for 'private press' limited editions of a story – tarted-up productions, each copy numbered and signed by the author and 'collected' by abnormal customers who were blissfully unconcerned with the text. To be paid twenty pounds or so for a hundred signatures seemed dotty, though welcome, to me. I plodded on.

His main patrons at this time were the Kirks, Geoffrey and Eve, who gave him meals and a place to stay at their comfortable home in Hampshire whenever they were needed. He dedicated *Rings on her Fingers* to them. Another wealthy patron was the minor novelist Sarah Salt, who dedicated her novel *The Wife* (1932) to Davies. Frieda Lawrence took him to visit Lady Ottoline Morrell on one of her famous Thursdays in Gower Street, where they were well received. Such a visit presented opportunities for Davies, who, if he had been career-minded, might easily have inveigled his way further into the Bloomsbury set, but he did not take them. Hilary Spurling describes Bloomsbury as

a small, self-conscious and inward-looking society of intellectuals, waspish, hard-up and far from smart, almost all single and sexually on the make, fascinated by and madly curious about each other's ages, clothes, looks, incomes, sexual inclinations and changes of partner.[21]

Being both working-class, at least as far as their perceptions went, and homosexual, though not in manner, Davies might have been ideally suited to inherit the mantle of D.H. Lawrence. Although derided by some and praised by others by reason of their snobbery, Bloomsbsury was, after all, an important nexus of constructive and creative influence on English taste between the wars.[22] But the Welshman did not warm to literary circles, preferring to train his camera-like eye over his associates without ever wanting to join them.

Money was still scarce. In 1931 he and a few other writers, including A.E. Coppard, appeared in *The Georgian Confession Book,* a meretricious production consisting mostly of blank pages in which participants were asked to write answers to a series of trite questions about themselves.[23] Though the motive was entirely trivial, Davies's responses are interesting for the light they throw on his life at this time. To the question 'What is your worst fault?' he replied, 'Thinking the best of people'. His favourite recreation was 'music or darning socks, both being soothing to an irritable mind'; his life's greatest

118

sorrow was 'that I am not a painter'; his favourite poem was Blake's 'Ode to Spring', his favourite book the Old Testament, his favourite character in fiction Anna Karenin, his favourite food and drink, Welsh broth and beer; his ideal, '£500 a year' – though he did not add 'and a room of one's own', Virginia Woolf's precondition for a writer's life. The book, the purpose of which it is now difficult to divine, was published by Foyles, who in the same year issued a handsome limited edition of *Arfon,* an extended short story by Davies that had first taken the title *Aaron*, perhaps the most perfectly realised of his early work.[24] In the same year *A Woman* appeared, which became the opening of his novel, *Count your Blessings* (1932), and *The Woman among Women,* published by the ever-supportive Charlie Lahr.[25] [26]

As the Foyles compendium demonstrated, Davies was good at writing laconically about himself when the occasion demanded. A biographical note found among his papers lists, *inter alia*, some of his phobias: 'Taking a lease on a house or flat. The prospect of settling down. The thought of frontiers becoming difficult to cross. Hospitals. Prisons.' His contribution to *Ten Contemporaries: notes towards their definitive bibliography* was a little less lapidary but still provocative. In an article entitled 'Writing about the Welsh', he begins:

It is not a pleasant job to write stories of Welsh people. Writing in English, one is published in London and one has to battle with the ancient recoil of the English from Welsh life. Across the border, in Wales, books – and especially novels – are looked upon as frivolous unnecessary things that cost money to obtain, that frequently encourage sin and blasphemy and provoke indolence, that sometimes even dare to criticise the purity of Welsh life. There, who needs a book beyond the Bible?... So the sight of a Welshman buying a book is as rare as a Jew arrested for drunkenness.[27]

He then eulogises his compatriots, though many of his compliments treat them as little more than children who have been kissed by the fairies:

The Welsh are still bucolic and simple, they still have their priceless Celtic sense of wonder, they are still beautifully child-like, with a child's love of fantasy – i.e. their worship of death, the world of supreme fantasy – and a child's antics, often immoral and shocking. There is no decadence in Wales. Life there is lived with the bright and hard colouring, and the definite simple principles of conduct, which one sees in a child's picture book. There are rogues and ogres, true, there is scandalous behaviour. But the Celtic simplicity and wonder is over all.

The article ends:

The life of their fairyland must not be told outside or to foreigners like the English. Alas, that there should be traitors like myself! But I cannot help myself – my passion for Wales, her beauty, her individuality, her quality of perpetual youth, her struggle to keep herself uncontaminated of industrial

blights, must be expressed, in the only way I know
– words – and as truthfully as I am able.

The same statement of Davies's attitude towards his
homeland and his aim as a writer also appeared in *The
Literary Digest* for 1947 and 'the Celtic sense of wonder'
would become one of his favourite phrases when writing
about the Welsh.[28]

Davies returned to more serious work in 1931 when he
published, under the title *A Pig in a Poke,* a collection of
his short stories that had appeared in magazines and
limited editions.[29] It includes the famous story 'Revelation'
in which Gomer Vaughan, a young collier, delivering a
message to the home of the pit's middle-class engineer, is
astonished when the man's wife, who is half-French, comes
to the door stark naked. Since Gomer has never seen his
own wife in this marvellous state, the apparition works
wonders for his marriage and turns out to be a life-
enhancing experience for them both. Gomer, like Davies,
yearns for a more open world in which the body and its
impulses can be taken as natural; Gomer's wife, too,
comes to a new awareness of her sexuality, with 'a slow
and wondering dawn in her eyes'. The book was followed
by *Daisy Matthews and Three Other Tales* (1932), an
elegant production by the Golden Cockerel Press that
includes, besides the eponymous story, 'The Wanderer',
'The Sleeping Beauty' and 'Lovers', some superb wood
engravings by Agnes Miller Parker. Over the years, and
despite his misgivings, Davies went on allowing his work
to appear in limited editions of this kind.

Mainstream success still eluded him, however. Having
set out to earn his living by his pen, the idea of a career

in which he would be published only on fugitive imprints and by companies with no access to the mass market, a prospect that had seemed so attractive while he was under Lawrence's influence, was beginning to pall. He began to feel the Welsh character of his stories militated against commercial success and that, in any case, the novel was not an art form which found particular favour in the England of the day. After writing *Count Your Blessings*, set partly in the Rhondda and partly in a discreet brothel in suburban Cardiff, he would choose Italy as the setting of his next novel.[30]

It must have been galling for Davies that his first book from a mainstream publisher, Putnam, was so poorly received. But worse was to come. R.L. Mégroz, a short-story writer who had been associated with *The New Coterie*, was commissioned by Gilbert Fabes to write a critical sketch of him. Unfortunately, Mégroz, with whom Davies was invited to collaborate in the writing of the monograph, took exception to both *Tale* and *Count Your Blessings*. It is difficult now to read either work as 'shocking' but Mégroz was certainly shocked, ending his little book thus:

> He is still young, moreover, and if he has responded to some of the invidious influences belonging to our epoch, that is not a damning fact for a writer with a future that looks so promising as his. One can believe, fervently, that he will not enter the field at present occupied mainly by some women writers, and give us sentimental pornography which passes the censor but is much more repulsive than the banned work of our Joyces and Lawrences.[31]

Mégroz was not the only critic to see Davies's book in a negative light. H.E. Bates thought he had real talent but disliked his latest work so much that he tried to get out of reviewing it. Eventually he wrote an uncomplimentary review for the magazine *Everyman*:

> Lawrence, having suffered much, began to look at the world with bitterness, writing of it with sneers and in an anguish of wrath. Mr Davies, twenty years younger, fancies he can do the same, though he cannot have suffered as Lawrence did. The result is that there is nothing in *Count Your Blessings* which is externally or spiritually beautiful, and little that is original.

Lahr sent the review to Davies in Blaenclydach but the Welshman was unimpressed:

> Master Bates has had his opportunity at last. It's nice to have his tribute. The only thing that's provoking us is that grown-ups should be submitted to the printed opinion of such an adolescent. He ought to be turned over and have his mean little bottom smacked.

It was to be many years before there was contact between the two writers again.

In *The Red Hills* it is the industrialism of the south Wales valleys, contrasted with the natural beauty of upland Glamorgan, that entraps the hero, Iorwerth, who subsists by scratching a living from a small, private coal level. The book, which began life in Nice, takes as its theme the revolt against the forces compelling Iorwerth to accept a subordinate role in life, which was one close to Davies's heart. In this respect the novel may be read as a symbolic rendering of his struggle to assert himself as a writer. Iorwerth seeks freedom through his love for Ceinwen, but she wants to settle down, and so she is rejected for the more passionate and rebellious Virginia. The novel ends on a hopeful note as the couple prepare to leave the Valley for an unknown destination. In its message of liberation through sexual allure, this is perhaps the most Lawrentian of Davies's novels, a fact that bothered Curtis Brown, who were also Lawrence's agents. Davies meekly accepted their view and agreed that he would have to shake off Lawrence's influence and write in his own voice. From this point on, the scope of his writing widens, the characters become more complex and the language less biblical. The detached, mature novelist begins to appear.

Very little is known about Vincent A. Wells, to whom *The Red Hills* was dedicated.[32] He was at least fifteen years older than Davies and the wealthy director of a City brewing firm, unconnected with and apparently uninterested in, literature. He lived alone save for a manservant at Bush Wood, a beautifully appointed thatched cottage in Stoke Row in the exclusive environs of Henley-on-Thames, where Davies joined him intermittently between 1932 and 1946. Few of the writer's friends ever met Wells, however. Neither Louis Quinain nor Colyn Davies could remember much about him when interviewed by David Callard in the 1990s. The writer's brother, Lewis, who was put up by Wells when his flat in central London was damaged by a bomb during the war, remembered a tall, bespectacled figure who was something of a recluse, but who would hire a Daimler whenever he and Rhys went on holiday. Wells was, it seems, one of a loosely associated group of homosexuals who thrived in a city that was, according to Lewis Davies, 'the safest city in Europe for gay men'.

Much of their world of 'rough trade' revolved around the Guards barracks in Knightsbridge. Guardsmen were poorly paid and many, including some of an otherwise heterosexual inclination, would turn to homosexual prostitution to supplement their pay. Davies became familiar with certain of the pubs where these soldiers gathered. The encounters were erotic rather than emotional. 'He would talk about Guardsmen he had picked up,' Davies's friend, the writer Fred Urquhart, recalled, 'but never seemed to remember their names.' [33] This arrangement suited Davies's temperament, which shrank from any involvement that might lead to a permanent commitment: paying money for sex was much less threatening because it had no strings attached. He favoured masculine, good-looking men, often heterosexuals, and kept photographs of some of them among his papers, though it is impossible to put names to any of them now. It is probable that Davies and Wells were not lovers, merely men of similar inclination who found it agreeable and, in Davies's case, highly advantageous, to share the same domestic arrangements.

Although Davies took care to avoid becoming embroiled in controversy, he did not always succeed. In July 1929 he was a bystander during a police raid on the Warren Galleries when a number of paintings by D.H. Lawrence were seized, though not before the artist had given him one of the canvases. The painting of pubic hair in some of the pictures was deemed offensive and, notwithstanding the testimony of Sir William Orpen, Augustus John and Sir John Rothenstein, the exhibition was closed down. Now, in 1932, Davies was again a witness to one of the most bizarre trials in the long tragi-comic history of censorship in Britain. Count Geoffrey Wladislas Vaile Potocki de Montalk, poet and self-styled pretender to the Polish throne – his brother, Count Cedric, had a rival claim – was a familiar if outlandish figure in the Soho of the 1930s.[34] He was often to be seen parading through the streets in a long, wine-coloured cloak and sporting a mane of blond hair that fell around his shoulders. Uniquely among the Lahr group, Potocki was extremely right-wing. He was also deluded in his estimation of himself as a poet: he regarded himself as inferior to Shakespeare but at least as good as Byron. His magazine *The Right Review* had been singled out for praise by Charles Maurras, leader of the *Action Française*, and in T.S. Eliot's journal *The Criterion*. To Davies, his extreme views and personality were a source of fascination: he saw in him a figure akin to the moon-struck Dr William Price and, unlike almost all those who were acquainted with the fractious eccentric, was able to remain on friendly terms with him until 1949 when Potocki left for the South of France.

Potocki, who was of Polish extraction but in the real world an architect's son from New Zealand, had prepared a small sheaf of poems, including translations of Rabelais and Verlaine, and three bawdy verses of his own, to which he gave the provocative title 'Here Lies John Penis', and had taken them to a printer with a view to publication.

This man, who as it happened also printed *The Methodist Recorder*, was horrified at the use of four-letter words, and thought it his moral duty to go immediately to the police. Despite the fact that the poems had not yet seen printer's ink, Potocki was arrested under the Obscene Publications Act and sent for trial at the Old Bailey. On the morning Potocki's case came to court, Davies found himself in Charlie Lahr's bookshop, where he ran into Hugh MacDiarmid, and together they decided to attend the trial. In an unpublished account Davies wrote:

From our position there I noticed the Count waiting to be called at the bottom of the stairs in a well-like aperture, and he might have been Jokanaan about to make his entrance from the cistern in Strauss's opera *Salome*. Waiting, the Count most carefully arranged his long hair and the folds of his wine-coloured mantle. From the moment of his entrance he was doomed.

Worse was to follow. The Count refused to take the oath on the Bible, declaring himself a pagan, and asked to swear by Apollo. Surprisingly, the judge agreed, and Potocki, lifting his arms and cloak above his head, proceeded to mumble something inaudible. The judge, who had published a privately-printed volume of execrable doggerel far removed from Potocki's robust sexual imagery, was not impressed and the Count was sentenced to six months in prison. His appeal against the verdict was supported by an extraordinary array of the great and the good, and his defence was paid for by T.S. Eliot, Aldous Huxley, Walter de la Mare, J.B. Priestley,

Hugh Walpole and H.G. Wells, among others. Leonard Woolf defended the royalist anti-Semite's right to free speech in the pages of the left-wing *New Statesman*. But it was all to no avail.

Potocki served his full six months in Brixton Prison, during which the offending verses were published in a very limited edition. On his release, the ardent polemicist, now embittered but still true to form in his determination to flout English orthodoxy, published a number of pamphlets abusing those who had tried to help him. Embarrassment at ever having been associated with the Count resulted in the case, a landmark in the campaign against censorship, being almost entirely forgotten. But disquiet in legal circles saw to it that, in future, expert witnesses in obscenity trials should be allowed to give evidence on the literary merit of the book in question, a precedent that was to have a bearing on the *Lady Chatterley* trial of 1960.

The brouhaha of the Potocki trial over, Davies returned to work in Vincent Wells's home in Henley. There, in 1933, he collected some of the stories which had appeared in limited editions, such as 'Daisy Matthews' and 'A Bed of Feathers', under the title *Love Provoked*[35] and worked on the novel that was to be one of the better-kept of his many secrets: in the same year Jonathan Cape published the only novel of a writer calling himself Owen Pitman, namely *Two Loves I Have*. The reason for his use of this punning pseudonym probably had to do with Davies's feeling that an abrupt shift from his home ground to the Italian Riviera might have been too much for his readers who were more used to 'those bleak and ugly fastnesses' of the Rhondda.

Anthony, the book's hero in whom there is much of Davies, is a moderately successful playwright temporarily resident on the Italian coast. He is suffering a sense of alienation that may have been akin to what Davies felt during his years in suburban London. Walking the streets and visiting low dancehalls,

> sometimes he did suspect that it was a sense of spiritual shame that sent him delving on those quests... at other times he wondered if there was little else in him but a deep and terrible fear of life.

It is perhaps more than chance that Lucy, Anthony's mistress for the last seven years, is fifteen years his senior, for this was the age difference between Davies and Vincent Wells. Anthony, once a Socialist with ambitions to produce a great work, is bored by the facility of his success in producing 'entertainments', while Lucy, the vestiges of her youth begining to fade, is turning to drink. The hero's attachment to Lucy is shattered in the book's opening pages by the sight of a young peasant girl bathing. His pursuit of the girl, who he believes can deliver him from stultification as a man and writer (Chekhov's *poshlost*), takes up much of the book. By the end he has lost both women but gained the desired sense of fulfilment as an artist.

The novel was generally well received and later reissued in a cheap format, though not everyone recognized the quotation from one of Shakespeare's sonnets, 'Two loves I have, of comfort and despair', in which the poet speaks of the Dark Lady on the one hand and the Earl of Southampton on the other. 'Mr Pitman's brilliance is softer and considerably less dazzling than Aldous Huxley's, but it is definitely in the same tradition,' commented *The Daily Telegraph*: 'The poignancy of reluctant age is very delicately presented in the character of the mistress, and Mr Pitman's clear sparkling style makes the book deliciously readable.' This was a view supported by a reviewer in *The Times Literary Supplement*: 'The author undoubtedly writes with more than common competence and there are many passages which reveal a rare power of observation as well as a skilful use of language.'[36]

A last impression of Rhys Davies at this point in his life was provided by G.H. Wells, an early bibliographer and biographer of H.G. Wells, to whom he was not related, who also wrote as Geoffrey West. In his diary for 11 January 1932 West referred to a weekend Davies had spent at his home in Much Hadham in Hertfordshire:

I do like Rhys Davies who spent a weekend, his second, here from Saturday till this morning (Monday). He has a quiet humour, an amiability, a sincerity which all but put one at one's ease with him. But I am curiously struck by the limitations of his interests. History, pre-history, astronomy, social, even intellectual matters: he passes these by quite easily. He is, he says, interested in people, in men and women, in their personal actions and reactions, especially in their sexual reactions as, I suppose, their most intimate and revealing side. He is quite content to take a theme like the industrialisation of the coal valleys and make of it a Tchekov short story of a young man coming home ill to find his family selling the property to mining companies, seeing the trees cut down and dying. A simple soul... now I'd want the whole multitudinous activity of it all. That simply doesn't interest him. He looks on life as a spectacle, a play amusing or dreary as it happens.

West had been the reviewer in the *Times Literary Supplement,* a periodical Davies respected, and he allowed him to read several of his novels in typescript, including the Rhondda Trilogy.[37] Over a period of about six years they exchanged letters in which they discussed matters of mutual interest. Davies is almost certainly the novelist R – in West's book, *Calling All Countries: a Post-War Credo,* in which the two friends talk about the state of the English novel.[38] It is not quoted here because the doom-laden views put into Davies's mouth are clearly not his own but those of his interlocutor, a highly opinionated man with an idiosyncratic agenda for the course of politics, literature and religion in the inter-war period.

The friendship continued for a few more years, however, until West expressed a critical opinion of *The Red Hills,* suggesting that its main characters were seen in isolation, 'in hillside detachment', from their environment. Davies accused him of wanting to redirect his writing on more naturalistic lines: 'I see you are pining for me to produce a thousand-page novel, complete with every damned detail down to the lump of soap in the kitchen and the pattern of the linoleum under the beds.' The upshot of this brisk exchange was that he wished, above all, to preserve the writer's autonomy, free of political influence. He would go his own way, and please himself, in this as in everything else.

Notes

1   Liam O'Flaherty (1896-1984), a native of the Aran Islands, whose most famous novel is *The Informer* (1925).

2   *The Darling of her Heart* (William Heinemann, 1958). Contents: 'All Through the Night', 'A Spot of Bother', 'Afternoon of a Faun', 'The Darling of her Heart', 'A Man up a Tree', 'A Visit to Eggeswick Castle', 'The Wedding at the Lion', 'Period Piece', 'Tears, Idle Tears'.

3   *Rings on her Fingers* (Harold Shaylor, 1930)

4   *The Red Hills* (Putnam, 1932, Covici, Friede, 1933, Tauchnitz, 1934)

5   The tension between Lawrence and his wife is nicely caught by Lewis Davies (not the brother of RD but the Welsh writer and publisher) in his play *Sex and Power at the Beau Rivage*, first performed at the Sherman Theatre in Cardiff in March 2002. The play contains the memorable line, put into RD's mouth, that sex 'is an unwanted present from an old maiden aunt'.

6   John Worthen, *D.H. Lawrence: the Life of an Outsider* (Allen Lane, 2005)

7   Graham Samuel, when RD knew him, was parliamentary correspondent for the *Western Mail* in London.

8   Brenda Maddox, *The Married Man: A Life of D.H. Lawrence* (Sinclair-Stevenson, 1994)

9   The young American Brewster Ghiselin turned up in Bandol in January 1929 and was given hospitality by the Lawrences; his account of meeting them appeared in *The London Magazine* (December 1958).

10 D.H. Lawrence, *The First Lady Chatterley*, with a foreword by Frieda Lawrence (The Dial Press, 1944; William Heinemann,1972)

11 This, and similar insights, had appeared in the first, fuller, printed version of RD's account of his visit to Bandol which had been published in the magazine *Horizon*, but it was excised from the coyer text of *Print of a Hare's Foot*.

12 'Louvre' and 'Seine' appeared in the anthology *Modern Welsh Poetry* (ed. Keidrych Rhys, Faber, 1944)

13 'The Sisters', in *The Song of Songs* (1927) and *Collected Stories* (ed. Meic Stephens, vol. 3, 1998)

14 It was left to RD to explain the double meaning of 'pansies' to Lawrence. It is difficult to believe he did not know it could denote an effeminate man, but he claimed *his* pansies were a pun on the French *'pensées'* ('thoughts'), in the manner of Pascal, which is indeed the word's root.

15 *A Bed of Feathers* (The Mandrake Press, 1929). This story first appeared in *London Aphrodite* (2, 1928). RD's friendship with Raymond B. Marriott began after the latter made a kindly reference to the story in *Era*, a theatre newspaper.

16 RD would have been mollified to see his novella in distinguished company in H. Gustav Klaus's anthology, *Tramps, Workmates and Revolutionaries: working-class stories of the 1920s* (Journeyman Press, 1993)

17 Matthew Arnold, Professor of Poetry at Oxford University (1857-67), whose 'Lectures on Celtic Literature' first appeared in *The Cornhill Magazine* in 1866 and in book form in 1867.

18 The *Western Mail* (1 February 1927)

19 *Tale* (E. Archer, 1930)

20 *The Stars, the World and the Women* (William Jackson, 1930); 'Of this book there have been printed at the Chiswick Press 550 copies, signed by the author, of which 500 only are for sale'.

21 Hilary Spurling, *Secrets of a Woman's Heart: the Later Life of Ivy Compton-Burnett 1920-1969* (Hodder and Stoughton, 1984)

22 See, for example, Stephen Spender, *World within World* (Hamish Hamilton, 1951)

23 *The Georgian Confession Book* (Foyle, 1931) was compiled by Gilbert H. Fabes, the rare books manager at Foyles.

24 *Arfon* (Foyle, 1931); 'numbered one to four hundred, and twelve copies lettered A to L'.

25 *A Woman* (Capell at the Bronze Snail Press, 1931). 'Of this first edition there have been printed 165 copies for sale, each numbered and signed by the author. Seventeen copies for presentation have also been printed and lettered A to L'.

26 *The Woman among Women* (E. Lahr, 1931); a Blue Moon poem for Christmas 1931; 100 signed copies for sale and 100 with drawing by Frederick Carter.

27 John Gawsworth, *Ten Contemporaries: notes towards their definitive Bibliography* (Ernest Benn, 1st series, 1932). This book contains a short article by RD, 'Writing about the Welsh', and an annotated bibliography of twelve of his books up to 1932; an article with the same title appeared in *Literary Digest* (2, 1947). John Gawsworth was one of the pseudonyms of T.I.F. Armstrong who, *inter alia*, ran the Twyn Barlwm Press, a name suggested by Arthur Machen, whose work he admired.

28 For this reason RD may be seen as a late exemplar of the Celtic Twilight launched by W.B. Yeats in 1893 and of which the only significant Welsh writer was Ernest Rhys (1859-1946). In the latter's *Readings in Welsh Literature* (1924) Davies had read a foreword by Elfed (Howell Elvet Lewis), with whom he thought he had a family connexion. The Archdruid had written of Ernest Rhys: 'Carmarthen, its scenes, its memories, its traditions, to him is the gateway of ancient romance, standing in the magical Celtic twilight.' The concept was ill-defined as it was misleading, then as now, and was usually taken up by people who were not familiar with literature in the Welsh language, but it resonated in RD's mind because of its connexion with Carmarthen. He would also have been familiar with Ernest Rhys's companion volume, *Readings in Welsh History* (1901), a book popular in the schools of Wales in the first years of the 20th century.

29 *A Pig in a Poke* (Joiner & Steele, 1931). Contents: 'Revelation', 'Death in the Family', 'A Pig in a Poke', 'The New Garment', 'Conflict in Morfa', 'The Song of Songs', 'The Stars, the World and the Women', The Lily', 'Mrs Evans Number Six', 'The Sisters', 'A Gift of Death', 'Evelyn and Ivor', 'The Doctor's Wife', 'Blodwen', 'Hunger'. First edn. limited to 1,000 numbered copies and a signed edn. numbered 1 to 50 for sale in Britain and 51 to 70 in the United States.

30 *Count your Blessings* (Putnam, 1932; Covici, Friede, 1932)

31 R.L. Mégroz, *Rhys Davies: a critical sketch* (Foyle, 1932)

32 It has proved impossible to trace Vincent Wells. Lewis Davies thought he went to live with or near his sister in New Zealand *c*.1947. The present writer has two of his letters to RD bearing the address Stanmore Bay, Silverdale, Auckland, New Zealand, and dated 1948. But all enquiries, including those of Jennifer Sturm, who lives near Auckland, have been in vain.

33 Fred Urquhart (1912-95), Scottish short-story writer.

34 Potocki was reputed to be the father of the child called Theodora who was adopted by T.F. Powys and his wife. For a full account of this extraordinary man see D.[avid] A. Callard, 'The Trial of John Penis', in *London Magazine* (39, 5 and 6 (August-September 1999) and Stephanie de Montalk, *Unquiet World: The Life of Count Geoffrey Potocki de Montalk* (Victoria University Press, 2001).

35 *Love Provoked* (Putnam, 1933). Contents: 'Daisy Matthews', 'The Romantic Policewoman', 'Lovers', 'Doris in Gomorrah', 'The Journey', 'The Wanderer', 'The Bard', 'The Sleeping Beauty', 'A Bed of Feathers', 'Faggots', 'Arfon'.

36 Even so, RD was reluctant to admit to his brother that he had written the book and even more unwilling to let him read it. For a fuller account of this novel see D.[avid] A. Callard, 'Rhys Davies and the Welsh Expatriate Novel', in *Planet* (89, 1991).

37 G.H. West, reviews of *The Things Men Do* in the *TLS* (4 July 1936) and *The Red Hills* (15 December 1936)

38 Geoffrey West, *Calling All Countries: a Post-War Credo* (Routledge, 1934)

Five

Among bohemians

Rhys Davies met and, in his genial manner, became acquainted with a wide range of people in the Fitzrovia of the mid-1930s. Foremost among them was the novelist Anna Kavan, who would become in due course his closest female friend. She had been born Helen Emily Woods in Cannes in 1901, the same year as Davies (though she kept her age a closely guarded secret), and was the only child of a wealthy English couple whose ancestral pile, Holeyn Hall, with its vast estate, was in Wylam, near Newcastle upon Tyne. Her mother's grandfather was Dr Richard Bright, sometime physician to Queen Victoria and discoverer of Bright's Disease (an older classification for several types of kidney disease).

During her unhappy, loveless early years – Helen saw her socialite mother for only ten minutes before dinner and knew herself to be an unwanted child – she was introduced into the emotionally cold world that would affect her personality for the rest of her life. Her parents took her to America, an uprooting that left an indelible mark on their vulnerable daughter, and then to Lausanne in Switzerland, where she was schooled privately. Her father drowned himself when she was eleven by jumping from the stern of a ship bound for South America, his death the ultimate act of abandonment in her young mind. She had built a fantasy round him, believing that, one day, he would make her his companion and give her the affection of which she was starved. With his suicide she felt herself alone in the world and could not forgive her neurotic mother 'for her indecent haste in putting him under the ground'. At 18 she was offered a choice between going to Oxford or staying at home in the country with an allowance of £600 a year, and was persuaded by her mother to choose the latter course. Helen Bright had struck it rich by marrying a very wealthy man at 18 and was determined her daughter should do the same.

Prior to meeting Davies, Helen had disastrously married a glamorous older man and dilettante artist called Donald Ferguson who took her to live in Burma, where the colonial lifestyle only added to her isolation and sense of alienation from social norms. In one of her most powerful novellas, *Who Are You?* (1963) Ferguson appears as Mr Dog Head, on whom she lavishes all the scorn and pity at her disposal, producing a portrait of a man driven to sadism and violence by an unhappy marriage. Their marriage lasted six years and they divorced in 1926.

Her first six novels, published between 1929 and 1937, were in the name of Helen Ferguson. From 1940, having taken up with a dissolute painter named Stuart Edmonds, she called herself Helen Woods Edmonds but wrote as Anna Kavan, a pseudonym taken from a character in one of her own novels, *Let Me Alone* (1930). There are several parallels between Kavan's life and that of Jean Rhys, another writer admired by Davies. As Elizabeth Young points out in *Pandora's Handbag* (2001), both women had been damaged in infancy and both had grown up gifted, suspicious and alienated, and as writers they both suffered long years of obscurity. For most of her adult life Anna was addicted to heroin.

Davies gave an account of meeting Helen Ferguson for the first time in the early 1930s in an article published in *Books and Bookmen* (March 1971):

My first glimpse of her had been when she arrived with her equally personable second husband at the Lechlade fishing cottage he had lent to a mutual friend and myself. She was a young woman coming over the pretty bridge spanning the young Thames where a trout stream joined it and where swans came to be fed below a window of the stone cottage. In this quiet-voiced, quietly smiling authoress – I already knew her books – there was no hint of the dark future, the mental breakdowns, the drugs, the desperate egotism, the ferocious battle to live alone, the wretched attempts at withdrawal from drug addiction in nursing homes, the compulsions to suicide. Later I saw her gambolling in Bledlow with her cherished bulldogs, animals that always seemed to me to conquer a high-strung temperament or neurosis by sheer weighty power of muscle and flesh. She and her husband lived luxuriously in Bledlow. There were social exchanges, a country pond placidity, and the village cricket team as captained by Helen's generous husband. She painted in thick oils, wrote her well-controlled novels; she had a son by her first husband.

Davies was prescient enough to hint at the dark currents moving under the smooth surface of life in the Chiltern village of Bledlow Cross in Buckinghamshire. Helen had been an addict since about 1925; she was also a depressive given to moods of the blackest despair. Davies did not particularly admire her work as a novelist, yet something drew him to Helen and a friendship would blossom that was to be his most lasting relationship.

On the collapse of her marriage to Edmonds, Helen, who had already had several abortions and given birth to a daughter who had lived only a few hours, tried to gain custody of a child they had adopted, but the little girl's guardians discouraged her from visiting and her attempts proved unsuccessful. The child, to whom they had given the name Susanna (her real name was Violet Turner), did not stay with Edmonds for very long and did not take his name, so that it has proved impossible to trace her. Helen made one of her several suicide attempts, entered a Swiss psychiatric clinic and twice went into hospital for detoxification. When she emerged it was with a new identity. She had not only dyed her hair platinum blond, she made it known that henceforth she wished to be called Anna Kavan, changing her name by deed poll. Having refused to have anything to do with the outside world, she had lost contact with Davies during her time in hospital, but then, in 1938, out of the blue, she wrote to say she was living in London and wanted to see him. Davies recorded their meeting thus:

Helen Ferguson had vanished. This spectral woman, attenuated of body and face, a former abundance of auburn hair shorn and changed to metallic gold, thinned hands restless, was so different that my own need to readjust to her was a strain. She had not long been discharged from her second period in a hospital and later I came to understand why she called one of her Anna Kavan books *I am Lazarus*.

Davies and Kavan saw each other regularly until she left England in 1940 – she travelled abroad in the company of an aspiring playwright of private means named Ian Hamilton and spent two fairly happy years in his native New Zealand, where she drank heavily in the hope of becoming less reliant on heroin. She and Davies resumed their friendship when she returned in 1943, but Kavan was plunged into a further bout of despair by the death of her son, Bryan Ferguson, while serving with the RAF in the year following. Between 1944 and 1946 Kavan worked as an assistant to Cyril Connolly, editor of the influential magazine *Horizon*.

Davies is the character 'R' in Kavan's story 'The Summons', which was included in her book *Asylum Piece* (1940); it begins:

R is one of my oldest friends. Once, long ago, we used to live in flats in the same building, and then, of course, I saw a great deal of him. Afterwards, the circumstances of our lives altered, wider and wider distances divided us, we could only meet rarely and with difficulty – perhaps only once or twice in a whole year – and then only for a few hours or at most for a weekend. In spite of this our friendship – which was purely platonic – continued unbroken, although it was naturally not possible to maintain quite the original degree of intimacy. I still felt that a close and indestructible understanding existed between R and myself: an understanding which had its roots in some fundamental character similarity and was therefore exempt from the accidents of change.[1]

There were undoubtedly similarities between the characters of the two solitaries. Not only were they the same age, both having been born in 1901, but Kavan, prior to her name-change, had been drawn to the masculine type favoured by Davies, particularly racing drivers with whose nonchalant attitude to death she was able to identify. But when she became Anna Kavan she abandoned heterosexual relations – she had lost any sexual drive during her years of heroin abuse – and lived surrounded by a mostly homosexual retinue which made no demands on her. Davies, too, as much as Kavan, was his own self-creation. Both possessed a well-concealed streak of narcissism that expressed itself in a liking for expensive clothes, and both were essentially shy people concerned almost exclusively with themselves. One of Kavan's favourite pastimes was staring into a mirror for hours on end and many of her paintings were of herself. The precise nature of the curious bond on which the unusual relationship between Davies and Kavan was based, and which lasted until her death in 1968, is now lost. Seeing each other so frequently and privately, they exchanged only the most perfunctory of letters, and sometimes postcards, and so there is very little correspondence that might otherwise have shed light on what they felt for each other.

They were also secretive: Kavan destroyed her correspondence and most of her diaries, and those remaining she doctored, hoping she would become 'the world's best-kept secret... what a thrilling enigma for posterity I should be'. Her first biographer, David Callard, whose book, *The Case of Anna Kavan* (1992),[2] is an account of her bleak life, found his way barred by the evasions, half-truths, fantasies and identity shifts of a deranged mind that concealed her benighted inner self. Jeremy Reed, in his fuller and more perceptive biography, *A Stranger on Earth* (2006),[3] found himself up against the same problem but managed to throw more light on the darker secrets of her life. Davies, no stranger to editing his own life, accepted Anna's hatred of her father, her sense of abandonment and betrayal, and her self-absorption, as essential factors in her personality and writing. He also understood, quite instinctively, her need to evade the truth about herself and hide it from others.

Neither was a particular admirer of the other's writing. As Helen Ferguson Kavan she had written six rather conventional, semi-autobiographical novels in a traditional mode. Davies called them, rather snootily, 'Home Counties novels', adding that he thought she had been wise 'to give a dose of arsenic to Helen Ferguson'. Indeed, reading her novels one after the other is like hearing the same story repeated over and over again, in plots that grow ever more nightmarish from book to book, their 'nocturnal writing' – the phrase is Anaïs Nin's in *The Novel of the Future* (1968) – involving a lexicon of dreams and addiction, mental instability and alienation from the real world. Kavan lived in a state of extreme subjectivity not unlike Nin's, exploring the mental torture of which her addiction was both symptom and palliative rather than the cause. She was hailed during her lifetime as inheriting the mantle of Virginia Woolf and Djuna Barnes, and Nin called Kavan's collection of stories *Asylum Piece* 'a classic equal to the work of Kafka', difficult though that is to see now. In a foreword to the posthumous novel *Mercury* (1994) Doris Lessing wrote, 'This glittering hallucinogenic novel is surely one of the best of the books inspired by drug-taking.'[4] A rather more critical assessment is found in an undated letter from Davies to Charles Burkhart, a mutual friend:

> Anna is a limited writer and I always had my reservations about her. However, I think she wrote less in a 'tunnel' than in a cell with a small window looking out on a wild, mad world... She was true to herself, however limited that self was. There is room for the interesting waifs in literature.

Kavan, for her part, although often referring to Davies as 'Wales's greatest novelist', had little time for his fiction because she thought it too conventional.

Yet this strange relationship, the details of which are invisible to posterity and irretrievable now, was to endure until Kavan's death. Numerous witnesses have confirmed her lack of even the most basic social skills. She disliked nearly all women, and women writers especially. On one famous occasion, at a small dinner party, she turned her back on Olivia Manning, read a magazine over the coffee, and fixed her strange eyes on some distance visible only to her. Her heroin addiction masked a deeper personality disorder that, to a lay person, appears to resemble bipolar manic depression of an extreme kind. But although she sorely tried the patience of her friends, including Davies, he never cut her off as he did so many of his acquaintances. He could even put up with it when she made one of the characters in a short story say, 'Human beings are hateful. I loathe their ugly faces and messy emotions. I'd like to destroy them all.' The world had given Anna Kavan nothing but grief and she did not much like living. She had looked at humanity and decided to keep it at a distance, where it would hurt her least. Davies found her battle against despair, in David Callard's estimation, 'heroic'. A copy of Davies's novel *Girl Waiting in the Shade* (1960), now in the present writer's possession, bears the inscription 'To Anna with love from Rhys'; of the many books he inscribed, no other has been seen that has the word 'love' on the fly-leaf.[5]

Davies was still virtually homeless at this time, always on the move between Blaenclydach, Henley and a variety of rented or borrowed flats. Although he often went to see Kavan, he rarely stayed overnight and there was no question of his moving in with Anna because both cherished their independence too much. His visits to the Rhondda in the mid-1930s became more frequent and of longer duration, since he had by 1932 decided on a new direction for his writing. He had been encouraged by a number of articles about him, notably one by Glyn Roberts in the *Western Mail*:

The observation is diabolical, the sense of a phrase perfect. Davies's technical control over English as a medium of expression for his very subtle and unusual mind is remarkable. In addition, he has humour, sincerity, and understanding. His insight into feminine psychology is possibly unique among living British writers. He is young, yet of the technique of his craft, which many men still struggle with at sixty, he has little to learn.[6]

After bringing out *One of Norah's Early Days*[7] in 1935, and *The Skull*[8] in 1936 both limited editions intended for the upper echelons of the bibliophile market, he would now pour much of his energy into writing a loosely connected trilogy of novels tracing the history of Blaenclydach from the pre-industrial days of 'sylvan Rhondda', before the discovery of coal, to the coming of boom, slump and industrial strife of the Depression years. These books, sometimes known as the Rhondda or Glan Ystrad Trilogy, were *Honey and Bread* (1935),[9] *A Time to Laugh* (1937)[10] and *Jubilee Blues* (1939).[11] Romantic though they are, the novels are the most sustained literary examination of Welsh industrial history ever published and certainly the least ideologically distorted. Although not always treated with the political realism that has become a stereotype of Welsh industrial fiction, among the recurrent features of the Trilogy are strikes, disasters and, above all, the impact of heavy industrial work on individual lives.

From time to time Davies expressed a sense of revulsion against the ugliness of industrial society as he had known it in the Rhondda. He was not alone in this aversion since no Welsh writer has seen the valleys of South Wales in any other way; it has been left to the painters to reveal the stark beauty of their industrial scenes: Josef Herman, George Chapman, Ernest Zobole, Will Roberts, Charles Burton, David Carpanini, and others.

As for the mindless violence of some sections of the workforce during times of industrial strife, Davies tended to see it as the expression of the resistant spirit of the mining communities, and as continuous with an older Welsh tradition of coping with a harsh terrain and difficult living conditions. His response to the decline of the Rhondda in the inter-war years, when unemployment soared to more than 40 per cent and large numbers of people left in search of work, is to be found at its most eloquent in the novels of the Trilogy. Even so, it was not the economic conditions or their political implications that exercised his imagination, but the drama of human lives under severe stress. He understood the quick pace of Rhondda society as no other writer has done, not even Gwyn Thomas or, later, Alun Richards and Ron Berry: its closeness and local rivalries, its social life revolving around pub, chapel, club and cinema, its back-lanes and terraces, the smoky panoramas and the wild hillsides, and more than all, the ebullient character of its people in the face of hardship. It says a great deal for his pre-eminence as a Rhondda writer that Thomas, Richards and Berry all admired his work and were influenced by it.

The first book in the Rhondda Trilogy, *Honey and Bread*, set in Glan Ystrad, a fictionalised but distorted version of Blaenclydach, focuses on the sale of an ancient estate dating back to Tudor times to one of the railway companies opening up the Rhondda for the purpose of extracting coal and taking it down the Valley to the docks in Cardiff. The Llewellyn family are cultured, eccentric but, by the end of the book, in terminal decline, their wealth squandered by Owen Llewellyn, the tubercular and irresponsible son who is no match for the new age of capital and steam.

In the second book, *A Time to Laugh*, of which an American edition appeared in 1938, the strongest character is Dr Tudor Morris, grandson of Owen Morris in *Honey and Bread*, who abandons his class and finds salvation in his work among the Valley's poor. On the eve of the twentieth century he salutes the revellers as 'obeying some wild liberated impulse of their ancient blood' and concludes that, despite everything, it is 'a time to laugh!'. The novel ends on a positive, lyrical note of which Davies was eminently capable when the need arose. Standing on the mountain top looking down into the Valley, a favourite spot in romantic fiction, and not only in South Wales, Owen Morris thinks to himself:

Tumult and disorder, frustration, wages, strikes, riots, debts – were these to be his world? The architecture of his earth was a muddle of low squat evil dwellings in which lived an aboriginal race dispossessed of any original dignity it may have held. What right had he to extravagant flights of idealism about these people? Ugliness, squalor and meanness was their portion. And yet, and yet... He would stay, struggle, go among them with an intent watching. They were the world with its beauty, mystery and pain; they fought and yielded, they were garlanded and they were battered. They had the full tarnished brilliance of life in them... And he began to laugh, with a soft low sound, half caught in his throat. He was laughing at himself, and at the people who were about him. Oh, life... rich, yes, it had all the soul demanded. Luxuriously, preposterously, abandonedly rich. And always a new earth and a new heaven to discover.

Set two generations on from the first book, this novel grapples with the nascent urban world that replaced pastoral Rhondda so quickly, and in a distinct move towards historical realism, opens with a strike and a riot that draw, though not quite accurately, on the Hauliers' Strike of 1893 and the Cambrian Combine Lock-out that led to the Tonypandy Riots of 1910, here set in December 1899. Although expressly radical in its sympathy for the working class, it also finds a place for local tradespeople, the small shopocracy to which the Davieses belonged: they remain neutral, non-political, with their livelihoods threatened, but hapless bystanders in the social conflict of the day. The book's emphasis is on collective responsibility rather than personal revolt as depicted in Davies's earlier novels. Even so, Davies remains wary of Socialist ideology and the collectivist mentality it breeds. As for the Communists, they are seen merely as propagandists and rhetoricians, rather than the socially vital force they actually were in places like Blaenclydach, so that *A Time to Laugh* cannot, any more than the other two books in the Trilogy, be considered a 'proletarian novel' in the strictest sense of the term.

As one of the unfortunate coincidences that plagued Davies's career as a writer, the theme of *A Time to Laugh* was echoed uncannily in a novel which was published in the same year but achieved greater commercial success, namely *The Citadel* by the Scottish writer A.J. Cronin. The book, set in industrial South Wales, was made into a film in 1938 and this, though more authentic than the Hollywood version of *How Green Was My Valley*, did much to establish the stereotypes of the mining valleys far beyond the borders of Wales. That two novels so similar in theme and treatment – though the doctor in the latter book leaves the Valley for Harley Street – should appear in the same year might suggest that a real-life model for the heroes of both books existed in the South Wales of the day. It may be that Dr Tudor Morris was suggested by Dr Martyn Lloyd-Jones, the Evangelical leader who had left his prosperous Harley Street practice to work as a missionary in South Wales – before he, too, returned to more lucrative work in England. Davies had heard him preaching in a packed Rhondda chapel at about the same time as he was writing *A Time to Laugh*, an experience he had described in *My Wales* (1937):

> The opening of his sermon had almost an intellectual primness; his sincerity had a cold ruthlessness, very attractive, at least to me... Dr Lloyd-Jones's fine violin-like voice was exquisite enough in its entreating. And there was one thrilling moment when, by use of that magic which all the great preachers of Wales possess, he called on the name of God with tremendous passion and, opening wide his arms, he seemed like a great black bat swooping down over the congregation.[12]

Even so, Lloyd-Jones was the very type of preacher of whom Davies disapproved and, ever alert to signs of the decline of religion in South Wales, he noted there had been no response to the preacher's invitation to any member of the congregation who felt the need for further guidance, or who wanted 'to give himself anew to God', to remain behind after the service. The writer was nevertheless disconcerted when, as he was about to leave the chapel, someone asked him, 'Well, Mr Davies, I suppose we'll find all this in your next novel?'

In the same year, 1937, another novel appeared that treated similar themes: *Cwmardy*, by Lewis Jones. Although he was only four years older than Davies and must have been at the village school at the same time, there is no evidence to suggest they ever met as adults or held opinions of each other's work. The Communist writer's book deals with the crisis in the mining valleys towards the end of the nineteenth century, especially the conflict over wage cuts, the sliding scale and the struggle to form a miners' union. Strike meetings are described in both books, as well as violence, notably that of the owners against their employees and of the miners against scabs who go to work in defiance of the union. But they differ in one important respect: while Lewis Jones is wholly on the side of the workers, so that his novel often reads like sheer propaganda, Davies identifies Dr Morris as the focal character in his book. Like the author, the doctor strongly sympathises with the miners, doing all he can to help their cause, but he is not one of them. There was a world of difference between the viewpoints of the two Blaenclydach men, Davies the grocer's son and Jones the collier, Marxist militant, Glamorgan County Councillor, street-orator and defender of the Spanish Republic.

Reviewing *A Time to Laugh* in the inaugural number of *Wales* in 1937, Glyn Jones, one of the first among Davies's compatriots to recognize his mature talent, wrote:

> Rhys Davies is undoubtedly a bigshot, a good bit of a pioneer, one of the first to get the valleys across on the English in the face of indifference, prejudice and a good deal of press-engendered hostility. He has written some of the best short stories ever published about the valleys; and his virtues, well-known by this time (fancy, salty dialogue, grotesque humour, a robust masculinity of style) are all present in this his latest novel... Only philosophy is missing.[13]

By 'philosophy' Glyn Jones undoubtedly meant political ideology. He went on to regret the lack of a unifying principle, or tension, that held the characters together in an imaginative world where their co-existence might be more credible. Although this stricture is much less true of Davies's short stories than of his novels, it does contain some perceptive criticism of his work as a whole. As for his lack of 'philosophy', Davies defended himself thus in an interview with Denys Val Baker in *John O'London's Weekly* (24 October1952):

> I become uneasy when a novelist begins to expound, preach or underline, state a case, even briefly, or when he douses his characters with over-personal wealth of vision. This sort of philosophising must be kept, with me, incidental.

In the third novel of the trilogy, *Jubilee Blues,* the heroine is the servant Cassie Jones who, with her husband Prosser, takes the licence on a pub based on the Central Hotel in Blaenclydach. Her common sense, thrift and generous heart are in stark contrast to her husband's profligacy. But, like the Valley, the pub is bankrupt and she decides to leave her husband and return to the 'white farm sitting on top of a hill under the sky' where she resumes her old life. John Fordham singles Cassie out for a key role in the novels:

> As the revolutionary zeal of the younger generation of Morrises dissipates in the frustrations and failures of collective action, Cassie Jones, the one-time simple farm worker, assumes her central role as the moral heart of the whole trilogy.[14]

Her departure marks the end of Davies's preoccupation with the Rhondda as the setting for his novels, although he would return to it as a source of material for some of his short stories. For reasons he never explained, Davies considered the three books of the Glan Ystrad Trilogy unsatisfactory and, like much of his early work, he expunged them from his bibliography. They are, nevertheless, among the best of his novels.

Rhys Davies was for a decade the only writer of any stature who dealt with the Welsh industrial experience and so was 'a good bit of a pioneer'. However, in 1934, he was to be joined by Jack Jones, whose *Rhondda Roundabout* was published to public acclaim in that year. Jones's background, as one of the fifteen children of a miner and who had begun work underground at the age of 12, was far more typical of Rhondda life than Davies's, even though he had been born and brought up in Merthyr Tydfil, a few miles to the east. As miners' agent for the Garw Valley and an experienced platform speaker, and often unemployed, he had long been in the thick of industrial struggle rather than an observer on the sidelines. But Davies, to his regret, found little to praise in Jones's book. To Charlie Lahr he wrote:

> I had been looking forward to reading *Rhondda Roundabout*. It begins with a rather attractive flourish and sweep. But I had to make an effort to get through it. It's good reporting, and makes a cheap afternoon excursion to the Rhondda for people. But reporting is not enough to make a real novel. Jones's vision is limited: he reports what he's seen of today's behaviour and throws it down loosely and carelessly. There's no background or pattern to this book... Jones seems to have not the slightest amount of imagination to aid him. I'm disappointed. It would be nice to have a fellow writer to sit beside me. I feel lonely about Wales sometimes!

Jack Jones, who wrote much as he spoke – except, as Gwyn Jones once remarked, he needed a pencil in his hand – was to become a prolific and popular author, achieving a best-seller status that eluded Davies, though he was never quite able to repeat the charm of his first book which made up in energy what it lacked in formal structure. That said, the unworthy suspicion lurks that Davies was unsettled at seeing a new novelist, albeit seventeen years his senior and a Merthyr man at that, moving into territory he had hitherto thought his own.

Be that as it may, he persevered with his stories. Wooed away from his publisher, Putnam, by Dwye Evans, Davies joined the Heinemann list, a new imprint whose rising star was Graham Greene. Fred Urquhart sensed that Davies and Greene would not get on very well because, over a lunch at which they were introduced, the Welshman was rather too forthright in his opinion of his fellow writer's work. Nevertheless, Greene, reviewing *The Things Men Do,*[15] a collection of Davies's stories, in *The Spectator* in 1936, was complimentary:

> Mr Rhys Davies is very readable, he writes well. And, he has an agreeable inventiveness: if one had to edit a volume of the best short stories of the year, one would certainly include at least two from the latest volume.

Greene may have been thinking of the stories 'Resurrection', which extracts delicious humour from the rituals of an old woman's death, or perhaps 'Cherry-Blossom on the Rhine', the story that managed to goad Davies's monocled pick-up Franz, now a Stormtrooper in Nazi Germany, into writing to accuse him of insulting his country because it made fun of the Hitler Youth. None of the book's reviewers noticed that, despite its title, *The Things Men Do* was almost exclusively concerned with women trying to maintain their dignity in the face of poverty and neglect by their menfolk.

That Davies was regarded as the Welsh writer *par excellence* in the eyes of London publishers, a status he did his best to cultivate despite kicking against the traces sometimes, was confirmed when, in 1936, Jarrolds commissioned him to write *My Wales*, a personal view cast in the form of a travelogue. He was not used to working to commission but he put his Rhondda Trilogy to one side to produce a surprisingly patriotic, but highly idiosyncratic, reading of his country's history. As a guide, he used *The Chain of Events*, *a Chronology of Welsh History from 1509 to the Present Day* by C. Leonard Ross Thomas assisted by Ifor H. Roberts, published by the *Western Mail and Echo* in 1936, his tattered copy of which has survived. The book was also influenced in its emphasis on the heroic and romantic aspects of the Welsh past by Owen Rhoscomyl's *Flame-Bearers of Welsh History* (1905), a book widely used in the schools of Wales in the first decades of the twentieth century. He also dipped into Owen M. Edwards's hefty volume on Wales in the series *The Story of the Nations*, an influential work in its day, marking the following passage in pencil:

> The wild and rugged outlines of the mountains are mirrored as intense but broken purposes in the Welshman's character, always forming great ideals, but lacking in the steady perseverance of the people of the plain [i.e. the English]. The silent and majestic solitude of the mountains has sunk into the Welshman's character as the fatalism which is the basis of his life and thought. The mountains, his mute but suggestive companions, strengthen his imagination. His imagination makes him exceedingly impressionable – he has always loved poetry and theology; but this very imagination, while enabling him to see great ideals, makes him incapable of

realising them – he is too impatient to be capable of organisation.[16]

Davies's book is clearly, in the words of Huw Edwin Osborne, 'an extended narrative act of tourism', intended for English readers rather than the people it purports to describe.[17] Much of it is about the relationship between the two countries as he tries to place Wales in a context that will be comprehensible to an English audience. In this respect he adopts the role of 'native informant', addressing 'the English colonial gaze' that regards the Welsh as child-like, stupid, ignorant, impractical, immoral and corrupt – just as the Blue Book commissioners had done in 1847.[18] The opening pages include a number of piquant extracts from London schoolchildren's essays about Wales:

> The Welsh men are very rough and they can't play cricket... I like to hear them speach [*sic*]... They are famous for singing and poetry... Some of them has [*sic*] ginger hair... They speak funny and always have a smile on their faces... We are great friends now, England and Wales.

Clearly Davies had a very complex, and often contradictory, relationship with his native land. Yet, for all his physical removal from Wales, he was very proud of being what he called '100% pure Welshman', by which he meant, not quite that he belonged to *gwŷr y gloran*, the autochthonous inhabitants of the parish of Ystradyfodwg before the discovery of coal, but that, as far as he knew, his forebears had all been native-born and long resident in Wales. Though his Rhondda accent had been refined in the manner of 'the cultured Welshman', the up-market version so many educated Welshmen acquire, there was something quintessentially Welsh in his appearance, especially his Iberian head, sallow complexion and high cheekbones: he was clearly, or so he believed, a descendant of the Silures, 'the small dark people' who were in south-western Britain long before the coming of the taller, fair-headed Celts. In *My Wales* he showed he was familiar enough with the racial theories of H.J. Fleure,[19] Professor of Geography at Aberystwyth, who had made a renowned anthropological study of racial types in Wales, and produced a book which, *faute de mieux*, served as a useful introduction to its subject until the publication of Ll. Wyn Griffith's more authoritative book, *The Welsh,* in 1950.[20] Even so, Davies's book lacks the documentary rigour of James Hanley's study of the distressed areas of South Wales during the Depression, *Grey Children,*[21] commissioned by *The Spectator* and also published in 1937, but it proved popular and an American edition appeared a year later.

Although most of Davies's book is taken up with a tour around several parts of Wales, including a visit to Llanfyrnach (the next village to Cilrhedyn) in Pembrokeshire, the most sombre note is struck when he arrives in the Rhondda Valley, now a 'brutal ruin' at the nadir of the Depression that had gripped it since the General Strike of 1926. During the course of a long historical survey, in which he was able to use much of the research that was to go into the Rhondda Trilogy, Davies could find little cause for optimism:

Such a landscape as the Rhondda today is a spectacle satisfying the pessimist and the satirist – the blemishes of civilization are revealed in all their gruesome squalor.

As Dai Smith has pointed out, Davies's account of the Rhondda in *My Wales*

is particularly intriguing since it oscillates so dramatically between the raucous world which had cradled him but not held him, and the despairing society whose quiescence in the downtrodden 1930s he deplored. It is as if, at one and the same time, he is driven to acknowledge the (vanished) power to fascinate which the Rhondda of his first two decades so abundantly possessed and the (evanescent) pity which its humanity could invoke in him.[22]

Moreover, Davies could not let an opportunity pass to let fly some of his grapeshot about Wales and the Welsh:

Wales is a beautiful mother, but she can be a dangerously possessive wife... Other nations have things the matter with them. Not Wales... It is well known that Welsh people are vigorously unable to tolerate any criticism of their land from their native writers... There is something sadistic about a Sunday in Aberystwyth... The fanatics for the language have a heavy task: which is not to say it will not be achieved.

Such strictures were doubtless meant as a dose of salts for his compatriots but if so, there was no response in the periodical press of the day.

As for nationalism, it had not yet taken root in the Valleys of South Wales. Indeed, Plaid Genedlaethol Cymru, the Welsh Nationalist Party, founded only ten years before, seemed irrelevant to the economic crisis then ravaging South Wales. Davies was unsympathetic to Welsh nationalism as a political force but was well enough informed to know that Plaid Cymru's leader, Saunders Lewis, was heavily influenced by the ideas of the French Catholic right. This seemed to him a guarantee of its not making much real headway in South Wales during the inter-war years, despite the personal following of such Rhondda Nationalists as J. Kitchener Davies, whose controversial play *Cwm Glo* ('Coal valley', 1935) had dealt with the dire social consequences of the Depression in South Wales. Indeed, Saunders Lewis had advocated that the mining valleys should be de-industrialised and their people returned to work on the land, a suggestion Davies found to be as preposterous as it was offensive.

The book ends with a fierce attack on what Rhys Davies called 'rabid Nationalism', which he attributed to 'too much inbreeding, both physical and spiritual', a criticism expressed in terms of the racialist discourse that is to be found in so much of his work – and, for that matter, in D.H. Lawrence's. As Daniel Williams has pointed out, racialism for Davies sprang from his fundamental belief in artistic freedom and individualism but has nothing to do with modern Welsh Nationalism.[23] More bluntly, George Ewart Evans, flabbergasted by

Davies's analysis of industrial unrest as based on ideas of race, called the book 'fascist-fodder':

> Rhys Davies attempts to take a detached view of the conflict between miners and owners since the beginning of the last century. He sees the struggle isolated in South Wales, not as a world-wide phenomenon. As a result he has startling theories of its cause. The strife in South Wales is a natural outcome of the presence of mixed breeds in the coalfield. What a notion![24]

The archetypal Welsh people singled out by Davies in *My Wales* were three who loomed large in his personal pantheon. With Dr William Price of Llantrisant, neo-Druid, Chartist and pioneer of cremation, the author seemed to have what came close to being an obsession, for he appears in no fewer than five of his books. Indeed, Davies once told his brother Lewis he had saved Price from obscurity and that, prior to his researches in Cardiff Central Library, he had been known only to students of the history of Pontypridd and the British Cremation Society. That is an exaggeration, but it is nevertheless true that Davies did a good deal to popularise the figure of Price, who until then had been alive only in the oral mythology of South Wales. Davies had first heard about him from his father, who had actually clapped eyes on Price, and first read about him in Morien's *History of Pontypridd and Rhonddu Valleys* (1903), a curious hotchpotch of local history, druidism, biography and mythology that had been popular when he was a schoolboy and from under the influence of which he did not wholly extricate himself.

What commended the rebellious doctor to Davies was that he had kept up a sustained assault on chapel morality, culminating in the cremation of his infant son, whom he had named Iesu Grist (the Welsh for Jesus Christ), in a field at Llantrisant in 1884. A qualified surgeon, Price was said to have treated the poor free of charge but demanded high fees from the better-off. He claimed to be a Druid and often performed fantastic ceremonies of his own devising on the rocking-stone above Pontypridd. He had set out at the head of a contingent of Chartists in the march on Newport in 1839 and when the rising proved a failure – at least twenty-two of the marchers were shot by soldiers outside the Westgate Hotel, and their leaders transported to Van Diemen's Land – Dr Price fled to France disguised as a woman. He was also an enthusiastic proponent of vegetarianism, nudism, moon-worship and free love, having sired a number of children by different mothers. The cremation of Iesu Grist, whom he had fathered at the age of 83, changed British funerary practice: at his trial at Cardiff Assizes the judge ruled that cremation was not illegal provided there was no threat to public order.

To Davies, Price was the complete Welsh hero, an example of 'the Old Adam', the pagan spirit that the writer sensed lurking beneath the staid surface of Nonconformist Wales. There was also something approaching a political slant to his view of Price:

> He was a descendant of the warrior-bards who were always at the side of those nimble Welsh kings and leaders incensed by the attempts of invaders to obliterate the ancient heritage of this small race.

Instead of foreign soldiers he had coalowners and iron-masters to grapple with – more subtle invaders. His task was to ensure that these did not utterly 'possess' the spirit of his people... He saw that a fatter wage packet was not enough: the ethos of his people required a more durable preservative.

In an interview with Glyn Jones in 1950, Davies remarked: 'It seems to me that Welsh writers have been fascinated too much by eccentrics... the trouble is perhaps to find the commonplace people of Wales'.[25] Yet few of his contemporaries wrote about eccentricity as often and in as much depth as he did, nor did they make such extensive use of the eccentric as a narrative strategy. Indeed, Davies relished it in all its forms, finding in its subversive power a way of overturning cultural norms and social conventions. The eccentrics in his stories are seized by a subversive idea, as in 'Conflict in Morfa'[26] and 'The Farm',[27] or possessed by an obsession, as in 'A Woman'[28] and 'The Bard',[29] or simply bent on murder, as in 'The Chosen One'.[30]

Eccentricity, for Davies, was associated with impropriety, lawlessness and crime, and he made it the cornerstone of his fiction. His depiction of it is invariably based on resistance to externally imposed labels and to an authority that denies the provisionality of all 'meaning'. He saw that South Wales, in the nineteenth century, had given rise to communities which were eccentric in that they were different from the metropolitan standard, in both language and social structure. After reading Davies's stories and novels, we are left wondering who the real eccentrics are, what exactly is meant by 'unacceptable behaviour', and what is 'abnormal'. The world, he suggests, is capable of a multiplicity of interpretations. It was thus, in writing about eccentrics, deviants, criminals and outcasts, that Davies – described by M. Wynn Thomas as 'a multiple outsider' – made room for his own form of sexuality and, at the same time, wreaked vengeance on a world that had excluded him from its 'normality'. For this reason Wynn Thomas has described Davies's career as 'a prolonged act of cultural sabotage' and suggested that he is 'a disquietingly bleak writer' who can be best characterized as 'the Strindberg of Wales'.[31]

The other two figures who exercised Davies's imagination were the Maid of Cefn Ydfa and Twm Shon Catti. The first of these was a tragic heroine, a high-born young woman from Llangynwyd in Glamorgan. At the age of 21 in 1725, she married a rich lawyer, and from this recorded fact has been spun a sentimental tale for which there is little or no foundation but which still exerts its fascination not only in 'the Old Parish' but also in a wider Wales. Ann Thomas, so the story goes, was in love with a young poet named Wil Hopcyn, and died from a broken heart because her parents would not allow her to marry him, though not before hearing her sweetheart singing *'Bugeilio'r Gwenith Gwyn'* ('Watching the white wheat'), which he had composed for her. Davies, who was no doubt drawn to the Maid because she was a victim of society's disapproval of her natural feelings, found the story in Isaac Craigfryn Hughes's fanciful but popular book.[32]

It was also the melodrama of this story that appealed to Davies, who based a play on it, *The Ripening Wheat*, which opened at the Royalty Theatre in London's West End in 1937. Among the principals were Sarah Erskine as Ann, Edith Sharpe as her mother, and Geoffrey Keen as Wil Hopcyn. The performance was something of an event in the cultural life of the London Welsh. No fewer than twelve Welsh MPs attended the premiere. The author was said to be too shy to take the customary curtain-call, although he was reported as having enjoyed the party given at the Savoy Grill afterwards. The play toured South Wales after the Second World War as *The Maid of Cefn Ydfa,* opening at the Empire Theatre in Tonypandy on the 20th of October 1952 with a young David Lyn taking the part of Wil Hopcyn. A copy of the programme was kept among the writer's papers, doubtless as a souvenir of an evening that had given the local boy a peculiar pleasure. It went on to the Town Hall in Pontypridd where, in the local newspaper, it was described as 'a new experience in serious theatre for Pontypridd', and then to the Astoria Theatre in Llanelli. A Welsh version by T.J. Williams-Hughes was performed at the Grand Theatre, Swansea, in 1936 and published as *Y Ferch o Gefn Ydfa* two years later.[33]

Although it was favourably reviewed in *The Times* and *The Daily Telegraph,* Davies took against the play and rarely mentioned it. It may be that he was piqued by the far greater success of Emlyn Williams's play *The Corn is Green,* which had its premiere in 1938 and went on to enjoy huge success both in Wales and England. The two writers never met and there is no record of Davies's opinion of Emlyn Williams, but the latter, in his introduction to an English translation of T. Rowland Hughes's novel, *O Law i Law,* published in 1950, referred to two strains of contemporary Welsh writing: the chocolate-box confections of the school of Allen Raine and

the more up-to-date and pretentious school of bogus
Welsh, not on chocolate boxes this time, but
presumably on sackloth with a pen dipped in ashes
... neither Welsh nor English but the rag-doll
offspring of Tchekov and D.H. Lawrence.[34]

It was clear from these strictures that Williams, who was
himself no slouch when it came to the chocolate-box view
of Wales, meant to convey the 'school' had but one
member and his name was Rhys Davies.

The third figure to capture Davies's imagination was
Twm Shon Catti, a highwayman whose heroic exploits had
first been popularized by T.J. Llewelyn Prichard in 1828.
Said to be the Welsh equivalent of the Scottish Rob Roy
or the English Robin Hood or Dick Turpin, Twm, who may
have had his origins in real life, took from the rich and
gave to the poor in the vicinity of Tregaron in the south
of Cardiganshire and, like the Maid of Cefn Ydfa, had
entered the oral culture of South Wales as a hugely
popular folk-hero. The section of Davies's book begins:

In remote pre-Nonconformist days, when hilarity
was more naturally abundant in Wales than it was
later, that is, before the Great Blight... Twm Shon
Catti was a rascal... he brings with him into the
museum an earthy, non-spiritual air of scoundrelism;
he grins a little, cynically...

and it ends:

He is a figure selected by us for the encrusting of
those unlawful desires which most of us suppress.

Someone must be their receptacle. Twm is a much admired and beloved figure in Wales, more familiarly and affectionately Welsh than our saints and warriors. We would all like to be a Twm, but to be a saint or warrior does not really attract. No wonder the rascal is also, traditionally, handsome, a poet, merry, a helper of the poor, and a great lover who married wealth and beauty. No wonder he became a justice of the peace and a mayor. He is an Ideal of all good Welshmen.

Thus, with tongue in cheek, Davies continued to bait his fellow countrymen by harking back to 'merrie Wales', that is to say pre-Methodist Wales, and to the representative figure of Twm, whom M. Wynn Thomas in his seminal study, *In the Shadow of the Pulpit* (2010), calls 'a heroic symbol of the Welsh artist liberated from the cultural shackles and mental inhibitions of Nonconformist culture'.[35]

Davies, like other Welsh writers who were among the first to mount a sustained critique of Nonconformity, wrote several stories designed to confront preachers with figures representing the suppressed instincts of their flocks. In a late story, 'The Old Adam', a theological student named Tudor Edwards is accused of being a Peeping Tom, after having been caught watching the buxom Jane as she sun-bathes in the nude.[36] Anxious to avoid scandal, the village of Clawdd offers him the alibi that he was simply poaching for salmon on the day in question. The cudgels are taken up by the families of the young people and an uneasy truce is eventually reached, though not before Tudor decamps, and his mother, with one eye on the wedding presents, succeeds in grabbing a figurine of Christmas Evans, one of the luminaries of the Welsh pulpit, clasping it to her ample bosom like a sexual fetish. The pagan god Pan triumphs over the chapel at the very end of the story.

But Davies does not stop there. His survey of the arts in *My Wales* hurls a fistful of barbs at what he perceived as the parochialism of writing in Welsh:

> Writers in the Welsh language hide, in a worldly sense, their light under a prickly bush. The members of this select, exclusive band labour for love; the ancient, strong, but sunset-tinted language is their passionate possession and they protect it zealously ... Welsh is a beautiful sensitive language and invites quiet literary experiment. But surely it must for ever remain subdued . . . Wales cannot afford a language of its own except perhaps for domestic use, holiday sprees such as the Eisteddfod, and dilettante poets who love the past...

It never seems to have occurred to him that as a Welshman who knew almost no Welsh, having been virtually deprived of the language by his parents and having made no attempt to learn it, in short, one who to all intents and purposes had lost contact with the native culture, he was hardly qualified to make such sweeping pronouncements. But, in M. Wynn Thomas's phrase, in this respect Davies was 'unabashed by his ignorance'. The anonymous reviewer in *The Catholic Herald* (16 July 1937) thought his remarks on the Welsh language 'contemptible'.

He was on firmer ground in his treatment of his countrymen writing in English. He was percipient enough to know that the work of Allen Raine, the only Welsh writer to have achieved best-seller status in Edwardian Wales with her 'nice fairy-tales about a beautiful land', would no longer pass muster. They drew from him a little of the acerbic sarcasm of which he was capable from time to time:

Sunshine's in her books, though, speaking for myself, I'd rather spend a cold and wet week in the waiting-room of Pontypridd railway station than read one of her books again. The utmost gloom seems preferable to Allen Raine's lurid optimism.

On the other hand, Caradoc Evans comes in for his meed of praise:

A thorn in the flesh of the Welsh, he has offended them more than anyone by refusing to see Wales as a bit of Heaven set down for a while in the world as an example to other nations. Hypocrisy, lying, fraud, dishonesty, miserliness, brutal lusts – these are the human characteristics Evans find best inspire him... But for all that, Evans's odious characters, his rascals and sluts, are depicted with a truth, fidelity and art that place him far above the moral standard.

Even so, Evans had his weaknesses as a writer in Davies's view:

His chief limitation is that he takes the short local view of Wales; he has never really escaped the chapel and is as much a deacon in the Big Seat as any of those faithful, grim wardens of the country's village life and mannerisms... A lesser limitation is his literary style. Imitative of the Bible and mock sing-song, it was attractive in his first book, but too much of it becomes wearisome.

Davies was fully aware that he wrote his early stories in the long shadow cast by a writer he had first read as a youth in Blaenclydach and he could recognize Evans's faults because they were his own. Evans, for his part, made clear what he thought of Davies when he was quoted in an article by Raymond Marriott published in *Wales*: 'I never heard him [Evans] praise a Welsh writer, apart from Machen, and a Welsh short-story writer generally considered one of the best of the day [he meant Davies but did not name him] he thought a feeble imitator of himself'.[37] It was to be a generation or two before Welsh readers, thanks mainly to the efforts of his editor John Harris, came to a better appreciation of Caradoc Evans's work as literary constructions of a high order.

Among other Welsh prose-writers in English given perfunctory mentions in *My Wales* are Arthur Machen, Richard Hughes, Hilda Vaughan, Geraint Goodwin, Margiad Evans, Jack Jones, Eiluned Lewis, Gwyn Jones, and Goronwy Rees; Emlyn Williams is not mentioned. All these made significant contributions to what was called then Anglo-Welsh literature and all have kept their places in the canon. Of Welsh poets in English Davies could mention only four: Edward Thomas, W.H. Davies, Huw Menai and Dylan Thomas. Of the last-named he wrote:

The young poet, Dylan Thomas, another dark horse, whose furious wealth of imagery is as wild and fearsome as a Welsh preacher involved in transports of *hwyl,* promises that a considerable poet has again come out of South Wales.

Dylan Thomas, who had already made his spectacular entrance on the London literary stage, was a familiar, if not omnipresent figure in the pubs of Fitzrovia in the 1930s. The warmth of what Davies had to say about him in *My Wales* (if that is what it was, since on other occasions he took a dim view of the obstreperous Thomas), was not reciprocated by the poet, who had himself been toying with the idea of a travel book about Wales. Writing to Mervyn Peake in 1938, he remarked, 'I feel I can't go on with the idea of a Welsh travel book; for one thing Rhys Davies has just done it, and a feeble job it was.' Cattiness and professional jealousy, it seems, was rife in the republic of letters, then as now.

The two writers had almost certainly met by this point and were to cross paths frequently over the coming years. While they are not recorded as having quarrelled, it soon became obvious they had very little in common. Davies's clean, smart appearance, moreover, gave the impression of a degree of prosperity, though in fact he was often much worse off than the unkempt Thomas, and his quiet, reserved manner sat ill with the rodomontade that Thomas kept up in company. Furthermore, his upbringing as the grocer's son in Blaenclydach had instilled in him the virtues of thrift, a horror of debt, and an insistence on paying his own way, while the spendthrift Thomas violated all these principles. At their first meeting Thomas had touched Davies for a few pounds and for that reason alone he was someone to be avoided. The novelist later learnt the poet had repaid his debt by leaving a cheque for him with a bookseller, where it was collected only after Thomas's death.

Lewis Davies told the present writer that, while drinking in The Salisbury, he and Fred Urquhart had once seen Thomas coming into the pub by the front entrance. Realising they were the only ones at the bar who knew him, which meant they would have to spend the evening buying him drinks, they quickly left by a side entrance. On another occasion, late at night, Rhys Davies was buttonholed by Thomas, who told him he had nowhere to stay. He was offered a bed in the novelist's Maida Vale flat, only for Thomas to wet it during the night, a situation not improved by the fact that the two men were sharing it at the time. Always drawn to extreme characters, Davies was fascinated by the poet's bohemianism, but preferred to remain at a distance – 'not too far away, not too close'. They were clearly not made for each other, yet he remained an admirer of Thomas as a writer, if not as a man. In a review of the latter's *Portrait of the Artist as a Young Dog* (1940), Davies wrote: 'It contains the true acrid scent of young life, magically distilled'.[38]

The year 1937 was a milestone in the history of Welsh writing in English, for this was when Keidrych Rhys, still only in his early twenties but highly energetic and influential in literary circles, launched his magazine *Wales*.[39] It was announced as 'an independent pamphlet of creative work by the younger progressive Welsh writers', on whose behalf it claimed, 'though we write in English, we are rooted in Wales'. Among the contributors to the first series were Dylan Thomas (who co-edited two issues), Glyn Jones, Idris Davies, Vernon Watkins, Caradoc Evans, and Rhys Davies.[40] The iconoclastic personality of the editor, who delighted in gossip, innuendo and controversy, was stamped on every issue of his magazine. Payment was nugatory and irregular, and Davies was a professional writer who expected to be paid for his work, yet such were his sympathy with the venture and his liking for Keidrych Rhys that he contributed frequently, both to the first series and the second. It was in *Wales* that he would publish his fond elegiac memoir of Nina Hamnett.[41]

He had met the painter in 1927, at a party given by Eve Kirk in Fitzroy Square. Born in Tenby in 1890, she 'invariably mustered up a nationalist sentiment for Wales' and had a special attachment to Welsh artists and writers, though she grew wary and censorious of Dylan Thomas: 'It was as though a king and queen trod on each other's toes', was Davies's non-judgemental comment. Hamnett at this time was a mainstay of Roger Fry's Omega Workshops – his portrait of her is in the Courtauld collection – and her talents as painter and draughtswoman made her an important member of the Modernist Movement. At this time she was still producing exquisitely tranquil drawings, particularly of old women and boys, at which she excelled, and still had the lithe figure captured in marble by Henri Gaudier-Brzeska in the sculpture known as 'Laughing Torso', which also became the title of her first volume of reminiscences.[42] She was not the easiest person in company, especially when the worse for wear, but Davies treated her, as he treated Count Potocki, with respect and infinite patience. 'Generous, good-humoured, loyal and witty', in Davies's view, she would sing bawdy sailors' songs in English and French to entertain anyone who cared to listen. She was one of the 'ruined characters' of whom Davies had such a rare understanding.

As time went by, Hamnett became a familiar figure who, for a drink or two, would relay the latest gossip or recount anecdotes of famous people like Augustus John and 'the Bloomsberries'. Gradually her talent atrophied and, with her ceaseless chatter and unwashed appearance, she became just one of the many drunks who frequented the pubs of Fitzrovia. In his essay the writer not only left a vivid impression of one of bohemia's most memorable personalities but also showed how a unique talent could be ruined by excess. To the young writer up from Wales in the 1920s such a lifestyle had seemed a liberating way for an artist to live, but the mature writer recognized it as potentially destructive.

Although Davies did not feel for Nina Hamnett what he felt for Anna Kavan, his affection for her was real enough and he had only kind things to say about her in his memoir: 'I felt that she still might become first and foremost Nina Hamnett the painter, rather than queen, paragon and very daisy of Bohemia.' He had been intending to visit her in the Little Venice area of Maida Vale in 1956 when he heard she was dead. It is believed someone had called at her house and, leaning out of a second-floor window to throw down the keys to her visitor, she had fallen forty feet to the ground, impaling herself on the railings and dying in hospital shortly afterwards. The mysterious caller was never identified and the official verdict was accidental death, though some believed Hamnett had committed suicide after hearing a radio play, *It's Long Past Time*, by her old friend Robert Pocock, in which she thought she had been grotesquely caricatured. The truth of the matter will never be known.

The 1930s, Auden's 'low, dishonest decade', ended with the defeat of the democratically-elected Spanish Republic by the forces of General Franco, a conflict that, unusually, drew from Davies, in a review of an issue of *New Writing,* an unexpectedly passionate criticism of writing about the war:

> A section is devoted to the Spanish War. But there is little to arouse one here. The huge, malignant, savage, wretched subject of war needs huge, malignant, savage and heroic writers. There have been few masterpieces written on this subject. The contributors in *New Writing* make it seem like the brawling of sparrows... The emotion of rage, which should be in them, is not.[43]

But it would take a Hemingway, or an Orwell, or a Malraux, to write about the ideologically-driven conflict of the war in Spain. This was as far as Davies, unwilling to take sides as ever, and not given to 'the emotion of rage', was prepared to go.

Notes

1 Anna Kavan, *Asylum Piece and Other Stories* (Jonathan Cape, 1940)
2 David Callard, *The Case of Anna Kavan: a Biography* (Peter Owen, 1992)
3 Jeremy Reed, *A Stranger on Earth: The Life and Work of Anna Kavan* (Peter Owen, 2006)

4   Anna Kavan, *Mercury* (Peter Owen, 1994), with a foreword by Doris Lessing

5   *Girl Waiting in the Shade* (Heinemann, 1960)

6   Glyn Roberts, 'Rhys Davies's Polished Prose', in the *Western Mail* (12 September 1933); see also the same author's article, 'They interpret Wales – in English', in the same paper (28 July 1936).

7   *One of Norah's Early Days* (Grayson & Grayson, 1935); 285 copies, of which 250, numbered and signed by the author, were for sale.

8   *The Skull* (Tintern Press, 1936); 95 copies bound in buckram and 15 in pigskin

9   *Honey and Bread* (Putnam, 1935)

10 *A Time to Laugh* (Heinemann, 1937). The novel was reviewed by John Edwards in *Life and Letters To-day* (Summer 1937).

11 *Jubilee Blues* (Heinemann, 1938). The novel was reviewed under the heading 'Woman of Wales' in the *TLS* (15 October 1938). Lynette Roberts, in *Wales* (6/7, March 1939), wrote: '[Cassie] brings to discussions of the dole and the means test the naivete and religious innocence of the farming west... One feels that Rhys Davies, like his own Cassie, is detached, frightened of any real contact, terrified to sink himself into the sub-world of twisted and trampled lives lest he too should partake of the general deformity.'

12 *My Wales* (Jarrolds, 1937; Funk & Wagnalls, 1938)

13 Glyn Jones, 'The Ripening Davies', in *Wales* (1, 1937)

14 John Fordham, *James Hanley: Modernism and the Working Class* (University of Wales Press, 2002)

15 *The Things Men Do* (Heinemann, 1936). Contents: 'The Two Friends', 'The Contraption', 'Wrath', 'Cherry-blossom on the Rhine', 'The Friendly Creature', 'Glimpses of the Moon', 'The Funeral', 'Caleb's Ark', 'Resurrection', Half-holiday', 'The Farm', 'On the Tip'.

16 Owen M. Edwards, *The Story of Wales* (T. Fisher Unwin, 1901)

17 Huw Edwin Osborne, *Rhys Davies* in the *Writers of Wales* series (University of Wales Press, 2009)

18 The Blue Books (3 vols., 1847), a report published by the Government on the state of education in Wales, caused religious controversy and an upsurge of patriotic feeling which had lasting effects on the cultural and political life of Wales. The Commissioners, who were young, inexperienced Anglicans, blamed Nonconformity and the Welsh language, then spoken by the monoglot majority of the people of Wales, for the poor state not only of education but of the morals and even the intelligence of Welsh children. The report was known ever after as *Brad y Llyfrau Gleision* ('The treachery of the Blue Books'). See G.T. Roberts, *The Language of the Blue Books* (University of Wales Press, 1998).

19 Herbert John Fleure (1877-1969), who held the first chair of Geography and Anthropology at Aberystwyth, was noted for his work on cephalic indices; the subject fell under a cloud during the Nazi era.

20 Ll. Wyn Griffith, *The Welsh* (Penguin, 1950)

21 James Hanley, *Grey Children: a Study in Humbug and Misery in South Wales* (Methuen, 1937)

22 Dai Smith, 'Rhys Davies and his "Turbulent Valley"', in *Decoding the Hare*

23 Daniel Williams, 'Withered Roots: Ideas of Race in the Writings of Rhys Davies', in *Decoding the Hare*

24 [George] Ewart Evans, 'The Valleys', a review of books by RD, Jack Jones, Goronwy Rees, Gwyn Jones and Lewis Jones, in *Wales* (3, Autumn 1937)

25 Glyn Jones interview with RD, '"Every genuine writer finds his own Wales"', in *New Welsh Review* (35, Winter 1996/97)

26 'Conflict in Morfa', in *A Pig in a Poke* (Joiner & Steele, 1931); *Collected Stories* (ed. Meic Stephens, vol.1, 1996)

27 'The Farm', in *The Things Men Do* (Heinemann, 1936); *Collected Stories* (ed. Meic Stephens, vol. 1, 1996)

28 'A Woman', in *Collected Stories* (ed. Meic Stephens, vol.1, 1996)

29 'The Bard', in *A Pig in a Poke* (Joiner & Steele, 1931); *Collected Stories* (ed. Meic Stephens, vol.1, 1996)

30 'The Chosen One', in *The Chosen One and other stories* (Heinemann, 1967); *Collected Stories* (ed. Meic Stephens, vol. 2, 1996)

31 M. Wynn Thomas, '"Never Seek to Tell thy Love"', in *Decoding the Hare*

32 Craigfryn (Isaac Craigfryn Hughes), *The Maid of Cefn Ydfa; an Historical Novel of the 18th Century* (1881; 30th edn., The Western Mail Ltd, 1927); the cover design depicts Ann dipping a quill in her own blood.

33 T.J. Williams-Hughes, *Y Ferch o Gefn Ydfa* (Gwasg y Brython, 1938)

34 Emlyn Williams, introduction to T. Rowland Hughes, *From Hand to Hand* (Gwasg Aberystwyth, 1950)

35 M. Wynn Thomas, *In the Shadow of the Pulpit: Literature and Nonconformist Wales* (University of Wales Press, 2010)

36 'The Old Adam', in *The Chosen One and other stories* (Heinemann, 1967); *Collected Stories* (ed. Meic Stephens, vol. 2, 1996)

37 R[aymond].B. Marriott, 'Caradoc Evans', in *Wales* (7, Summer 1945)

38 RD, a review of Dylan Thomas, *Portrait of the Artist as a Young Dog*, in *Life and Letters To-day* (vol. 24, no. 31, March 1940)

39 Keidrych Rhys (1915-87), was born Ronald Rees Jones in Carmarthenshire, but later changed his name; the Ceidrych is a stream near the farm where he was born which joins the Towy at Bethlehem. A journalist and editor, he set up the Druid Press, which published, *inter alia*, the early poems of R.S. Thomas. He is remembered chiefly as the

editor of the Faber anthology *Modern Welsh Poetry* (1944) and of the influential magazine *Wales*. For details of his life and work see Charles Mundye's introduction to *The Van Pool: Collected Poems* (Seren, 2012); see also the next footnote.

40 *Wales* (1st series, 11 nos., Summer 1937 to Winter 1939/40; 2nd series, July 1943 to October 1949; 3rd series, September 1958 to New Year 1960); see also the previous footnote.

41 'Nina Hamnet [*sic*], bohemian', in *Wales* (3rd series, September 1959). Hamnett's portrait of RD, done in 1948, is in the National Library of Wales.

42 Nina Hamnett, *Laughing Torso* (Constable, 1932; Virago, 1984); sequel, *Is She a Lady? A Problem in Autobiography* (Allan Wingate, 1955)

43 A review of *New Writing* (Spring 1939), in *Life and Letters To-day* (21, 22, 1939). RD also wrote, for the same magazine, reviews of books by Mulk Raj Anand, Adrian Bell, Elizabeth Inglis-Jones, Dylan Thomas, Ruthven Todd, and Glyn Jones.

Rhys Davies c.1930 photo: Dora Head

Six

Boy with a trumpet

At the beginning of 1939, Rhys Davies was in Blaenclydach, short of money and glummer than usual. 'As you can see,' he wrote to his friend Raymond Marriott, 'I am once more returned to the gritty bosom of my native land. Still very black here, and a general air of sluggishness. The mines work off and on, but every other person out of work.' But what worried him most was the prospect of war, which filled him with foreboding and, he claimed, kept him from writing:

> During the first year of the war I wrote scarcely a line; the thought of the destruction to come stultified me. 'Chaos is come again,' I thought, and 'I am for the dark.' Yet after a while I heaved up, took my bearings and began anew. But it was hard, hard work... The physical destruction of war is antipathetic to that creative instinct which is the artist's reason for existence.[1]

'I've touched bottom as regards my belief and faith in mankind,' he informed Marriott. 'God knows what will happen to us all.' He felt, moreover, that the London in which he had grown to maturity as a writer no longer existed and that, in the event of a German victory, he and his sort would be among the first to be imprisoned or killed. In September 1939 he was living with an architect named Bevan in Maitland Park House, Maitland Park.[2]

The premonition that Davies was 'for the dark', a very real fate for a homosexual in the event of a Nazi victory, may have had to do with the trauma he had suffered at his brother Jack's death in 1918, though he expressed it by railing against the folly of governments, particularly the one in London. 'I think military life would amuse me, for a while – its squalor, coarseness and idiocy entertain me,' he wrote to Raymond Marriott in December 1940. 'It all depends, of course, how successfully one can see it objectively, and how much one is in control of one's reactions'.

By 1941 the likelihood of military conscription hung over his head, for he had received his call-up papers and was destined for the auxiliary fire-service – 'that fine body of men' in which Spender was to serve. It was one reason why he was in the habit of giving the year of his birth as 1903: Davies would have been liable for call-up in 1939 had his true age been known, although it is difficult to see how the authorities could have overlooked him for very long. His brother Lewis and his friends Raymond Marriott and George Bullock had registered as conscientious objectors but Davies was not inclined to do the same. While waiting for his call-up papers he grew more and more despondent at having nothing to do but wait. 'I get horribly depressed if I'm idle for more than a week or two – I've got a puritanic strain in me which makes me feel parasitic and inferior,' he told Marriott. Prone to what his brother called 'bad patches', he was now perilously close to a nervous breakdown similar to the one he had suffered in 1935.

In the event, both Rhys and Lewis Davies were declared medically unfit, Grade 4-F, the lowest category possible, by a doctor known to be sympathetic to homosexuals, though they were deemed fit for civilian duties. The interviewing clerk who filled in Davies's particulars was puzzled as to how to describe his occupation and when a form was later posted to him he was described as 'signwriter'. 'I suppose by rights I ought to be in khaki,' he wrote to Louis Quinain, one of his closest friends, in May 1940, adding camply, 'but I hate it as a colour.' The serious nature of the conflict was brought home to him, however, when Lewis's flat was destroyed by a German bomb and seven of his neighbours killed.

However, his claim that the outbreak of war depressed him so severely that he stopped writing was not strictly true. He may not have published any books in 1939, but he worked on *Under the Rose* and *Sea Urchin: Adventures of Jorgen Jorgensen,* both of which appeared in 1940.[3][4] In the first of these he gave a West Wales setting to the story of Rachel Lloyd, a frustrated spinster who murders Stephen Meredith, the man who had deserted her on the eve of their wedding, and then buries him under a rosebush in the garden. The book ends when Rachel, blackmailed by Stephen's lover when she comes looking for him, jumps to her death in best Gothic style. The reviews in *The Observer* and *The Times Literary Supplement* were not entirely favourable, prompting Davies to write twice to Raymond Marriott:

> Such rebuke! It seems that it's not for me to deal in dark murders[5]... As far as I can judge, people think I ought not to have left the woes of the workers to write this kind of book. A pox on such limited minds! [6]

When, in due course, Marriott read the book and did not like it, Davies wrote to him: 'It was the product of Rhys Davies no 2, who is not necessarily inferior to no 1, only different. I have a side of me which must be expressed in that type of work.' To George Bullock he wrote that he had thought the novel would sell and that he had one eye on a stage or screen version: 'But, alas, I'm beginning to see that it's not in me to write a best-seller.' He nevertheless kept his sense of humour when a woman reader wrote to say she thought him a fine novelist but a poor gardener who knew nothing about the cultivation of roses.

The second book published in 1940, *Sea Urchin*, commissioned by Duckworth, is a highly competent biography of Jorgen Jorgensen, a Danish sailor whose adventures in the early nineteenth century included a brief spell as Protector of Iceland, a title he had bestowed on himself, for which he was transported to Van Diemen's Land. The old-style synopsis printed on the book's title-page is a fair summary of its contents:

> Being a true narrative of the life of a Danish adventurer: his glory, infamy and sad decline: who

was a lover of England, sailor of the British Navy, Leader of a Revolution, Ruler of Iceland, convict, preacher, spy, author, policeman, newspaper editor, gambler, pioneer and explorer: together with extracts from his writings and letters, published and unpublished.

As research, Davies drew on the sailor's own 'confessions', his autobiography, memoirs, letters and journals. It is not known why he was given a commission to write this book or whether he was paid a generous fee, but he applied himself to the task and, professional to his fingertips, delivered a manuscript in good time.

It could not have been easy to write in a city constantly bombed by the Luftwaffe and with food in short supply, but despite his bleak foreboding, Davies found wartime London surprisingly congenial to his vocation. Looking back, he wrote, 'Yet after a while I heaved up, took my bearings and began anew. But it was hard, hard work.' If anything, the war seems to have spurred him on to write even more prolifically, though the only story directly about the conflict was 'Spectre de la Rose'.[7] Nor did his nomadic existence, with a change of address every few months, make for a steady social routine. He had never been a recluse, enjoying a pint and chat in congenial company. But he could not entertain in his cramped lodgings and tended to meet people in ones and twos in pubs. By 1939, most of the Lahr group had dispersed, some into the armed forces, and it was no longer possible (if ever it was possible) to speak of a Rhys Davies circle. The extraordinary range of people he knew were, for the most part, unacquainted with one another and he kept up his contacts with each and every one of them singly or in pairs, not in groups.

Again, many were women, who found him charming, witty and good company. In the interview he gave to Delyth Davies of BBC Wales in 1977 he said, 'I like having women around. I like them to come to see me and I like visiting their homes. But I don't want to tie myself to anyone, man or woman.' Two of the women he knew in the 1940s were Matilda Eeches, an actress who later went on to some small success in Hollywood, and Marie Lloyd Jnr, daughter of the famous music-hall star, who used to sing in some of East London's homosexual pubs. Another was Nora Wyndham, by all accounts a garrulous and strong-willed woman who worked as a Social Survey Supervisor and who, for a while, stalked Davies and made his life wretched.[8] Despite her unprepossessing personality, he kept up a friendship with her until, to his horror, he realized she was infatuated with him. Rebuffed, the woman went around making slanderous remarks about the writer until he threatened legal action against her, and so the friendship came to an abrupt end in 1942. 'I never discovered what the slander was,' Lewis Davies told the present writer, 'but I imagine it was of a sexual nature.'

It may very well be that by this stage of his life the restless Davies was unable to feel properly at home anywhere. Like Chekhov, he was 'a refined nomad', forever moving on because there was always something wrong with the place where he happened to be. Back in Blaenclydach for a few months in 1940, he wrote letters to London friends complaining about the rain, the boredom and lack of a social life, though he did enjoy

RD at 15 Russell Court, 16 June 1968
photo: Julian Sheppard / National Library of Wales

Clydach Vale in the 1920s

Peggie Davies (later Williams), the writer's youngest sister, schoolteacher

Arthur Lewis Davies, the writer's younger brother, librarian and patron of the Rhys Davies Trust

Gladys Davies, the writer's sister, nurse

Gertie Davies, the writer's eldest sister, headmistress

Charles Lahr (1885-1971), anarchist and RD's first
publisher, 'a rare boyo of a character' (Liam
O'Flaherty)

Anna Kavan (1901-68), c. 1950, writer,
RD's closest female friend

Raymond B. Marriott (1911-92),
journalist and RD's friend
photo: *The Stage*

Herman Schrijver (1904-72),
bon vivant and interior decorator
photo: Robert Horner

Philip Burton (1904-95), a friend of RD

Postcard inscribed 'Kind regards, Roy', a Guardsman, 1938

Miriam Karlin, RD and Flora Robson, discussing *No Escape* (1954)

Dodie (William Brown), one of RD's romantic crushes

Louise Taylor

Louis and Greta Quinain with son Peter in
Shamley Green c. 1946

reading stories to a small girl named Patsy who had come from Manor Park to stay at the Treorci home of his sister Peggie and her teacher husband Walt Williams for the duration of the war: 'Tell Greta,' he wrote to Louis Quinain, 'that we have a child evacuee here and I dandle her on my knee and she calls me Uncle! . . . She has a passion for stories but her ''Uncle's'' are not suitable for children.'

When in London, where he maintained his promiscuous lifestyle, haunting the pubs around Knightsbridge Barracks with occasional forays to the homosexual haunts of Limehouse and the East End, Davies complained about the crowds, the noise, and the shortage of good food. Vincent Wells's city warehouse had been destroyed in the blitz, and he was beset with financial troubles, which made Davies feel he had outstayed his welcome at the house in Henley-on-Thames, but he could still stay at Eve Kirk's studio at 19 Tavistock Place, near London University, and at Bevan's flat in Maitland Park whenever he wanted.

With only one of his closest acquaintances, Raymond Marriott, who became deputy editor of *The Stage*, could he indulge his passion for the theatre and opera. It comes as no surprise to learn that his favourite works were Richard Strauss's *Elektra* and *Salome*, their vengeful female figures striking a resonant chord in his imagination. With complimentary tickets provided by Marriott, Davies went to the ballet and opera at every opportunity and saw many of the world-famous orchestras and theatre companies that played in London during the 1940s. According to his brother Lewis, he later became obsessed with Maria Callas, attending the diva's every new performance on the London stage. Several of her recordings and theatre programmmes were found in the writer's trunk after his death.

Before leaving the leafy environs of Henley, Davies had met a man called Len Smith in one of the homosexual pubs in Reading, the nearest large town. He worked as a chauffeur for the McKenna family of Waltham St Lawrence in Buckinghamshire, but moonlighted as a car mechanic. Smith introduced Davies to a young couple whose car he worked on from time to time, namely Louis and Greta (Gertrude) Quinain, who were to be very kind to him. Quinain was a country policeman at Shamley Green, near Guildford, and wrote two popular books about the force before turning his hand to farming, as well as many articles about country living under the pseudonym Peter Froud. Although literate and book-loving, he was far enough removed from metropolitan cliques to make Davies feel comfortable in his company. The Quinains agreed to let him stay with them for the summer of 1941 and, after the war, when they moved to Jennings farm at Clayhidon in Devon, he continued to be a welcome guest.

It was in Shamley Green that Davies wrote *To-morrow to Fresh Woods*, his largely autobiographical book – the title is a part-quotation of the last line of Milton's *Lycidas* – which bids a fond farewell to his youth and was to be his last Rhondda novel. Louis Quinain recalled:

Every morning after breakfast, before sitting down to write, he would walk a mile or more round the country lanes. He would usually have returned by ten o'clock and would write until lunchtime,

continuing in the afternoon. He wrote very little of
an evening and said he could not work late since he
found it difficult to switch off at bedtime. He liked
to be free at weekends, perhaps working on
Saturday mornings but seldom after lunch or on
Sundays. On Saturday evenings he would always go
out, usually to Guildford.

By late August of 1941 Davies was back in Blaenclydach,
where, he told Marriott, he could get back to 'the raw
stuff of life, by which I mean the original simplicity in
man, that primal glow which gives him meaning in a
blind world'. After posting the corrected proofs of *To-
morrow to Fresh Woods* to the publisher, he went for a
break in Porthcawl.[9] The resort – 'my bucket-and-spade
idea of paradise' – seemed to draw him whenever he
wanted to enjoy some fresh air and experience again the
erotic thrills he had first encountered there as a young
man. Writing from 43 Esplanade Avenue to Louis
Quinain, one of the very few men with whom he was
open about his sexuality, he reported the town to be full
of military personnel and that he was hoping to find 'a
sink of iniquity' during his stay. A fortnight later, he
wrote to say he had found:

a couple of 'gayish' pubs, rather low, where the local
military and RAF foregather for singsongs etc, with
a sprinkling of their good-hearted, apple-cheeked, if
boisterous wenches. I sang with them – folk songs,
old ballads, hymns etc etc. I met an amusing RAF
boy from Yorkshire, very camp. Also two bits of
native nonsense (while the moon was shining), one

of which knew London very well indeed. As you may guess, I was last off the Promenade at night.

The use of 'gayish', denoting 'homosexual', in this letter, is one of a very few instances the present writer has found anywhere in Davies's correspondence. The adjective 'gay' had acquired its meaning of 'homosexual' by about 1935, but had been current in homosexual sub-cultures long before that as a password and code. Alberto Manguel and Craig Stephenson in their introduction to *The Flamingo Anthology of Gay Literature* (1994) dated this usage slightly later:

> Naked except for a fur-trimmed negligée and waddling about in bare feet, Cary Grant announced to an enquiring May Robson that he was thus attired because he had gone 'gay'. With this pronouncement in the 1939 film *Bringing up Baby*, the word 'gay' meaning 'male homosexual' publicly entered the English language of North America.[10]

That Davies had not yet begun to use it in this way by the late 1930s is suggested by his reference to 'gay parties in which people sit about and examine their sophistication' in his admiring review of *Last Stories* by Mary Butts, a lesbian, that appeared in the magazine *Wales*; there 'gay' means no more than 'merry' or 'carefree'.[11] 'Gay' may have been loaded with meaning in *Gay's the Word*, the title of Ivor Novello's last musical in 1951, but it was one Rhys Davies hardly ever used, even after the Gay Liberation movement got under way in the 1960s.

In early October 1941 Davies moved again, this time
to 4 Altar Cottages, Crowhurst, near Lingfield in Surrey,
where he had been offered a cottage for five shillings a
week by a writer friend called John Gray. But the
experience of living in the country and having to look after
the property, which was isolated, had no bath and only
an earthen closet, held little appeal for him. Although
Davies was emotionally and intellectually the most self-
sufficient of men, he was pretty helpless when it came to
practical matters. He sent his manuscripts to a typist and
his clothes to a laundry, and when living alone, as he did
most of the time, would eat out at corner cafés as often
as possible. He never owned property or furniture, never
learned to drive a car and for years had no telephone;
people wishing to contact him would leave messages with
his publishers or in the pubs and bookshops he was
known to frequent, which was one reason why he made a
regular round of those establishments. 'It really is almost
a full-time job,' he complained to Quinain about doing
household chores:

> I can get no time for reading, let alone writing of
> which I haven't done a stroke. I get a girl in to do a
> bit of cleaning, but there's all the cooking and 100
> other jobs: it's really not worthwhile for one person.

He began to slip away to London and, just before Christmas,
abandoning the cottage, moved back to Blaenclydach, where
home comforts were always to be found, his mother and
sister waiting on him and seeing to his daily needs. 'In my
parents' house I had a comfortable room for work on my
novel,' he wrote in *Print of a Hare's Foot*.

I had pleasing food and I paid nothing... I settled
into the dismal winter, going out less and less. The
solitary occupant of a lighthouse, or a spider
weaving a web in the rafters, I had one of the
loneliest jobs in the world. It was also self-chosen.
There was not a bounden duty for anyone else to
pay the slightest attention.

Even so, his future, he now decided, was going to be in
London, bomb-ravaged though it was and its social life
badly affected by wartime shortages. John Gray wanted
to move back into the Crowhurst cottage, and
conveniently passed on to Davies the basement room he
had been occupying at 131 Randolph Avenue in Maida
Vale. It was shabbily furnished and inadequately heated
but had a kitchen and its own side entrance, which
afforded Davies a degree of privacy. 'It's not my cup of
tea at all,' he wrote to Quinain on taking it over, but the
room was to be his base for the next twelve years. His
landlady was 'a faded actress, purply with drink and the
dramas of a succession of lovers', a Mrs Waugh-Brown.

Now, despite a severe cold that persisted all winter,
Davies lost no time in seeking out his old contacts in the
metropolis. No one reading his correspondence can fail to
remark the frequency of the colds, sore throats and high
temperatures to which he was prey. It may be he had a
congenitally weak constitution, but since his ailments
were invariably minor, a more likely explanation is a
degree of hypochondria approaching Proustian levels.
Writing to Quinain in April 1942 he reported 'a racking
cough, waves of something like flu recurring, with the
resultant mental wretchedness'. Soon afterwards he went

down with food poisoning and developed a kind of neurasthenia or nervous debility which may have triggered a mild nervous breakdown; the details were never divulged, not even to his brother Lewis.

However, it was not long before he was up and about again. He was offered a teaching job in the Near East but promptly turned it down. Then he began writing humorous, non-political sketches for *Tribune*, the journal of the British Left edited by Aneurin Bevan. He also found he could earn money from the plethora of magazines now publishing short stories. Commercial possibilities for the genre had improved immensely: the 1940s were the golden years for periodical literature in Britain, and there was an enthusiastic audience for the short story especially. Paper rationing had recently been introduced, a factor that had severely affected the quantity and production quality of books, but magazines were exempt. When Davies came to put together a collection of his recent stories, *A Finger in Every Pie* (1942) – 'This book is produced in complete conformity with the authorised economy standards' – he was able to acknowledge *Esquire, The Evening Standard, Horizon, Life and Letters To-day, London Mercury, Tribune, Star, Modern Reading, Selected Writing*, and E.J. O'Brien's annual anthology, *Best Short Stories*.[12]

This new collection, together with *The Trip to London* (1946) and *Boy with a Trumpet* (1949), represents the high water mark of Davies's mature style as a short-story writer.[13] [14] *A Finger in Every Pie* includes the story 'Nightgown', in which a wife with an unheeding husband and five strapping sons to feed, colliers all, goes without food so that she can provide them with the thick rashers of salted bacon and tinned tomatoes they crave. The wife, in her man's cap and son's boots and muffler, was based on a woman described as Mrs Hughes Number 8 in *Print of a Hare's Foot*, whose son's funeral was the first Davies had attended as a young man. At the last, emaciated but uncomplaining, she is taken by a stroke. But a neighbour lays her out in a silk nightgown she has secretly saved up for as the one luxury in her drab life and in which she wished to be buried. The husband and sons now come into the bedroom to view her:

> They slunk up in procession, six big men, with their heads ducked, disturbed out of the rhythm of their daily life of work, food, and pub. And entering the room for the last view, they stared in surprise. A stranger lay on the bed ready for her coffin. A splendid, shiny, white silk nightgown, flowing down over her feet, with rich lace frilling bosom and hands, she lay like a lady taking a rest, clean and comfortable. So much they stared, it might have been an angel shining there. But her face jutted stern, bidding no approach to the contented peace she had found.

The nightgown is not just a luxury but also the last vestige of the femininity she has been forced to conceal in the overbearing masculinity of her household (which her husband displays while bathing on the hearth). She can assert her femininity only in death. Even then the husband is unheeding, immediately looking for another woman to maintain himself, the house and the sons. Typically, Davies takes the woman's side.

Another story in the collection that illustrates Davies's

understanding of Rhondda society is 'The Pits are on the Top', which is almost a documentary account of a bus journey from Tonypandy Square up the hill to Blaenclydach. Some of the women passengers discuss, knowledgeably and volubly, whether the body of a miner, dead from 'the dust', should be dissected so that it can be established whether he has died from silicosis or pneumoconiosis (a disease of the lungs that was the colliers' scourge) and whether his wife is therefore eligible for compensation, and all the while a younger woman sits quietly with her fiancé, listening to his hacking cough. In less than five pages Davies sketches a scene that is precisely local and yet universal in its sympathy for human suffering. Dai Smith has called the story:

> a near-perfect cameo, so good for its passing moment that it could be wished Rhys Davies had never left his 'turbulent valley' at all so that... he might have stayed to capture its complete rhythm.[15]

The same feeling for ordinary lives is found in 'The Two Friends' in which colliers' wives risk being caught picking coal on a slagheap. This story is reminiscent of George Orwell's *The Road to Wigan Pier* (1937) in its observation and sympathy.

In June 1942, although unfit for the army, but because he was liable for civilian duties, Davies was obliged to take a full-time job at the Ministry of Information. It was his first regular employment since 1927 and came as something of a shock to his system. He was employed in the Curzon Street branch that dealt with the records of prisoners of war. The work was not too menial and the ambience was fairly pleasant, since the office was staffed mainly by married women, with whom he had always got on well, and by part-timers wanting to do their bit for the war effort. Some days there was nothing for him to do at all, so he read manuscripts for Michael Joseph in a quiet corner. The hours were long, however. He had to get up at half-past seven in the morning and work a full week with only every other Saturday afternoon off. The job left him too tired to write and he almost immediately began to plan his escape. His unease was brought to a head in July when he was transferred to a new department where the work was much more demanding. It had become obvious that he could not combine office work and writing, and somehow managing to get a discharge on medical grounds, he left in November of the same year. In the autobiographical entry he wrote for *Twentieth Century Authors* (1955) the five months he had spent in the Ministry were expanded into the years 1939 to 1942.[16] 'He liked to play it up, you know,' commented Lewis Davies tartly.

He was now anxious to return to his chosen métier. But, despite his efforts to shake off the tag, he was still perceived in London as 'the representative Welshman'. When the publisher Collins commissioned him to write *The Story of Wales* for the *Britain in Pictures* series, it was a good opportunity for him to fulfil a straightforward task and get back into the habit of writing, which he had been finding more and more difficult.[17] The blurb of this elegant little book, that was less substantial than *My Wales* but covered much the same ground, reads as follows:

In all the arts today, a high proportion of the best-esteemed names are those of Welshmen; among writers, Mr Rhys Davies is outstanding as a short-story writer of unusual talent, and he has also written several novels and plays. It is a tribute to the Welsh character that in spite of, or perhaps because of, having had no independent political existence for four hundred years or more, they [*sic*] have preserved a living language and tradition of their own and today both language and tradition are more alive than ever; Wales is still a very different country from England and the Welshman very unlike his neighbour the Englishman. In telling *The Story of Wales*, Mr Davies gives a masterly sketch of the earliest period of its history, in which already the strongly marked characteristics of the race are distinguishable, and from there he brings his narrative down to the present day. As he tells the story he fills in the landscape, draws in the character and evokes the very essence of his country and its people for in his own writing are apparent those qualities of sensibility, imagination, humour and vigour which are the inheritance of every true Welshman.

It seems the author was content with this description of his book, for all its hyperbole, since no remark of his to the contrary has survived; he may very well have written the blurb himself. He was paid £50 for a few weeks' work and an American edition appeared in 1943.

As might have been expected, the book was not without its critics in Wales. Foremost among them was

Pennar Davies who, using the name Davies Aberpennar, would shortly afterwards take the author to task in an article published in *The Welsh Nationalist*, one of Plaid Cymru's newspapers.[18] The polymathic Pennar Davies was usually sympathetic to those of his compatriots writing in English – some of his own poems appeared in Keidrych Rhys's anthology *Modern Welsh Poetry* in 1944 – but now he complained about Davies's 'sentimental and escapist patriotism' that amounted to 'racialism':

> To be Welsh, according to Mr Rhys Davies, means not to belong to a living nation like the Greeks or the Spaniards, but to be possessed of certain excitingly romantic qualities of mind and character, qualities possibly of immemorial antiquity and inexplicable origin, qualities that flourish in captivity more lustily than in freedom... But the most amazing piece of self-justification in the book is the curious doctrine that the essential Welsh life flourishes best under the domination of England. It is the menacing proximity of England, he argues, that has brought out all that is distinctively Welsh in the Welsh character; and the more aggressive the penetration of England's culture and outlook may be, the more stubbornly and wondrously Welsh we become.

Even before the Collins book appeared, Davies had begun work on the novel which was to be his only commercial success. But after such a long break from creative writing, progress on *The Black Venus,* which was written during his usual peregrinations between Maida Vale, Henley and

Blaenclydach, was slow.[19] On New Year's Day 1944 he wrote to Louis Quinain:

> 1943 for me seems to have been all turmoil and toil. My book refused to be finished and it seemed a dreadful and interminable task – or is age telling on me at last and I need twice the time for everything? I know I have been busier than ever before yet there was not much visible evidence of it.

The Black Venus[20] is a novel set in the fictitious village of Ayron in the Teifi Valley of Cardiganshire. His only known visit to the Valley had been in 1937 while researching *My Wales*. The novel is a fantasy based on the custom of *caru ar y gwely*, literally, 'courting on the bed' but known in English as 'courting in bed', or in Scotland and America, as 'bundling'. The custom, common among the peasantry of Wales in the 18th and 19th centuries, had caught the attention of many visitors to the country, including the infamous Blue Book commissioners of 1847, who had written it up with fascinated horror.

It had its origin in the tradition that maidservants, denied the use of the parlour, would sometimes entertain suitors in their own rooms. As a rule, the young people were expected to remove only their shoes and to spend the evening in conversation while reclining on, rather than in, the bed, which was often the only furniture in the room. Opinion seems to be divided as to whether the custom was observed under conditions of strict chastity, with a bolster placed between the sweethearts, or whether sexual contact was permitted. It was most common among the rural poor and often led to pregnancy, the woman's ability to bear a child being considered a prerequisite to marriage.

Davies may have found an account of the custom in an edition of Henry Reed Stiles's monograph, *Bundling: its Origins, Progress and Decline in America* (1871) which had been reissued in a fine format in 1934, a copy of which was found among his books.[21] Or he may have come across it in Wirt Sykes's celebrated study, *British Goblins* (1880), an equally rare book, about which Reginald Reynolds, one of the Lahr group, wrote in his witty, erudite study *Beds: with many noteworthy instances of lying on, under, or about them* (1951), as follows: 'A single paragraph on pp 301-2... appears to have suggested the theme of *The Black Venus* – a fact which I offer *gratis* to future biographers of my friend Rhys Davies.' The suggestion has been noted and is gratefully acknowledged.

Olwen Powell, the beautiful young heiress of Tŷ Rhosyn, the most fertile farm in the Vale of Ayron, uses the custom to test the eligibility of various suitors – 'A woman's testing of a man I am wanting to make it and not always a man's testing of a woman,' she says, thus turning the custom on its head. The novel, which ends with a marriage, is as concise and microcosmic as one of Davies's short stories, an intricate tale that illustrates not only the complexity of human relationships but the conservatism of Welsh rural society, of which the author clearly approved, and it makes the chapels a conduit for the continuity of life in the countryside. The book, for all its charm, is not one of Davies's best, but the seemingly insatiable taste of the British reading public for tales of bucolic sex during wartime ensured brisk sales. It was the only one of the author's books to be published as a mass-market paperback.

Once again some critics found more explicitly sexual symbolism in the plot of *The Black Venus* than those who have read it simply as an amusing yarn based on an old Welsh custom. Although it is for the most part the light-hearted story of how Olwen Powell searches for a suitable husband, much to the disapproval of the community in which she lives, the novel can be read, as Kirsti Bohata has shown, as a subtle, complex portrayal of female sexuality as something subversive that should be considered in atavistic terms, a narrative that uses the vocabulary of racial purity, breeding and miscegenation, savagery and civilization, linking it to primitive impulses that are relics of humankind's barbarous and even bestial origins. Bohata, in her *Postcolonialism Revisited*, even goes so far as to suggest that the nude statue of the black Venus, which is draped in a muslin apron on Sundays in deference to gentleman callers, may have been suggested to the author by 'the Hottentot Venus', a genitally malformed Khoikhoi woman with very protuberant buttocks who had been exhibited in London and Paris in the early nineteenth century.[22] If it was, there is nothing in Davies's papers and correspondence that alludes to any of this.

There was now a new man in Davies's life. Desperate for, as he put it to Quinain, 'that salt which gives taste to life', he had walked into the Wheatsheaf pub one evening in November 1943 and there met a young man named Colyn Davies. Having been brought up in an orphanage, Colyn had been conscripted in 1939, and trained as a military trumpeter, but had suffered a nervous breakdown that precipitated a suicide attempt. Invalided out of the

Navy, he had gravitated to Soho in the vague hope of finding work as an actor. Smitten by his good looks, Davies doted on him. Colyn was both penniless and homeless. The writer took him back to his Maida Vale lodgings and put him up for a few weeks until he found a room in a house in the same street that was part-boarding house and part-brothel. Through theatrical friends like Raymond Marriott, Davies soon found Colyn small parts in West End repertory, where he was said by wags to stand out as the only heterosexual in the chorus line. He also sang Victorian ballads and music-hall songs, on which he was something of an expert and some of which he can be heard singing on the internet.

Colyn Davies was undoubtedly the great love of Rhys Davies's life, after Anna Kavan. He was also the subject of the celebrated story 'Boy with a Trumpet', one of Davies's best, that was, according to Colyn, a substantially accurate portrait of him at this stage of his life. In the story, the 19-year-old waif is befriended by the whores who live and work in the house where he lodges, finding release from his depression only by practising on his trumpet, an instrument he plays badly. The story has been described by Barbara Prys-Williams as 'a most compassionate picture of narcissistic pain'. Davies himself was aware of the effect it might have on its readers, writing to the Quinains, 'Hope the gloom of this story won't put you and Greta off your food. But I never could believe in silver linings.' It is, in short, an intense study of human loneliness at its most harrowing.

The boy is incapable of love: 'he had no instinctive love to give out in return for attempts of affection: it had never been born in him'. He tells one of the prostitutes, 'I have no faith, no belief, and I can't accept the world – I can't feel it.' This may very well be Davies admitting his own lack of feeling for the suffering of others. Dejected by hearing another man play a tune on the trumpet with superb mastery, the boy realizes he has no power to redeem the world and is plunged into the despair that Davies felt throughout the war: 'There's no such thing as victory in war. There's only misery, chaos and suffering for everybody, and then the payment.' When one of the women, the tender-hearted Kathleen, refuses to let the boy put his mouth to her breast – his request is not sexual but stems from his loveless childhood – he is overcome by loneliness. The story ends:

> He rolled over and over on the bed. Shuddering, he pressed his face into the pillow. When the paroxysm had passed he half rose and sat looking out of the window. In his movement the trumpet crashed to the floor, but he did not pick it up. He sat gazing out into the still world as if he would never penetrate it again. He saw grey dead light falling over smashed cities, over broken precipices and jagged torn chasms of the world. Acrid smoke from abandoned ruins mingled with the smell of blood. He saw himself the inhabitant of a wilderness where withered hands could lift in guidance no more. There were no more voices and all the paps of earth were dry.

Whereas it is definitely known that the boy with a trumpet was, in real life, named Colyn Davies, who died in 1991, no one has suggested who Caerphilly Jones might have been.[23] He is said in *Print of a Hare's Foot* to have been a Household Cavalryman whom Davies claimed to have met on a Paddington train while returning from the Rhondda. Jones, a perfect alias for a Welshman, had married a London girl and was to die in action during the war, according to Davies. Although a whole chapter is devoted to him in *Print of a Hare's Foot*, there are no real clues as to who he actually was, except that his home was 'over the mountain' from the Rhondda. The writer never mentioned him to his brother Lewis. But if Caerphilly Jones ever existed, and if Davies did have a sexual relationship with him, the chapter is the nearest this most unreliable of narrators ever came to describing a homosexual partner.

Colyn Davies remembered Rhys as 'very kind, very generous', but had no illusions as to the nature of his interest in him. That was a problem, since he was entirely heterosexual. When David Callard, in 1990, asked him whether Davies had ever made advances to him, he replied that he had on one occasion, when the two were sharing the same bed. Colyn had made it clear he was not interested in a physical relationship and the older man had taken the matter no further. Nevertheless, he seemed keen to give the impression to others that he and Colyn were lovers, and most of their friends assumed them to be so. The two remained friends for several years though, after the war, they met less frequently. Writing to Louis Quinain in November 1944, Davies told him: 'Colyn is now going his own way. I saw him briefly in London... but have not had any contact with him for months.' Rigorously heterosexual then and thereafter, in 1954 Colyn Davies had a son by the then unknown Fay Weldon, who grew up to be the novelist Nick Weldon, and later he married and had two more children. In her autobiography, *Auto da Fay* (2002), Weldon remembered Colyn as

> an inveterate hanger-outer and if he could do nothing rather than something, chose to do nothing ... He told terrible jokes and wrote terrible, wonderful, rude, crude poems... He was a troubadour and I ran off with him, pitter-pat bare feet by night through the long hot summer streets to his place up at Belsize Park (where else?) and pretty soon I was pregnant.

Acting and busking proved too uncertain a way of life, however, and Colyn eventually became an executive in the Post Office. He held no animus against homosexuals and remained, moreover, a lifelong friend of Quentin Crisp whom he had met when the latter was only a Soho gadabout. Entering into a sexual relationship with Rhys Davies would have given him a small degree of financial and emotional security. As Nina Hamnett once archly remarked when he complained of poverty: 'You missed your chance with Rhys.' But in truth, Colyn Davies was just not interested. This must have been a severe blow to the writer but he left no recorded remark as to the hurt it caused him.

Perhaps he hid his disappointment in the writing of a musical play, though not even that would have proved a remedy for his heartache. The play, *Jenny Jones*, which was based on his short story 'Abraham's Glory', was not a success.[24][25] Writing about it more than a decade later, Davies recalled:

This is not the place for me to dwell on my bruises or fallings-by-the-wayside, or on odd by-products of work, such as George Black of Moss Empires producing a 'musical' based on one of my stories at the London Hippodrome just as the first rockets began to drop, disturbing the exotic ballet, the live dog, the boy soprano, the French acrobats and other things not in my original Welsh story.[26]

He was not the first, or the last, writer to see his work traduced by the dictates of theatrical whimsicality. Despite indifferent reviews, the play was broadcast on radio on the 23rd of November, which helped ticket sales but not enough to prevent the show from closing in mid-January 1945 after a three-month run.

Nevertheless, it made Davies some money, as had the commercial success of *The Black Venus*. For the rest of the year he was engaged in putting together his *Selected Stories* for publication by Maurice Fridberg, a small firm specialising in cheap paperbacks for the mass market. He was also writing new stories for his next collection, *The Trip to London* (1946).[27] This volume contains the short story 'The Benefit Concert', one of his funniest, in which a collier discovers Horeb chapel has a hundred pounds left over from a concert that has been held to raise funds to buy him a new artificial leg. In the row that ensues, the deacons emerge victorious but the narrator remains perfectly non-committal, takes no side and leaves judgement to the reader. Before the year was out he had written 'Spectre de la Rose', his satire on the Wheatsheaf bohemians that was inspired by the V2s which had rained down on London, and completed the long story 'Orestes', that brings the book to a masterly close.[28]

Davies's work continued to attract favourable comment. In an article entitled 'The British Short Story' published in the well-regarded magazine *Voices* Michael Williams compared it favourably with that of Glyn Jones and Gwyn Jones, concluding: 'there are no other short-story writers better equipped than Rhys Davies and H.E. Bates for adding their imprints to the pioneering footsteps of D.H. Lawrence'.[29] C. Day Lewis praised Davies's writing for its vitality and exuberance and for 'the gift, uncommon today, of story-telling: his stories have plot, we wonder what is going to happen next, we are startled or amused by a dénouement.'

The years immediately after the end of the war in 1945, which he did not record celebrating in any way, were a chance for Davies, like the rest of Britain, to recuperate and take stock. His first response was to write about the timeless beauty of the Welsh countryside where he saw, once again, a continuity uninterrupted by war and still resisting the tentacular invasion of an alien industrialism. This was a theme that was to appear in several novels over the next few years, most notably *The Perishable Quality* (1957) and *Girl Waiting in the Shade* (1960).[30] [31]

He had spent two days staying at a farm in 'Carmarthenshire' that belonged, he claimed, to some relations of his and which, in an essay in *Countryside Character* entitled 'Time and the Welsh Mountains', he calls Arosfa.[32] However, ten years before, Davies had written to Raymond Marriott: 'Stayed for a day or two on a most primitive farm in Cardiganshire, with distant relations. Life and faces there much the same, I should think, as 500 years ago. It was so cold that I sat most of the time under the hams in the enormous ancient fireplace. If I had been rubbed in salt first, I should have turned into a lean bit of bacon myself. Very little English spoken there and gradually I found my own mind beginning to work in Welsh.'

This farm cannot be identified, nor can the other homesteads he names as its neighbours: Nantcellan, Frondolau, Derwyn Llas, Lechryd, Erw-isaf. Yet Davies claims to have been a frequent visitor and to have family roots in the district, though there is nothing here that points to the area immediately around Cilrhedyn or Cilgerran, which are, moreover, not in Carmarthenshire or Cardiganshire but Pembrokeshire. Arosfa is said to be 'on the shoulder of a ravine' and situated twenty miles from a seaside town, which sounds rather like Aberystwyth or Aberaeron, to which he takes his hostess, Rhoda (a name he used in another context), on a day's jaunt. The local chapel is called Soar and belongs to the Independents. The farm's name, signifying a place to stay or stopping place or dwelling place, is a very common one in all parts of Wales. The other farms Davies mentions are scattered over a wide tract of land between Cardigan, Llandysul, Newcastle Emlyn and Cynwyl Elfed, and were probably chosen, it must be concluded, for the euphony of their names: 'they too have something of the streams' music'. Impossible, then, to say where exactly the writer spent his brief holiday.

It is not long before Davies, after praising the idyllic life of Arosfa, spots a man who is 'of the long-skulled Iberian type'. His blue-eyed wife with her heavier mould and her tendency to a reddish blondness is, for him, of the later Celtic stock. He goes on:

> It is in such isolated districts as this, protected by mountains, that the pure racial types are found untarnished by time. Now and again, with a start of recognition, one comes across them in the industrial parts of Wales, but there they have an accidental and almost alien look.

He is so smitten by the rustic charm of his hosts that he even suspends his antipathy towards the chapel:

> The Nonconformist movement, with its first itinerant preachers penetrating determinedly into lonely folds and more domestic in their appeal than the priests of the proud Established Church, performed a great work in uniting the people socially.

As for the language the family speaks, it 'makes England seem very far away'. He even puts up with having his leg pulled on account of his bachelorhood: clearly, they do not suspect the true nature of his sexuality.

In short, Davies seems to like everything he sees and hears during his two days in the lamp-lit quietude of Arosfa. The essay, which may be construed as a longing for roots and identity, ends with a panegyric to the continuity of rural, Welsh-speaking Wales:

> May this country never die, may it never be broken up by more of these appalling arterial roads, brazen

'holiday camps', and the thing that asbestos huts, gun-sites and refugees symbolize. May that fallow field with its skimming birds, the pasture quiet with musing cattle, the moist hillside patched with sheep, remain unmolested.

Wales would have to wait a few more years before R.S. Thomas wrote about the harsher realities of life in upland Wales.

Davies did very little literary journalism, even when he was short of money. Apart from a stint during 1939 when he wrote a few book-reviews for Robert Herring's *Life and Letters To-day*, the only periodical to which he was a regular contributor was Keidrych Rhys's *Wales*. On the occasion of the magazine's tenth year of publication in 1947, he was one of several eminent Welshmen – they included Wyn Griffith, John Cowper Powys, Vernon Watkins, George Ewart Evans, R.S. Thomas, Arthur Machen, Glyn Jones, and Idris Davies – who wrote to congratulate the editor:

It is a pleasant coincidence for me that I am in evergreen Carmarthen and able to bring my congratulations to your office in Lammas Street. I know how unselfishly you have worked to make *Wales* sing during ten difficult years and if it went to sleep for a while and you disappeared into battle-dress the fault wasn't yours. I would like, too, if I may, to pay a tribute to this work of yours which I feel sure has brought you little, probably nothing, in the way of material reward. But such a tribute may surprise and even annoy you, I suspect, perverse editor that you are, that the arrival of a fine poem, story or truthful article nourishes you much more than a profitable balance-sheet. So I'll say no more and only stand admiring the laurel wreath. Your ever faithful subscriber and contributor, Rhys Davies.[33]

Davies contributed to all three runs of *Wales*, more for patriotic than for pecuniary reasons, sending Keidrych Rhys material that was specifically about Wales and the Welsh. Between 1943 and 1946 he wrote three articles entitled 'From my Notebook' that are the nearest he ever came to writing a literary manifesto.[34]

In the first he was at his pithiest and most provocative best:

A man is greater than his country. Therefore I do not exist for Wales, but Wales exists for me... Directly a man becomes self-conscious about being Welsh he ceases to be a Welshman... Never carry a flag; be yourself quietly; as a human being you have no need of a flag... Be a full-time writer. Amateurs are the curse of art in Wales... When you are of sufficient size to deal with them, make enemies. They are essential to your well-being... Do not preach, do not lecture, do not attend banquets, conferences, or sit on committees, or submit to the propaganda lure... Do not read the Welsh classics if they bore you or if they refuse to light a little enchanted fire in your being... There is only one classic: Wales... Be malicious when you are faced by cant, humbug and sentimental patriotism. Be rude, but not ill bred, to persons who beat their breasts and shout about their Welsh nationality; they may possess a small genuine light in them... If asked (in that offensive suspicious way!), I always say I am not Welsh to the Welsh, just as I say I am not English to the English... Why are the Welsh so undisciplined, why do they ravage the delicate magic of our country with such clumsy hands?... Beware of Welsh sentimentality. It is of the worst kind, but seductive... I am in favour of self government for Wales... Commit the wrong sort of crimes; i.e. do not thieve, murder, commit arson or adultery, but attack the complacent, the greedy, the mundane and the materialists in their lairs.[35]

In the second 'Notebook', he was less prescriptive but just as caustic. Commenting on Flaubert's famous statement, *'Madame Bovary, c'est moi!'*, he observed that the French author was mostly a woman during the six years he had been writing his masterpiece, just as Tolstoy had been Anna when writing *Anna Karenin*, and that Flaubert's measure of his disciplined control over this metamorphosis was that Emma was depicted with such perfect objectivity:

We can also conclude that even the bearded Tolstoy must have 'become' Anna Karenina before he could have given that marvellously living delineation of a woman.[36]

On the other hand, Davies found it hard to 'become' a child:

Children are so aloof, locked, original and pure in
their world; a corrupted adult feels lost in it;
children frighten me.

Yet this too does not accord with the observations of
others. In a letter to the present writer one of the
daughters of Charlie Lahr, Sheila Leslie,[37] remembered
how good Davies had been with her and her sister
Oonagh, playing with them and reading their homework.
He had called at their home, 9 Wilton Road in Muswell
Hill, on a day when the little girls were holding a funeral
for a broken doll, and wrote a story about it, 'The
Funeral', which appeared in *The Things Men Do* in 1936.
As for Welsh short-story writers, Davies had this to say:

During the last three or four years I have read some
dozens of these stories, in print and manuscript.
And when stripped of their nationalistic decorations
nearly all of them were unoriginal in conception,
trite in theme, commonplace in execution... *First
rule for a new writer*: Stop thinking of yourself as a
Welsh writer. Consort as much as possible with
people who dislike Wales or, better still, are
completely indifferent to her.

This was Davies at his most oracular, not to say self-
justifying.

The third article begins with a meditation on the urban
landscape of the Rhondda:

I cannot escape the feeling that this historic Valley
is always thrashed by a gritty ceaseless rain, an

erosive rain gnawing like a hungry dog at a bone. The rows of houses look stark, denuded, bitten. Architecturally it is certainly the ugliest place I've seen... But what about the 'hearts of gold' that beat in this famous mining valley – if some poets, novelists and journalists are to be believed? Well, they are still there, more's the pity.[38]

To the question, 'What should be done to encourage the people of the Rhondda to be less impervious to their surroundings, or is it best to leave them to their insensitivity?' he replied, 'I cannot answer these questions. I am not a sociologist or a propagandist.' He then proceeded to laud a performance of Racine's play *Phèdre* given by the *Comédie Française* on a recent visit to London.

Davies's condemnation of the Rhondda as a place of no hope was roundly contested in the *Western Mail* by such worthies as A.P. Glanville JP, Chairman of the Rhondda Urban Council, who declared, 'Rhondda's family life, standard of cleanliness, and moral tone, will compare favourably with those of any highly industrial area'. Will John, the Labour M.P. who represented the Rhondda between 1920 and 1950, then leapt to its defence. While agreeing the Valley needed modern housing and better urban planning, he declared it was still a place of beauty:

A man finds what he seeks. Evidently Mr Rhys Davies has not on his visit seen Rhondda's beauty spots. It appears that he had not walked the mountain tops or walked the Nantgwyddon road from Llwynypia to Gelli Colliery... My experience is that the ambition of the large majority of Rhondda people, who because of circumstances have been forced to leave the locality, is to return as speedily as possible.

The response prompted Davies, then living in Wigginton near Tring in Hertfordshire, to write a letter to the *Western Mail*, published on the 11th of July 1946, the only time he was to write to a newspaper, in which he defended his article and attacked the complacency of those in authority, but it must have inflamed local pride still further: 'I must point out to Mr Glanville that the trend of my article was a protest against Rhondda residents having to endure such drab surroundings.' If this eirenic note was meant to mend fences, the impression was soon dispersed:

I am not ashamed. There are placid and romantic writers enough who shut their eyes to the unpleasant things... Finally, as one ex-Rhondda native, I feel no desire to settle there again. At least not yet.[39]

In the same notebook in *Wales* he turns to a questionnaire that Keidrych Rhys had sent to a number of writers. To the question, 'Do you consider yourself an Anglo-Welsh writer?' he replied, 'No. I am only a writer. Does one (if I may make so bold) think of Henry James, or T.S. Eliot as Anglo-American writers? Down with passports to Art!'[40] To the question, 'For whom do you write?' he gave a typical response: 'Primarily myself. But if persons, of either sex, wish to look over my shoulder at what I am writing, I do not discourage them; in fact, I positively welcome them.' Asked whether 'Anglo-Welsh'[40] literature should express a Welsh attitude to life and affairs, or whether it should merely be a literature about Welsh things, he responded,

> Neither, consciously. If a writer thinks of his work along these lines it tends to become too parochial, narrow. But if he is Welsh by birth, upbringing, and selects a Welsh background and characters for his work, an essence of Wales should be in his work, giving it a national 'slant' or flavour. But no flag-waving. A curse on flag-waving.

Lastly, he declared himself perplexed by the question, 'Do you believe that a sense of Welsh nationhood is more consistent with one particular attitude to life and affairs than any other?':

> Offhand, I should say that Welsh nationhood is consistent with an attitude of minding one's own business, self-sufficiency, a certain elemental instinct and appreciation of the poetry of life; vitality, humour; an attitude containing a vision of small range but intense within this restricted orbit.

Davies's posture of indifference to literary fame and fortune, adopted by so many writers, was for him real enough. He did not seem to care very much whether his books sold well or badly and, excepting the strictures made by his old friend H.E. Bates about *Count Your Blessings*, seemed genuinely unconcerned by adverse criticism of his work, even from his peers.

As the war in Europe came to an end, Davies was invited to renew his support for the Freedom Defence Committee, a group formed 'to uphold the essential liberty of individuals and organizations and to defend those under threat of persecution for exercising their rights to freedom of speech, writing and action'.[41] He was asked to take an active part as a member of the Committee, that was now revived in response to a police raid on the offices of the Freedom Press, which published an anarchist periodical, at the end of 1944, and the prosecution of the editors of *War Commentary* in early 1945 for attempting 'to undermine the affections of members of His Majesty's forces'. Davies, encouraged by the old anarchist Charlie Lahr, had lent his name as a sponsor in 1944, but it is not known whether he renewed his subscription; there was nothing among the papers left at his death to confirm his continuing support. He never mentioned the matter to his brother Lewis, perhaps because it was the nearest he had ever come to committing himself politically.

By 1945 Davies had begun to enjoy much wider renown as a writer of short stories, helped by his frequent appearance in prestigious anthologies of the day. This process had begun when one of his stories, the much-anthologised 'Revelation', was included by Alan Steele in *Selected Modern Short Stories* published by Penguin in 1937, and continued throughout the following decade. In 1945, for example, he was represented by 'The Nature of Man' in *Stories of the Forties*, edited by Reginald Moore and Woodrow Wyatt, and by 'Spectre de la Rose' in the sixth series of *English Story*, edited by Wyatt alone.[42] In 1946 his story 'Harvest Moon'[43] was included in Denys Val Baker's *Little Reviews Anthology* and the ever-popular

'Canute'[44] in Aled Vaughan's *Celtic Story*. Other stories of his were to be found in what must be kindly described as fugitive publications among which Davies was in the habit of scattering examples of his work.

The last-named story, 'Canute', which was included in *Boy with a Trumpet*, is rather more coarse-grained than is usual for Rhys Davies but it is enjoyable for all that. It features a rugby match between Wales and England at Twickenham that Wales wins by 6 points to 4.[45] The scene on the platform at Paddington after the match is described with relish:

The big clock's pallid face, which said it was a quarter to midnight, stared over the station like an amazed moon. Directly under it was a group of women who had arranged to meet their men there for the journey back. They looked worried and frightened. As well they might. For surely they were standing in a gigantic hospital-base adjacent to a bloody battlefield where a crushing defeat had been sustained. On the platforms casualties lay groaning or silently dazed; benches were packed with huddled men, limbs twitching, heads laid on neighbours' shoulders or clasped in hands between knees... Most of them looked exhausted, if not positively wounded, as from tremendous strife. But not all of them. Despite groans of the incapacitated, grunting heaves of the sick, long solemn stares of the bemused helplessly waiting for some ministering angel to conduct them to a train, there was singing. Valiant groups of men put their heads doggedly together and burst into heroic song. They belonged to a race that, whatever the cause, never ceases to sing, and those competent to judge declare this singing something to be greatly admired. Tonight, in this melancholy place at the low hour of midnight, these melodious cries made the spirit of man seem undefeated.

In the mean while, one of the fans falls asleep atop a shoe-shine dais deep in the subterranean gents' toilets and becomes marooned there when the water mains burst, and has to be rescued by his collier butties. Ever after he is known as Rowland Canute.

Also in *Boy with a Trumpet* is the small gem of a story, 'Fear', in which a boy is mesmerized by an Indian snake-charmer on board a train. It is a story full of sexual imagery as the over-friendly man tries to fix the boy's attention on the cobra swaying up out of its basket. From the very first sentence we are given to understand this is a story about sexual initiation: 'As soon as the boy got into the compartment he felt there was something queer in it.' Sensing the presence of evil, the boy says nothing throughout the story but the man persists in trying to hold his interest. The last paragraph reads:

But the train was drawing into the station. It was not the boy's station. He made a sudden blind leap away from the man, opened the door, saw it was not on the platform side, but jumped. There was a shout from someone. He ran up the track, he dived under some wire railings. He ran with amazingly quick short leaps up a field – like a hare that knows its life is precarious among the colossal dangers of the open world and has suddenly sensed one of them.

Although no evidence has been found to suggest this story was based on its author's own experience, it is difficult not to believe that something similar had happened to him, so palpable is the fear it describes. But in the present writer's copy of *The Boy with a Trumpet* the author wrote the inscription: 'To P. H. Burton who told me about the boy in the train'.[46] Clearly, the story created enough imaginative resonance in Davies to enable him to get inside the sexual tension that is so potent in the incident. The story is significant, too, in that it includes the first reference in Davies's work to a hare as a creature threatened by the alien world it inhabits. The story was given the accolade of being reprinted in the pages of *The Evening News* on the 7th of May 1946.

A modicum of critical prestige came Davies's way at this time. In his book *The Modern Short Story* (1941), H.E. Bates singled out Rhys Davies who,

> though never shaking off the influence of Lawrence, has substituted for the rather erotic poetry of his earlier stories a quality of humour, partly robust, partly ironical, which has something in common with folklore. This gift, still not developed fully, is possibly the best part of himself. But his virtue is that, following Lawrence, he went back to his own people, to whom he remained tied by the equal bonds of sympathy and hatred. And for some years Davies showed – to an audience that was either not completely there or not completely listening – that there was, in Wales, a life as remote from life in England as the life in the Ohio valleys was remote from the life of New York. By his example, Davies

urged its re-discovery. That re-discovery was delayed by two factors: first, by the long economic depression, which paralysed so much of Welsh life and inevitably sterilized the little artistic impulse that remained; and secondly, by English prejudice, which eagerly grasps at any interpretation of Irish life, even though it springs directly from hatred of England, but which rejects the corresponding interpretation of Welsh life with blank or sour indifference. An Irish play in London is an event; a Welsh play (with exceptions like Mr Emlyn Williams's *The Corn is Green* and the film *Happy Valley*) gets its London production, if it gets it at all, in a back-street little theatre, and is then shipped back to Wales in the next empty coal-truck. This is true also of Welsh novels; truer of short stories. In defence of the English attitude it must be said that Welsh writers, depressed, appalled, and angered by that sour parochial gloom which the very sensitive feel as they cross the border, used for many years a stereotyped pattern, of which colliery valleys, chapels, meanness, avarice, the dole, the sacred front room, revivals and revolts and love-in-the-entry were the inevitable parts. Readers began to know what to expect; and they had a right to expect, if they were to be interested in Welsh literature at all, a change of mood. There is no doubt this change has come.[47]

Bates then mentions the Welsh writers Margiad Evans, Geraint Goodwin, Glyn Jones, Gwyn Jones, Alun Lewis, and Dylan Thomas, all of whom had contributed to *The*

Welsh Review, and in Welsh, Kate Roberts. These were the writers who, in Bates's estimation, had contributed to the revitalization of the short story form in Wales, and he ended with the recommendation:

> In contrast to the present state of Irish literature the rebirth of Welsh literature is a remarkable thing... Towards Wales, then, the English short story may perhaps begin to look for a new influence.

This view was confirmed by William J. Entwistle and Eric Gillett in their book *The Literature of England* (1943) which refers to Davies as heading 'a noteworthy Welsh school' of fiction-writers:

> Davies is completely at home with the ironical humours and tragedies of his own people, and nothing like so much at home when he has crossed the Welsh border.[48]

In 1944 Davies's short story 'The Wages of Love' was selected by Cyril Connolly for inclusion in his Faber anthology *Horizon Stories,* where he referred to the 'picaresque' Davies as 'well known for his stories of odious Welsh people'.[49]

But if 1945 had been a good year for Davies, the year following opened disastrously. At the end of February, Vincent Wells's thatched cottage in Henley-on-Thames was destroyed by fire and with it most of the writer's manuscripts, clothes, gramophone records, documents, letters and books also went up in smoke. Ironically, he had removed most of his papers from his flat in Maida

Vale lest they be damaged in the Blitz. Hardly anything of Davies's survived, which makes a biographer's task all the more difficult in following his peregrinations during this part of his life. The writer even had to go looking for copies of his own books in London's secondhand bookshops.

Vincent Wells, who had recently retired, now decided to go and live near his sister in New Zealand, though not before falling out with Davies over insurance compensation to which the writer felt he was entitled, having lost everything in the fire. There followed an acrimonious correspondence, of which only the letters from Wells have survived. With a heavy heart, Davies considered taking his claim to law but decided against it in the end. Bush Row had been a retreat since the early 1930s and he had done a good deal of uninterrupted work there. Davies felt the loss of friendship keenly. Vincent Wells was, after Charlie Lahr, his oldest friend. Davies now needed somewhere to live and work. His parents, having retired from Royal Stores in 1942, had moved to live at 70 Jones Street, a stone's throw from 6 Clydach Road but much less congenial as a source of fictional inspiration because there was no daily contact with customers who provided him with material for his stories.

In June 1945 he was introduced to the Scottish short-story writer Fred Urquhart, whom John Betjeman had described as being 'to Scotland what Rhys Davies is to Wales'. The two men hit it off immediately and began a friendship that was to last the rest of their lives, even surviving after Urquhart, in May 1947, was introduced by Nina Hamnett to Peter Wyndham Allen, a dancer, with whom he was to live until the latter's death in 1990. It was Allen who delivered the piquant verdict on whether Davies had ever been in love when he told David Callard in an interview in 1990, 'Rhys Davies never loved anyone but Rhys Davies'.[50]

Fred Urquhart never managed to get Davies to talk about himself in an intimate way, commenting, 'Rhys was not a man who bared his soul to anyone' – surely an understatement. According to Colin Affleck, Urquhart's biographer, he was a great admirer of Davies's stories and readily admitted that his own writing had been influenced by them. A conscientious objector during the war, he had been directed to work on the land and had been farm secretary on the Woburn estate of the Duke of Bedford but later became temporary literary editor of *Tribune*. Both he and Davies were from humble backgrounds; what is more, both men were able to write from a woman's point of view. They decided to share a cottage known as Wood House in Cholesbury Road, in Wigginton, near Tring, in the Chilterns, that belonged to the anthologist Denys Val Baker, which Urquhart described as 'a disused army hut', and so began yet another venture into rustic life which, complain as he might about London, did not suit Davies. Nevertheless, secure in the knowledge that the tenancy was for a summer only, the Welshman and the Scotsman moved there early in May 1946.

Notes

1   'From a Notebook' in *Wales* (5, Autumn, 1944)
2   It has proved impossible to identify H.E. Bevan. The only clue to his identity is that in a letter to Louis and Greta Quinain dated 15 January 1943 RD informed them that Bevan had had a bad stroke and was not expected to live.

There is no trace of him in the records of the Royal Institute of British Architects.

3   *Under the Rose* (Heinemann, 1940)

4   *Sea Urchin: adventures of Jorgen Jorgensen* (Duckworth, 1940); Icelandic edn., *Jörunder hundadagakongur, aevintyri hans og aeviraunir* (Bókfellsútgáfan, 1943)

5   Letter to Raymond Marriott (23 September 1940)

6   Letter to Raymond Marriott (August 1940). The letter continues: 'Alas, though, that the Big Three (*Times Lit.,* *Observer* and *Sunday Times)* were so dreadfully hostile – all together soon as the book was out, worse luck. The strange thing was that I didn't feel in the least bruised. I really felt I knew so much more than these reviewers... But of course it was unfortunate for the books; must have affected sales.' There was also a hostile review by Daniel George in *Tribune* (27 September 1940). Even so, the reviews in 'the Big Three' were not entirely negative. The novel attracted several more favourable reviews: Wilfred Gibson in *The Manchester Guardian* (27 September 1940) thought Davies 'had taken his place in the front row of contemporary story-tellers'. Kate O'Brien in *The Spectator* (4 October 1940) wrote, 'He draws character with an ease which suggests full reserves of novelistic power'. Norah Hoult in *John O'London's Weekly* (14 October 1940) thought 'Such books are not often written these days, for Mr Davies combines a medieval ruthlessness with the tenderness of complete comprehension.'

7   'Spectre de la Rose', in *The Trip to London* (1946); *Collected Stories* (ed. Meic Stephens, vol. 3, 1998)

8   Louis Quinain told David Callard that he and Greta were never quite sure whether Nora Wyndham was 'after' RD or Lewis, though this must have been meant lightheartedly, since the Quinains were aware of RD's sexual orientation, if not of his brother's. In a letter to Louis and Greta dated 20 August 1943 RD refers to Wyndham as 'a half

demented and totally silly woman... she caused me a lot of mental distress', and informs them the friendship is at an end. The Quinains never discussed Davies's sexuality with him, pointing out to Sarah Leigh Mabbett that the topic of homosexuality was 'not in the public eye as it is today' (6 March 1996).

9   *To-morrow to Fresh Woods* (Heinemann, 1941). A review in *The Spectator* (7 November 1941) praised the novel: 'Mr Davies has gathered lavishly for his book, and with his eye for the odd, the spirited and the gallant, his long chronicle is kept lively and exciting.' Not all the reviews were favourable, however. The anonymous reviewers in the *TLS* (25 October and 6 December 1941) were unimpressed: 'The general effect is of a rather unillumined work of fiction. The trouble seems to be that he has difficulty in sustaining the pace and tension of a full-length novel. The best of his short stories, gay and impulsive in their realistic manner, capture an alert humanity and an unblinking comic vision. In the novels his vitality seems to be thinned out and his dramatic sense is in abeyance or else artificially whipped up.'; 'The novel tends to dissipate its strength through want of the discipline of narrative design.' Pamela Hansford Johnson made much the same point in *John O'London's Weekly* (7 November 1941): 'It is too loosely-knit... too cluttered, a collection of vignettes rather than a consistent work.' George W. Bishop, on the other hand, wrote in *The Daily Telegraph* (14 November 1941): 'After the disappointment of his last book, *Under the Rose*, the rich humanity of Mr Rhys Davies's new novel is the more noticeable... The grocer and his family are beautifully drawn and the whole book pulses with life. The story passes through drab times, but there are no grey passages; it is a fine and understanding piece of work.'

10   Alberto Manguel and Craig Stephenson (eds., *The Flamingo Anthology of Gay Literature: In Another Part of the Forest*

(Flamingo/Harper Collins, 1994). For discussion about the
evolving use of 'gay', including its often pejorative
connotations (two of its current meanings are 'rubbish' or
'stupid'), see the article by Steph Power, 'What Does Gay
Mean?' in *Planet* (205, February 2012).

11 *Wales* (6/7, March 1939)

12 *A Finger in Every Pie* (Heinemann, 1942). Contents: 'The
Wages of Love', 'Abraham's Glory', 'Charity', 'Mourning for
Ianto', 'The Nature of Man', 'A Pearl of Great Price',
'Nightgown', 'Alice's Pint', 'The Dark World', 'Ancient
Courtship', 'Over at Rainbow Bottom', 'The Pits are on the
Top', 'Weep Not, My Wanton', 'The Zinnias', 'Pleasures of
the Table', 'Tomos and the Harp', 'The Parrot', 'Queen of
the Cote d'Azur'. The novel was reviewed under the
heading 'Welsh Tales' in the *TLS* (12 September 1942).

13 *The Trip to London* (Heinmann, 1946; Howell Soskin,
1946). Contents: 'The Benefit Concert', 'A Dangerous
Remedy', 'The Last Struggle', 'Price of a Wedding Ring',
'The Trip to London', 'Gents Only', 'The Public House',
'River, Flow Gently', 'Spectre de la Rose', 'Death of a
Canary', 'Orestes'. The collection was banned in Ireland,
together with books by Somerset Maugham and Eric
Linklater. 'The Last Struggle' was made into a film for
American television in 1953 under the title 'The Red
Dress'.

14 *Boy with a Trumpet* (Heinemann, 1949); Doubleday, 1951.
Contents: 'The Dilemma of Catherine Fuchsias', 'Boy with
a trumpet', 'Canute', 'A Human Condition', 'Fear', 'The
Fashion Plate', 'A Man in Haste', 'Tomorrow', 'One of
Norah's early Days', 'The Foolish One', 'The Beard', 'Wigs,
Costumes, Masks'. German edn., *Der Junge mit der
trompete* (Nymphenburger Verlagshandl, 1960). Reviewing
the collection in *The Daily Telegraph* (11 November 1949),
Pamela Hansford Johnson wrote: 'It is apparent from *Boy
with a Trumpet* that Mr Rhys Davies's comic gift is in the

ascendant. When he is making his own kind of comic poetry he is superb... Every story in this book has its own fascination... It is a delight to read writing so beautiful, so sure, so perfectly judged.'

15 Dai Smith, 'Rhys Davies and his "Turbulent Valley"', in *Decoding the Hare*

16 *Twentieth-century Authors: a biographical dictionary of modern literature* (ed. Stanley J. Kunitz and Vineta Colby (Wilson, 1955)

17 *The Story of Wales: Britain in Pictures* (Collins, 1943). Writing as a 'Cymrophil', John Betjeman reviewed the book in *Wales* (3, January 1944): 'The interesting fact about all Celtic countries to us who live in England is how each country has put up with the English... [The Welsh] have remained a nation, not a nation within a nation, but a nation apart. Why and how have they, of all Celtic races in this island, done this? That is the first question to which I would have liked an answer... But Mr Rhys Davies has told me a lot about Wales which I did not know.'

18 Davies Aberpennar (Pennar Davies), 'Anti-Nationalism among the Anglo-Welsh', in *The Welsh Nation* (February 1946)

19 *The Black Venus* (Heinemann, 1944); Howell Soskin, 1946; Danish edn., *Den sorte Venus* (P. Branner, 1947); Swedish edn., *Den svarta Venus* (Fritzes Bokförlag, 1948)

20 *The Black Venus* (Pan Books, 1950)

21 Henry Reed Stiles, *Bundling: its Origins, Progress and Decline in America* (Peter Pauper Press, 1934); a modern edn., 'Reprinted for the Enlightenment of the Present Generation', in a box with decorated board covers (n.d.).

22 Kirsti Bohata, *Postcolonialism Revisited* (University of Wales Press, 2004). A more appropriate response was that of Gwyn Jones, reviewing the novel in *The Welsh Review* (vol. 3, no. 4, December 1944): 'Where Caradoc Evans threw gravel and fetched a ladder, Rhys Davies slides over the windowsill: he

has written a whole novel about courting in bed... I don't know that this is Rhys Davies's best novel: there are sections where he appears to ride his theme somewhat determinedly, as though the best length here would be that of a "long-short" rather than a novel, but it displays most of his gifts in full measure: his eye for character and characters, his mischief, fancy, and humour, his unsentimental love for his people, his poetry and lovely use of dialect, and above all, his exciting mastery of words... his paragraphs have the rich ripe glow of late-September blackberries, his images are plumped with juice... every page carries matter that delights with its truth or charms with its novelty.' The woman known as 'the Hottentot Venus' was Saartjie Baartman, who was taken to London by Dr William Dunlop, who exhibited her in shows to paying audiences, and then to Paris where she died and was dissected and embalmed. Her remains were finally laid to rest in the Gamtoos valley in South Africa on 9 August 2002.

23 The most diligent enquiries have failed to identify this man, who may have been a figment of the writer's imagination or else a means of tantalising and misleading the prurient; see also Chapter 8. The only clue to his identity known to the present writer may be the inscription in a copy of *A Finger in Every Pie*: 'Kenneth Johnstone Welsh Guards October, 1942', above which RD put his own name. Unfortunately, the only soldier of this name for whom the Welsh Guards have a record was an Eton-educated Lieutenant-Colonel with a fashionable address in London, and he was not killed in the war. Another clue, perhaps, is that among the dozen photographs of men kept by the writer there is one of a Guardsman dated 22 April 1938 that bears the inscription, 'Kind regards, Roy'.

24 The play *Jenny Jones* opened in the London Hippodrome in 1944.

25 'Abraham's Glory', in *A Finger in Every Pie* (1942); *Collected Stories* (ed. Meic Stephens, vol. 1, 1996)

26 *Wales* (September 1958)

27 *Selected Stories* in the *Hour-glass Library* (Maurice Fridberg, 1945). Contents: 'Resurrection', 'The Contraption', 'Revelation', 'Death in the Family', 'Conflict in Morfa', 'Wrath', 'Arfon', 'The Bard', 'The Journey', 'Cherry-blossom on the Rhine'.

28 'Orestes', in *The Trip to London* (1946); *Collected Stories* (ed. Meic Stephens, vol. 3, 1998)

29 *Voices* (ed. Denis Val Baker, new series, no. 1, Autumn 1946)

30 *The Perishable Quality* (Heinemann, 1957)

31 *Girl Waiting in the Shade* (Heinemann, 1960)

32 Richard Harman (ed.), *Countryside Character* (Blandford Press, 1946). Either Davies had more Welsh than he let on, or he was trying to impress his English friend; it is unlikely that a day or two in a Welsh-speaking home would have enabled him to start thinking in Welsh unless he already had some at his command.

33 *Wales* (26, Summer 1947)

34 RD is not known to have kept such a notebook, certainly not a *journal intime*, or if he did it was destroyed before his death.

35 *Wales* (2, October 1943)

36 *Wales* (5, Autumn 1944)

37 Sheila Leslie in a letter to Meic Stephens (1 March 2012)

38 *Wales* (22, June 1946)

39 *Western Mail* (11 July 1946), in response to letters in the same paper (4 July 1946)

40 Sincerely though this view was held in the 1940s, RD was to change his mind towards the end of his life, by which time there had been a good deal of discussion about the term: 'I am an Anglo-Welsh writer,' he told Delyth Davies of BBC Wales in 1977, 'but it's not a term I'd use by choice.'

41 Among the Committee's supporters were Bertrand Russell, George Orwell, Harold Laski, Benjamin Britten, E. M.

Forster, Augustus John, Osbert Sitwell, and Herbert Read. The paper was renamed *Freedom* in 1945 and edited by George Woodcock.

42 'The Nature of Man', in *A Finger in Every Pie* (1942); *Collected Stories* (ed. Meic Stephens, vol.1, 1996)

43 This story is set in the fictitious village of Brwmstan; the name is Welsh for 'brimstone', denoting sulphur, as in Genesis 19:24 in which God rains brimstone and fire on Sodom and Gomorrah. RD was in the habit of using place-names of this kind, though none so telling as the one in this story.

44 'Canute', in *Boy with a Trumpet* (1949); *Collected Stories* (ed. Meic Stephens, vol. 2, 1996)

45 This result may have been suggested by the game played at Twickenham on 16 January 1937 when, *per contra*, England beat Wales by the same number of points.

46 Philip Burton was the man who nurtured the talent of the young Richard Jenkins, the twelfth of a miner's thirteen children, who became his ward, took his name and won fame as Richard Burton. For an account of his life and work see D[avid]. A. Callard, 'The Other Philip Burton', in *Planet* (122, April/May 1997). In Burton's autobiography, *Early Doors: My Life and the Theatre* (1969), he wrote: 'I had come to know, like, and admire Rhys Davies very much. His early courage in staking all on his writing ability did much to shame me in my days of doubt and fear... He was the first Welshman to make such a decision without compromise. One or two others before, and several since, have become writers but with the safeguard of a private income or another profession, such as journalism or teaching. Rhys made a total decision, and abided by it... He shrewdly observed the follies and hypocrisies of men with a wry twinkle, but was himself generous and thoughtful.'

47 H.E. Bates, *The Modern Short Story* (Thomas Nelson, 1941)

48 W.J. Entwistle and Eric Gillett, *The Literature of England A. D. 500-1946* (Longmans, Green, 1946)

49 Cyril Connolly (ed.), *Horizon Stories* (Faber, 1944)
50 Quoted in David Callard's article on RD in *Dictionary of Literary Biography: British Short Story Writers, 1945-1980* (1994)

Seven

The perishable quality

Once again Rhys Davies found that country life, despite his panegyrics, did not suit him. 'The countryside drove Rhys mad,' Fred Urquhart recalled, remembering how he would slip away to London for weekend visits that grew longer and longer as time went by. Conditions in the Tring cottage really were pretty basic. The pair had to gather their own firewood and bathe in a zinc tub, and gas for the cooker and geyser was always in short supply. The bedroom furniture was made of orange boxes covered with strips of chintz. The two writers also got on each other's nerves from time to time: 'Fred can't get up in the morning,' Davies groused to Louis Quinain in May 1946, 'what *is* the matter with his generation?' Urquhart, in Davies's estimation, was 'undomesticated' and, a cardinal sin in his book, made pastry that was inedible. But Davies had a habit of complaining about other people, including his brother Lewis, whom he often described as lackadaisical and unable to make up his mind about anything. There was something prim, even priggish, in his character that insisted on tidiness, punctuality and scrupulous attention to the quiddities of everyday life. This was a kind of uptightness that was maybe related to his hiding so much of his sexual and emotional life.

Nevertheless, Davies and Urquhart had lots of visitors, including Lewis Davies, Raymond Marriott, Louise Callender, an editor at Heinemann, and a lesbian couple, Kay Dick and Kathleen Farrell, who were to become their friends. The women – Dick was a novelist and worked in publishing while Farrell had private means – entertained many of the most famous writers of the day in their home at 55 Flask Walk, Hampstead, including C.P. Snow, Angus Wilson, Stevie Smith, Olivia Manning and Muriel Spark, and Davies was often invited to dinner parties there. Like Anna Kavan, Dick was a difficult woman of the type Davies was usually drawn to and their friendship was to be a stormy one. He thought her 'ruthless' on their first meeting. According to Michael De-la-Noy, who wrote her obituary in *The Guardian* in 2001, Dick expended far more energy in pursuing personal vendettas and lesbian affairs than in writing books, and 'for crudity, vulgarity and foul language she had few equals'. But once again Davies made her his friend and enjoyed her company.

Of Davies Dick remarked that 'calm in public may denote hysteric in private', and she accused him of deliberately causing rows. This was far from the truth, for Davies could not stand bickering and confrontation, and rarely lost his temper: he had had enough of it in Royal Stores where his mother and eldest sister were constantly at loggerheads. Dick lacked the femininity of her partner Kathleen Farrell, who was Davies's favourite. On one occasion, Dick, Farrell, Urquhart and Davies were in a tea-shop where they were offered a choice of cream cakes or cheese and biscuits. Dick was the only one to choose the savoury option. 'That was to show,' Davies remarked waspishly, 'that she was the only man among us.' Dick, however, remained in contact with Davies, to whom she inscribed copies of three of her books, 'For dearest Rhys, in friendship and love', though she did not include an interview with him in her semi-autobiographical book *Friends and Friendship*, published in 1974.

By July 1946 Davies was anxious to escape the rural rigours of Tring, reporting to Quinain that he intended curtailing his stay by two months and vacating the cottage in August. He was at this point working on his novel, *The Dark Daughters,* which appeared in the following year.[1] This book, a modern-day reworking of the Lear story, opens among the London Welsh but soon moves to West Wales and, a new departure for Davies, a largely middle-class milieu. The central character, Mansell Roberts, is a smooth, handsome hypocrite who deceives his wife, neglects his daughters, and takes as his second wife a music-hall artiste who bears him another daughter, Laura. The three sisters from his first marriage grow up to blame him for their mother's death and their own spinsterhood. Laura returns to the dreadful house where Roberts, in the third part of the novel, lives as a recluse, thus precipitating the final tragedy. The result is a rather more credible West Wales than the fantastic, even grotesque setting for the goings-on in *The Black Venus*, and Davies thought it his best book.

It was at this point Davies seems to have taken the decision to downplay the Welsh content in his stories. He believed writing about Wales had become hackneyed and unmarketable, a view that may have been influenced by the huge success of Richard Llewellyn's novel *How Green Was My Valley* (1939), in which most of the clichés used in writing about the Welsh had been exploited to full effect. For years thereafter, London publishers wanted another *How Green Was My Valley*, but Davies refused to compete with other writers and had no intention of writing to formula. In a letter to Arnold Gyde of Heinemann, he told him that he no longer wished to write 'too much Welsh semi-folk-lore stuff' and explained in a synopsis of *The Dark Daughters* that the action could be in any country:

> There is no building of Welsh atmosphere or flavour (except what is intrinsic in the father's character with its blending of mysticism and materialism). My usual Welsh 'inverted' dialogue is not used, since the daughters were born and educated in London and nearly all the other characters are English.

His next eight novels avoid the working-class Rhondda communities that had won him a loyal readership and with which his name had become so closely associated. Nevertheless, it was ironic that some reviewers, particularly in Wales, went on treating Davies as 'a Welsh proletarian writer'. This was a dilemma for him. On the one hand, he wanted respect as a 'pure artist' and resented being marketed as a Welsh writer; on the other, he knew his Welsh material was what had made him a writer in the first place, and it was difficult to shake off the Rhondda dust.

The novel was given what can only be described as a glowing review in the *Western Mail* by Gwyn Jones, soon to become the grey eminence of Welsh writing in English, who described Davies's stories as 'extraordinarily alive' and with 'a leaping quality':

> He has a sharp eye for the broad trend and the minute particular, his dialogue is trenchant and exact, his sentences are juiced and shapely as summer fruit. His prose is a poet's, his vision sensual but humorous, amoral but compassionate. His best work is deeply felt but unsentimental. One doubts whether he can ever become a really popular author. So far he remains a prophet less honoured than he should be in his own country. This is not so much, I imagine, because of the marked eroticism and pagan exhiliration of much of his work, or even his flaunted disrespect for time-worn prejudices, but he never gives his reader that warm, stupid, amorphous, 'nice' feeling which is the equivalent in literature of the cinema's *vox humana*.[2]

Despite his huge output, Davies's career was scarcely rewarding in financial terms and, if money had been his prime motive, he had enough talent to produce a follow-up to *The Black Venus*. He might have emulated his erstwhile friend H.E. Bates, who, after a lifetime of writing artistically fine but unremunerative work, hit on a winning formula with his Larkin books during the 1950s, including *The Darling Buds of May*, which gained a fresh readership in the early 1990s following its successful adaptation as a television series.[3] Davies was by no means a lesser talent. In a review of *The Best of Rhys Davies*, a selection made by the writer shortly before his death, Eric Partridge wrote:

> I have always maintained that Rhys Davies was a better short-story writer than H.E. Bates; time has borne out my early judgement.[4]

If Davies had been interested in making money, he could easily have followed Bates's example.

Back in London, Davies complained once more about urban living as he had about life in the country, but his furtive erotic lifestyle continued much as before. In pubs such as the Paxton's Head in Knightsbridge, Guardsmen could be picked up for the cost of a few drinks, with the tariff in the immediate post-war years set at ten shillings. One of his casual pick-ups who turned into a regular partner was a young Scots Guardsman based in Caterham Barracks who was known as Dodie, or perhaps Doddie; both versions of this nickname (perhaps a diminutive form of Dorothy or George) appear on the signed photographs he affectionately sent to Davies, though his real name was William Brown. He was blond, good-looking and from a tough Gorbals background. On the Guardsman's visits to London, Davies would entertain him at the flat belonging to Redvers and Louise Taylor in the King's Road. Such is the discretion, or subterfuge, with which Davies conducted his private life that it is impossible to date the affair accurately, but it appears to have started in the late 1940s and to have ended at some point during the early or mid-1950s when the intellectual gulf between the two men became too great for it to continue amicably. Once again, the man married – and sent Davies a photograph of himself with his wife.

Davies was now moving constantly on the periphery of a dangerous world. Guardsmen were known to beat up and rob the men they met in public lavatories. Len Smith, the mechanic who had introduced him to the Quinains, was found dead in the Thames in 1945. The official verdict was suicide, but he was to have appeared at the Old Bailey as a witness in a trial for assault and robbery. Davies had been worried about Smith's mental state for some time, suspecting that his period of military service had unhinged him, and was concerned he had taken to frequenting the homosexual haunts of the East End, a far more dangerous milieu than Soho. Furthermore, a friend of Dodie's, whom Davies had met and liked, had been murdered in Glasgow by one of that city's razor gangs. There was, too, the ever-present possibility of blackmail, which was rife in those days before the Sexual Offences Act of 1967, and of prosecution for public indecency, though Davies was never known to have been blackmailed or prosecuted for 'cottaging' – the practice of seeking homosexual partners in public conveniences, an offence for which the actor John Gielgud was arrested in 1953.[5]

An element of security in Davies's social life was provided by his friendship with Redvers and Louise Taylor, which was warm, genuine and long-lasting. Red Taylor, an Englishman, had been a Lieutenant-Colonel in the War Office, where the two had met during Davies's brief stint of war-work. Taylor, who was the same age as the writer, had retired from the army in 1937, was then recalled for war-service and retired again in 1946. He had then made the unusual career move from soldiering to the practice of avant-garde art. He painted, but became best-known for 'junk sculpture', a forerunner of *Arte Povera*, the kind of art practised by Antoni Tàpies in Barcelona and Alberto Burri in Italy. Davies wrote the introduction in the catalogue of his exhibition at the Lefevre Gallery in 1948, after which Taylor was taken up by Gimpels, one of the more enterprising avant-garde dealers in London.[6]

The career of Louise Taylor was even more unusual. She never revealed her true age, even to Davies, but some of their friends thought she could have been as much as twenty years older than her husband. Born in Seattle, she was musically gifted and as a young woman had worked with the celebrated pianist Isidor Philippe in Paris. She had renewed her friendship with Alice B. Toklas, with whom she had been at school, at some time before 1907 and, during the years *entre deux guerres*, had been part of the great expatriation of writers and artists to the French capital, where she had been one of the circle around Gertrude Stein. She had also lived for a while in Mallorca, and had got to know Robert Graves, with whom she kept up a correspondence. After Stein's death in 1946, Toklas had inherited her estate and, in turn, she named Louise Taylor as her heiress, although by that time there was little money left to inherit.

The Taylors were well-off, at least by Davies's standards. They had a flat at 31 King's Court North in Chelsea, which the writer, following his usual practice, frequently occupied while the couple were away. They also had a country house known as Revere in Bishops Lydeard near Taunton in Somerset to which he was often invited. When in London the Taylors ran a literary and artistic salon, of which the two most longstanding members were

Davies and Bill Naughton, later to find fame as the author of *Alfie* but then a struggling writer of stories of working-class life. Though Davies would invariably write to 'Red and Louise' out of politeness and inscribe copies of his books in affectionate terms to them both, it was to Louise he was drawn and he seemed to his brother Lewis to have been fonder of her than he let on.[7] He was allowed to stay at their house in Mallorca, from where in February 1950 he wrote to say how much he disliked Sartre's novel *The Age of Reason*.

Although Davies's output of short stories now began to diminish in quantity if not in quality – he maintained the form was really better suited to younger writers and he was no longer young – he continued to attract the attention of critics, mostly from outside Wales and some from overseas. In 1947 his famous story 'The Benefit Concert' was included in the prestigious anthology *Best World Short Stories* edited by John Cournos and Sybil Norton and his portrait of Dr William Price of Llantrisant was chosen by Geoffrey Grigson for inclusion in the miscellany *The Mint*. His story 'Canute', first published in *The Welsh Review*, appeared in Denys Val Baker's *Little Reviews Anthology* in 1948. He became a regular contributor to *Argosy*, one of the most popular magazines of the day. A monograph by Gustav Felix Adam also appeared in 1948 from a publisher in Bern in Switzerland, where Adam had been a student.[8] Although the section on Davies, with whom the author was acquainted, contains a number of factual errors, he was pleased it paid him the compliment of serious critical consideration.

Davies's appearance in most of the best anthologies and little magazines of the day continued throughout the late 1940s. It did not pay very well but kept his name before the literary-minded and book-buying public. If in 1949 he was overlooked by John Pudney, editor of *The Pick of Today's Short Stories*, an anthology that included work by his peers H.E. Bates, James Hanley, Eric Linklater, Frank O'Connor, V.S Pritchett, Fred Urquhart, and Seán Ó Faoláin, he was represented in Woodrow Wyatt's *English Story* in the company of William Sansom, A.E. Coppard, and Angus Wilson.

In *55 Short Stories from The New Yorker* (1949), which included 'The Dilemma of Catherine Fuchsias', the company was even more illustrious: John Cheever, James Thurber, Irwin Shaw, J.D. Salinger, Mary McCarthy, John O'Hara, Sylvia Townsend Warner, Carson McCullers, and Vladimir Nabokov. Wales had at last produced a short-story writer whose work could be seen alongside that of the best practitioners in the United States. Davies's reputation was confirmed in Britain when his story 'Fear' appeared in *The Pick of Today's Short Stories* in 1950, alongside stories by Olivia Manning, V.S. Pritchett, Osbert Sitwell, Monica Dickens and Evelyn Waugh, the only other Welsh writer to be represented being Margiad Evans. Stories by Davies were also included, much to his satisfaction, in three editions of the handsomely-produced *American Aphrodite*, 'a quarterly for the fancy-free', published in New York.

But by 1950 the golden age of the short story in Britain was beginning to draw to a close. The magazines that had published writers like Davies started to fold, and even *Horizon*, which Cyril Connolly had founded in 1939 and which had first published Davies's memoir 'D.H. Lawrence in Bandol', came to an end. Davies now had to look for a market elsewhere and, in common with other British writers, found it in America. One story from his collection *Boy with a Trumpet*, namely 'The Dilemma of Catherine Fuchsias',[9] had been accepted by *The New Yorker* which, with its generous rate of a dollar a word, more than made up for the comparatively measly fees paid by British magazines.[10] Davies was very fond of Catherine Fuchsias – 'Alas, characters like her come along too rarely,' he wryly observed. He regarded the story's opening paragraph as among the best he had ever written:

> Puffed up by his success as a ship-chandler in the port forty miles away, where he had gone from the village of Banog when the new town was rising to its heyday as the commercial capital of Wales, Lewis had retired to the old place heavy with gold and fat. With him was the bitter English wife he had married for her money, and he built the pink-washed villa overlooking Banog's pretty trout stream. And later he had set up a secret association with an unmarried woman of forty who was usually called Catherine Fuchsias, this affair – she receiving him most Sunday evenings after chapel in her outlying cottage – eluding public notice for two years. Until on one of those evenings, Lewis, who for some weeks had been complaining of 'a feeling of fullness', expired in her arms on the bed.

Sex and death, especially their tragi-comic elements, were constants in Davies's work and here, within a few lines, he delineates the career of Lewis, his marital problems and need for a mistress, his social status, and Catherine's, and the faintly hypocritical observation that the liaison was conducted after chapel. To the writer's amusement, the book, together with works by Joyce Carey, Anthony West, Erskine Childers and Georges Simenon, was banned in Ireland in the year of its publication.

An interview Davies gave to Glyn Jones in 1950, in which he spoke of the 'dreadful resolve' required to produce a novel of 90,000 words, revealed something of his approach to the novelist's craft. He compared writing a novel with the role of an actor who is 'capable of impersonating anything and anybody, regardless of age, sex or class. This impersonation... certainly can be exhausting, though not for me loathsome. I don't wonder that most good writers I know look worn and somewhat battered, as most actors do off stage.' He went on:

I have rarely copied a complete character from life. My experience is that they become unconvincing in writing, flat, rather dull. But I admit to finding a personal satisfaction in using in a fictional character some part of an acquaintance's make-up or his idiosyncrasies... In writing one can rid one's bosom of much perilous stuff. But of course one must beware of extravagant glee and of injustice.[11]

Pressed by the blandishments of Glyn Jones, who in his usual polite manner apologised for being 'importunate', Davies was reluctant to say much more about his 'aesthetic aims': 'It's a bit like asking a man if he thinks he's brave, or handsome, or a saint. Let critics and readers decide the answer to that one.' He went on to acknowledge that by the age of twenty a writer 'has accumulated enough raw experience for a lifetime of artistic re-creation'. That was hardly true in Davies's case but at least it paid tribute to his twenty years in Blaenclydach. The interview drew to a close in a discussion about what was called in Davies's day Anglo-Welsh literature. Davies complained about

> the eternal preoccupation with the mining-valley saga, the chapel goings-on, sentimental evocations of rustic life with the characters smothered in Welshness like those awful flannel nightshirts one used to see, warm and durable, no doubt, but oh, so tormenting. I can understand these limitations in theme and character; I think Welsh social life does tend to be rather isolated, private, shut within its ancient spirit, though this of course is its great preservative virtue.

Challenged to say whether he believed a Welsh writer should live in Wales, he replied:

> Alien people and surroundings seem to sharpen and contract, to crystallise, one's memories and emotions of one's country... For myself, I must go on wandering. I know what feeds me best, and I have no intention of being a traitor to myself.

One of the frankest he ever gave, the interview ended after Glyn Jones asked whether Davies thought his work reflected 'the real Wales', at which he seemed to bristle:

> The 'real Wales'? What *is* the real Wales? Whose is it? Is there some final arbiter, is there some absolute

opinion of Wales? Surely every genuine writer finds his own Wales. I don't ask people to accept my picture of Wales as the real one; it is inevitable that as people differ in temperament, in views, in beliefs, many should reject my picture of our country, should find certain elements exaggerated, others omitted. A piece of writing is mainly a sort of flowering, a fulfilment of oneself.

In 1951 Davies had the satisfaction of appearing in *Who's Who* for the first time. Although the entry would grow over time, his 'recreations' remained the same: 'theatre; living in London; cultivating ruined characters', as did his fib about the year of his birth: '1903'.

Davies's next novel, *Marianne* (1952), was set in what appears to be the industrial town of Port Talbot, a place he was never recorded as having visited, but which appears to have been based on a true incident.[12] The mesmerizing plot revolves around a pair of twins, both pretty and one cleverer than the other. The less clever dies giving birth, breathing to her sister the name of her illegitimate child's father. Her sister then tracks the father down, marries him and, in revenge, drives him to his death, only to discover in the novel's denouement that she has killed the wrong man. She feels no remorse, in fact she feels nothing. All she finds is release, 'no longer outlawed, no longer shut in a close labyrinth of secrets, deceits and terrors'. Release was what Davies wanted from his writing, though for different reasons. In so much of Davies's work, not least in *Marianne*, Davies drew on what M. Wynn Thomas has called, a whole nexus of feelings that find expression in the fiction: a wish to defy society's prohibitions on sexual frankness and to uncover the secret acts and desires of the respectable; a yearning for a culture of openness, where the likes of Davies could, as it were, fully expose their identity; a mingled fear of and fascination with the female; an embarrassed and yet excited identification with the male... Art, then, can say one thing and mean another. It is in fact a wonderfully slippery medium, a veritable squirm of delicious possibilities.[13]

It may be, too, why Davies sublimated his sexual desires in his writing and why, as his brother Lewis remarked to the present writer, 'Most of Viv's sexual life went on in his head', and why many of his relationships with younger men were, in fact, platonic. There is also, according to his brother, the possibility that by this stage of his life Davies was, if not impotent, then finding his sexual powers were on the wane. The reviewer in *Books of Today* came near the mark in assessing his handling of the psychology of the novel's main characters when he wrote that *Marianne*

demands a considerable suspension of disbelief on the part of the reader. Revenge is a tricky subject for any author and the study in this instance is complicated by two factors which are probably outside the range of experience of the ordinary reader. The first is the intangible affinity between twins and the other the possibility of a young girl working out a subtly refined revenge which involves the deliberate destruction of another human being.

Perhaps the Celtic streak in Mr Davies and in his heroine makes credible what would otherwise strike the average English person as incredible conduct. If one can accept the psychology of the heroine then the whole story falls into line, and it is a tribute to the author's skill that however much one may question the motives which create the situation, the handling of the story holds one's interest... The writing is a little lush at times, some of the interiors are a little too cosy, but one senses the touch of fire and poetry, and it is this which transforms what could be a commonplace tragedy into something the size of life.[14]

John Betjeman praised Davies for being a 'full-size' novelist:

He can create round, complete characters. His people are neither caricatures nor are they types who show one side of themselves only. He likes a large plot involving birth and death and the purging of the reader with pity. He likes a joke, light or sardonic.[15]

Most importantly of all, the book was to open up a new friendship and the start of a new career for its author. Davies had done work sporadically for the BBC since 1937, most notably in 1945 with 'The Old House', an hour-long feature about the history of a mining community in South Wales over a period of half a century. In 1938 he had contributed a short talk, 'Incident in a Bookshop', that was broadcast on the Welsh Home Service of the

BBC, in which he accused his compatriots of having an inferiority complex when it came to novels in which they were depicted:

> A writer will, of course, be forgiven if he will flatter and prettify. He must not talk about sex, and if he deals with religion, he must be pious. He must drown the lovely country cottages in roses, he must sentimentalize over the Welsh miners and rhapsodize over the farms and farmers, he must make the women dewy daisies, the men clean and wholesome as pats of fresh butter. The Welsh are not the only people who prefer this kind of romanticism. But I think we are unique in the wrath we display when writers dare to touch on what some call, rhetorically, dirt, others truth. And we will not understand that a writer can be critical of the nation and still remain enamoured of it, that criticism does not always come out of sourness or hatred.[16]

But his career in radio had not been spectacular. Both *The Dark Daughters* and *Under the Rose* had been adapted for radio by Ross Cockrill in 1948 and 1949 respectively, though his own dramatic versions of both books were never used. But he had met Philip Burton, producer of 'The Old House', and the two men had got on well from the start. Burton admired Davies's dedication to the craft of writing to the exclusion of all else. Something of a legend in the BBC, even outside Wales, and before he took the actor Richard Jenkins under his wing, it was he who had commissioned Dylan Thomas's *Return Journey* in 1947, even writing a five-minute pastiche to extend it to the required length when it proved too short. Over the next two years five of Davies's stories were broadcast by the BBC.[17]

Burton's stern schoolmasterly manner and sarcastic tongue earned him a fearsome reputation among writers and the BBC's technical staff alike. But Davies was more than a match for his friend's superciliousness and, on one occasion, recorded that he was 'inclined to be snooty in reaction; at one moment I had to speak severely to him.' Both were solitaries, both were able to live a self-contained life, both were homosexual and both, moreover, were would-be playwrights. Burton did a fine job in adapting *Marianne* and it reminded Davies of his ambition to work in the theatre. It was a personal blow when, in 1954, the producer announced he was about to emigrate to the USA. The affectionate inscriptions Davies wrote to Burton in many of his books, all of which the latter sent back to the present writer from his home in Florida shortly before his death, attest to the warmth of their friendship. More's the pity that, for some unknown reason, he destroyed all the letters Davies had written to him over the years.

Not a great deal came of Davies's ambition to work in film, radio or television. An option on 'Gents Only' was sold for £150 in 1953 to Michael Powell, then at the height of his fame as a film-maker.[18] The film was never made, and over the years, even up to the 1990s, there were to be several more options and the outright sale of rights on Davies's stories and novels, none of which came to anything. But at least they brought in money for the writer, generating income for little or no extra effort.[19]

Davies's career in the theatre was scarcely more successful. He wrote dramatic versions of no fewer than six of his novels and two short stories, as well as two original scripts for radio, all to no avail. He never complained about any of this but towards the end of his life he confessed that, though bitten by the theatre bug, he had come to realise it was impossible for him to be both prose-writer and dramatist. The only consolation had been that, with the money from this source, he had been able to travel a little, to Malta, Switzerland, Amsterdam, Venice and especially Paris where he stayed once more at the Grand Hôtel de Versailles. On his fiftieth birthday in 1951, an occasion he spent alone – perhaps because his friends thought he was only 48 – he was able to take some satisfaction from the knowledge he had achieved a good deal of critical success and a modicum of commercial success that was enough to finance his bachelor lifestyle exactly as he pleased. From now on, there would be fewer trips to the Rhondda, either via Paddington or on imagination's train.

After the publication of *Marianne* in 1951, Davies entered one of the fallow periods that, copious though his writing was, he needed from time to time. But he did not twiddle his thumbs for long. Among his new friends was the American poet W.S. Merwin, who had contacted him after reading 'The Dilemma of Catherine Fuchsias' in *The New Yorker* and whom he later met at the home of Eve Kirk. Another was Herman Schrijver, a Dutch Jewish interior designer whose most prestigious commission had been the decoration of Fort Belvedere for Edward VIII and Mrs Wallis Simpson.[20] He had also worked on the houses of assorted aristocrats and millionaires, including, in 1936, the house of Hugh Tevis in South Africa. Tevis was the husband of convenience of Anna Kavan's mother, and many years her junior. Even vast wealth did not protect this platinum-haired homosexual, who kept a retinue of young epicenes in and around Monterey, his estate in the Constantia suburb of Cape Town, from the strict moral code of Boer society and he needed a 'cover'. Kavan's mother was more than happy with the arrangement, since it gave her access to a fortune enabling her to retain a permanent suite at Claridges on her visits to England. Anna Kavan both detested and depended on her mother, whom she blamed, with good reason, for her many psychological problems, yet they managed to be civil towards each other and the daughter enjoyed the mother's lavish hospitality. Writing to Davies shortly after arriving at Monterey, in an undated letter but during or soon after the Second World War, she described it laconically as:

Large, luxurious, and arranged with good taste although it's far too full of valuable objects for my liking. One has rather the sense of living in a museum; every time one sits down it seems to disturb the perfection of the arrangements. I have an enormous 4-poster Hollywood bed which makes me feel like Garbo at her most delapidated [sic]... Troops of coloured servants rather get under one's feet all the while – English butler and footmen very dignified and impressive. Personally I dislike being waited on to such an extent; it seems to impinge on one's freedom. But I suppose one gets used to it... I don't know if there are any 'intellectuals': I'm not likely to get a chance of meeting them anyway unless I make efforts to get outside the family aura... Shall I send you food parcels? Love, Anna.

Herman Schrijver had met Anna and it was she who introduced him to Davies. A man of immense culture, a wit and *bon vivant*, Schrijver was a member of the salon of Ivy Compton-Burnett. On the death of her companion, Margaret Jourdain, he was to become her closest confidant. Like Davies, he was a promiscuous homosexual, though he also had a regular partner, an American named Charles Burkhart, who wrote a memoir, *Herman, Nancy and Ivy* (1977).[21] Schrijver's style of decoration depended heavily on the use of mirrors and *trompe l'oeil* effects. He was also a narcissist, given to declaring that everyone is really homosexual because it is the closest one can come to making love to oneself. Burkhart said of him, 'The women he knew who he asserted were lesbians, Wembley Stadium would not hold.' A great admirer of Davies's writing, in 1952 Schrijver introduced him to Ivy Compton-Burnett.

The Welshman never expressed an opinion of Compton-Burnett's fiction but of the woman herself he wrote, 'She's not in the present day world at all and I don't know what to make of her.' He attended her salon on several occasions but soon gave up: 'She's soooo boring,' he confided to Burkhart. Once again Davies had spurned an *entrée* into the metropolitan literary world, as he had done once before when he turned his back on the home of Lady Ottoline Morrell. Compton-Burnett's retinue was almost entirely homosexual and most of its members were well-connected in London publishing circles. It is impossible to avoid the conclusion that Davies regarded literary friendships with the same distaste that he felt for exclusive human relationships.

He was not entirely oblivious to others, however, and could show a degree of sympathy for those he liked or admired. In 1953, for example, he recorded the death of Dylan Thomas in a New York hospital on the 9th of November with real regret. To the Taylors he wrote, 'Poor Dylan Thomas!... It quite depressed me (on my birthday too). I knew him slightly and he always said nice things of my work, to others, which came back to me... a brilliant and most original poet.' He gave £3 to the fund opened to bring Thomas's body back from America. But how thoughtless of the Rimbaud of Cwmdonkin Drive to die on Davies's birthday!

In 1951, Davies's landlady of many years, Mrs Waugh-Brown, died and the house passed to her lover, whom Davies disliked intensely. He therefore moved to 29 Castellain Road, a stone's throw from Randolph Avenue and still in Maida Vale. There his landlord was a Mr Gay, one of Mrs Waugh-Brown's former lovers, but this was far less satisfactory and he was soon looking for some alternative accommodation. It was about this time that he found a new romantic interest to warm his heart. Breakfasting almost daily at Lyons Corner House near Marble Arch, he spotted a young man clearing the tables: Ron Heggie, a Scot, was well-built, good-looking, and had theatrical ambitions. They saw each other regularly over the next few years, and in November 1954 Heggie moved in as Davies's flat-mate at 6 Belgrave Place in Brighton. The Scot, who had no real interest in literature, described Davies's routine thus:

He was a man of habit. After lunch (1pm until 5 pm), work. Always shopped at Sainsbury's. Never missed Selfridges sale... 'very good for bed linen'. Even to his writing: first draft in pencil on lined pads. Next day, correct/alter. Copy onto identical pad. Continue on first pad. Five o'clock... Earl Grey and digestive biscuits... He was a 'bed-sit' type... he seemed to prefer to live, work and sleep in one room. I was away working much of the time but, when there, I learned to be out of the flat each afternoon to allow him to work. Never to ask what he had written. 'Never ask a writer what he has written. If he talks about his book he will talk it out instead of writing it out'.[22]

Ron Heggie also recounted an incident in which a man occupying the flat directly above Davies's committed suicide by plunging head-first down the service shaft that led into the writer's bathroom. Davies, having heard the thump and groaning, called the caretaker and then watched, fascinated, while the panel was unscrewed and the body removed. It is a wonder he did not write a story about it because it was the sort of weird incident the writer relished.

Although Davies gave others a different impression, Heggie denied there was any physical relationship between them.

In all the years I knew him I never saw any indication of sexual activity whatever. He hinted at homosexuality in his youth and that the Boy with a Trumpet was someone he had known many years before. However, I now firmly believe that, by the time I met him, he was completely asexual. He never once made any overtures toward me or to any of my friends who met him... I think I was Rhys's status

symbol. I was at his side to show off to his friends
that he could still attract attention... Many of his
friends had lifelong partners, but he didn't. It could
just have been loneliness, to have a friend but no
commitment.

One of the visitors to the Brighton flat was Dodie, who
turned up with his wife and baby. 'We Scots got on
famously,' Heggie told David Callard. 'Would that have
been the case with a displaced lover?'

Although he refused at first to co-operate with Callard
who, in 1991, had approached him in the hope of an
interview, Heggie wrote five pages of notes in which he
set down what he could remember of Davies, asking that
such a complex and sad person, whose memory he held
in high regard, be treated gently. He did, however, express
the view that Davies, in his wish to be seen in the
company of younger men, himself included, was trying to
give the impression he too had someone in his life, but
that it was wrong of him to have accepted genuine
friendship and portrayed it as anything more in order to
satisfy his own ego.

In 1953 Davies's move to the flat in Brighton, at 6
Belgrave Place, meant he had many friends in the town's
homosexual community, including Kay Dick and Kathleen
Farrell who, until the end of their affair in 1962, lived
near by. There was also a constant stream of visitors from
London: Raymond Marriott and his partner George
Bullock, the antique dealer Tommy Gascoigne (with whom
Davies went on a motoring holiday in Italy), Herman
Schrijver, the novelist's brother Lewis, and the concert
pianist Lionel Bowman. His sisters, one of whom, Peggie,

lived in Lewes, visited him occasionally, and his mother came up from Wales – 'a tiny frail lady dressed all in black and very Welsh', was how Heggie remembered her.[23] Neither Lewis Davies nor Raymond Marriott liked Heggie and both wondered what Davies saw in him.

The pram in the hall may indeed be a sombre enemy of good art, as Cyril Connolly memorably remarked, but in Davies's case it was 'the ringing door-bell at 6 Belgrave Place that kept him from writing: 'I came to Brighton to lead a more secluded life,' he complained forlornly to the Taylors. Another irritation was that Davies and Heggie were soon bickering, something the Scot thought, mistakenly, the Welshman enjoyed. Things came to a head after Heggie, dining with Davies, Kay Dick and Kathleen Farrell in a Brighton restaurant, began flirting with Farrell, which caused a hysterical outburst from Dick which went on into the early hours of next morning.

Quite what Davies was working on in Brighton in 1954 it is difficult to say with any certainty. He had recently turned down a request from Heinemann to write his autobiography, telling the Taylors: 'I'm replying that it would be too gloomy and the truth (what use is a book without truth) wouldn't bear telling.' His novel *The Painted King*, based on the life of the Welsh matinée idol Ivor Novello, who had kept the home fires burning with his immensely popular song during the First World War, had been ready for some time, but publication had been held up while it was vetted for libel.[24] It includes a wickedly hilarious portrait of Guy Aspen's mother, Madame Annie, who was based on Clara Novello Davies, conductor of the Welsh Ladies' Choir which had won an international competition at the Chicago World Fair of 1893. It also shows the main character – Davies disliked Novello's schmaltzy music – unable to differentiate between reality and the tinsel world of his Ruritanian musicals.

The identity of the real-life model for Guy Aspen and his domineering mother did not escape Arthur Helliwell, a columnist with *The People*: 'Friends and admirers of the late Ivor Novello will be shocked and angered by a cruel book...' he began, before roundly attacking it (21 March 1954). James Harding, Novello's biographer, on the other hand, thought the novel 'brilliant', an acutely observed portrait of his relationship with women. Perhaps, Harding suggested, the author had known Novello, or else a woman who had kissed and told. In fact, neither was true. In depicting a narcissistic Welsh homosexual whose closest emotional ties were with women, Davies simply wrote a fantasy projection of himself: it was one way of coming out of the closet without incurring danger. Other reviews of the book were favourable without being enthusiastic. In *The Sunday Times*, for example, it was described as 'a novel highly accomplished and witty without malice', and in the *Birmingham Post* as 'a dynamic study of personality, entertaining, sustained, perceptive, the author's sharp wit softened but not dimmed by his awareness of the amazing but fascinating fools we mortals be.' A handsome American edition was published in the same year and sales across the Atlantic were astonishingly good.

In 1954 Davies was glad to be asked to help Archibald Batty to adapt his novel *Under the Rose* into a stageable play. It was given its premiere in Eastbourne as *No Escape* on the 5th of July and then taken on a provincial tour.[25] In a production note to the published text Batty wrote:

A play which begins with murder, deals in blackmail and ends in suicide, may strike the casual reader as providing a somewhat lugubrious evening's entertainment. The theme is horrific: public performance up and down the country has proved that the impact on the audience is not. There is always comedy in different people's points of view and excitement in the inevitability of crime coming home to roost. But, let every producer be warned, there are no comic characters here.

The play might have provided its author with a moment of *réclame* had not the production run into difficulties soon after its premiere. It happened to star the distinguished actress Flora Robson as the frustrated spinster Rachel Lloyd and the then unknown Miriam Karlin in her first major role as Violet Myers, a woman of easy virtue. Davies's adaptation was in the tradition of the well-made play but the producer, John Fernald, introduced a rather daring innovation that turned out to be a fatal mistake. Miriam Karlin made her entrance, not from the wings, but by walking down the theatre's central aisle and then going up onto the stage. This theatrical device, novel in its day, had an electrifying effect on the audience, which was not sure what to make of an attractive young woman in tight skirt and high heels walking into the drama in this way.

The character played by Robson, on the other hand, was highly unattractive in comparison and so Miriam Karlin had the best lines and, inevitably, the best reviews. Although Flora Robson had a rather sweet image in the eyes of the theatre-going public, she was 'something of a bitch' where young actresses were concerned, according to Miriam Karlin, later to win fame as the militant shop steward in the television series *The Rag Trade*. Be that as it may, it was too much for Robson's pride and, after a tour that lasted barely sixteen weeks, she called Davies into her dressing room and informed him she would not be in the cast if the play were taken to London. She would not, she insisted, be upstaged by 'this music hall technique'. Davies's friends were furious but he, with his usual sang-froid, simply shrugged it off and made no complaint, passive in this as in all things. In 1955 the BBC televised the play with a different cast and it was performed by amateur groups over the next decade, but that was effectively the end of Davies's career as a dramatist. Although he continued to make versions of almost every novel he was to write up to *Honeysuckle Girl* in 1975, none was ever staged.[26] Several of his short stories, however, were adapted for television, including 'The Dilemma of Catherine Fuchsias', directed by the distinguished Welsh film-maker John Hefin.

At something of a loose end, Davies now set about putting together his *Collected Stories*,[27] which was to appear in 1955. This book, in fact, contained barely half the stories he had published but all he cared to preserve. In his preface he wrote:

When a suitable period has elapsed a writer is entitled to exercise judgement of his past work, and from the eighty-odd of my published short stories I have chosen forty-three which yield me various degrees of satisfaction: the rest cause me various degrees of unease.

The present writer, when compiling Davies's *Collected Stories* in the late 1990s, was able to find well over a hundred stories which eventually occupied three substantial volumes, and several others have been located in obscure places since then.[28]

Davies's preface gives little away about his working methods, except the much-quoted sentence that appears in parenthesis on the first of its two pages: '(That instinct to *dive*, swift and agile, into the opening of a story holds, for me, half the technical art; one must not on any account loiter or brood in the first paragraph; be deep in the story's elements in a few seconds.)' He went on:

> Short stories are a luxury which only those writers who fall in love with them can afford to cultivate. To such a writer they yield the purest enjoyment; they become a privately elegant craft allowing, within very strict confines, a wealth of idiosyncrasies. Compared with the novel, that great public park so often complete with draughty spaces, noisy brass band and unsightly litter, the enclosed and quiet short story garden is of small importance, and has never been more... Another virtue of the short story is that it can be allowed to laugh.

Davies had already made clear how he viewed the short story form in Wales when he reviewed Glyn Jones's collection, *The Water Music*, in 1945:

> I think that there can be no doubt that the short story, often possessing intrinsic affinities with the poem, the picturesque oration, the hymn and even

the sermon, springs naturally from the Welsh
temperament, which perhaps is too volatile for the
sustained and plodding effort the long novel needs.[29]

He did not add, nor would he, that the short story is also
considered to be a 'refuge of the misfit and isolato', as
M. Wynn Thomas has called the form; the idea comes
from Frank O'Connor's influential study of the short story,
The Lonely Voice (1962).

As to whether he thought his short stories superior to
his novels, his definitive answer was given to Jean Pol Le
Lay, the student at the University of Brest who was
writing a dissertation on his work in 1967:

> I suppose my short stories give me more satisfaction
> than my novels, but really I have very little feeling
> about any of my work once a thing is written.
> Writing, although exhausting, yields a peculiar
> pleasure which completely vanishes once a piece is
> in print. Going through typescripts and proofs for
> correction is depressing and oppressive work. Only
> the act of writing – creating something new – is
> rewarding and worthwhile.

His *Collected Stories* drew praise from John Betjeman, clearly
a fan, who described him as 'the Welsh equivalent of George
Gissing': 'Rhys Davies is a first-class writer and every short
story in this book is a novel in itself.' His old associates from
the days of The Progressive Bookshop came forward to
praise him, too. H.E. Bates had been cut off by Davies after
his review of *Count Your Blessings* in 1933, but now the
Englishman wrote to the Welshman congratulating him: 'I

like the preface. It's all absolutely true, what you say about the short story, and it really is much more pleasure to write than a novel – I wholeheartedly agree.' Bates by this time was deeply disillusioned with post-war Britain, its politics and literature: 'There is so much that is piddling now.' Davies shared his disappointment, writing to the Taylors that he was unable to get excited about the General Election of 1955. As for his fellow writers, he dismissed Angus Wilson, who dealt with homosexual themes in a coded way, just as Davies did, as 'England's leading specialist in bitchery'.

In late 1955 Davies moved into a bedsitter in 15 Russell Court, Woburn Place, in the heart of Bloomsbury. This was to be his home for the rest of his life and here, at last, he had his own telephone, if not a television set.[30] It was in Russell Court, on the 16th of June 1968, that the present writer met him in the company of Julian Sheppard, who took a series of photographs of him for the Welsh Arts Council that remains the best pictorial record we have of the writer.[31] A reserved man in the presence of people whom he had only just met, Davies received us courteously, serving tea and biscuits and gladly adopting poses showing him relaxed but alert, even agreeing to sit chatting on his favourite bench in Woburn Place while the photographer snapped away. He had been able to afford the rent on the flat, he said, with the help of money he had inherited from his parents, who had left him a little more than their other four children because, and this with a mischievous chuckle, he had saved them the expense of higher education.

No sooner had he moved to Russell Court than he was faced with a family crisis: both his parents died within weeks of each other, his father in December 1955 and his mother in late January 1956. Davies had to return to Blaenclydach for their funerals and to administer their estates with Gertie, the eldest of his three sisters. He left no recorded response to his parents' deaths, though by now he had lost whatever nostalgia he had felt for the Rhondda. 'If only they'd leave, I'd never, never go near the place again,' he had written to the Taylors in June 1955. 'The thought of the Rhondda now fills me with dismay, if not despair.'[32]

It was shortly afterwards that Davies referred to his sister Gertie in a letter to Louis Quinain as 'a frustrated spinster' and 'a psychopath'. The latter was no doubt an exaggeration but the former may very well have been near the mark. Lewis Davies, who shared his misgivings about their sister, informed the present writer that she had not married because, in her day, married women were debarred from teaching in Glamorgan and she was not willing to give up her career for any man. He added, somewhat inconsequentially, that in middle age she had suffered from impetigo, which he thought was psychosomatic. Nor were relations between Gertie and Gladys of the most cordial, as the correspondence between Gladys and Lewis Davies reveals: Gertie hoarded her money, refused to leave the home they shared at 13 Fitzjohns Road, Lewes, for fear of intruders, did not lend a hand in running the house, and went for weeks without speaking to her sister.

It is not likely Davies was much use in settling his parents' estates for he was supremely incompetent in such matters, and he did not enlist the help of his brother Lewis. Nevertheless, the two months he spent in

Blaenclydach were put to good fictional use. Herman
Schrijver sent his commiserations:

> This always reminds me of that terrible day in the
> middle of the war when I got a telegram from the
> Red Cross telling me that both my parents had been
> murdered... I do think that to lose both of one's
> parents is a strange release. I think you will know
> what I mean, for the first time one feels really 'free',
> but don't ask me free from what.

Davies did not say whether he felt any release, but the
death of his parents meant he no longer had any pressing
reason to return to the Rhondda.

Davies's ruthlessness and his forensic, unsentimental
attitude to life's vicissitudes is perhaps best illustrated in
his famous entry in *Who's Who* which listed as his
recreation, 'cultivating ruined characters'. Ron Heggie
recalled that Davies would not come to his wedding and
would not agree to meet his wife or dine at their home:

> That hurt me very much... I occasionally went to his
> flat for tea and a chat. His entry in *Who's Who* read
> something like 'Interests: Collecting people' [*sic*]. I
> didn't like that. It equated people with foreign
> stamps or silver teaspoons, and told him so. He said
> that people were like that and had to be discarded
> in the end. That shocked me. One evening I called
> at his flat, sure that he would have finished work.
> He hadn't. He said, very exasperated, 'You can't
> come in, I'm working. Why didn't you phone to
> make arrangements?' I wondered why friends had

to make arrangements to meet. I remembered *Who's Who* and felt discarded and just walked away. I never saw Rhys again.

The book on which Davies was working when he turned Heggie away in 1956 was almost certainly *The Perishable Quality*, a novel that appeared in the following year.[33] His quotation of Flaubert's famous assertion, *'Madame Bovary, c'est moi!'*, which he always rendered as *'I am Madame Bovary'*, was a coded expression of his belief that he became, to some degree, the various women in his books. These were either wanton types corresponding to the promiscuity of his own private life, or frustrated spinsters, or viragos like his sister Gertie. The reader does not have to be a psychiatrist to understand that he was, so often, of all three types. As a homosexual who was attracted only to heterosexual men, he was bound to be frustrated and disappointed: it was a lifelong and inescapable condition. In *The Perishable Quality*, Davies was Eva Pritchard, at least in his imagination, a woman returning from London and the bohemian life of Soho-Fitzrovia to the fictitious town of Bylau, a name the author often used to denote Tonypandy. Eva is 'kindly, intelligent, discriminatingly loose, ageing but still attractive', and is in flight from an ardent younger lover whose libido is much greater than hers: the 'perishable quality' is sexual desire and youth, but especially the first of these. Davies at this time was in his mid-fifties but the young lover seems to have been entirely imaginary. The story draws on his last visit to the Rhondda at the time of his parents' deaths. Eva is struck, as Davies must have been, by the new optimism brought about by the nationalisation of the coal industry in 1947. Like Davies, too, she comes to stay in Bylau with her sister. Like her, Davies was now not only alone but also even more acutely aware of his loneliness. This sense of not belonging any more is nowhere more acute than in *The Perishable Quality*.

The story shifts between Bylau and London, where the central figure among Eva's bohemian friends is a hard-drinking poet called Iolo Hancock. He is so readily recognisable as Dylan Thomas that the poet's first biographer, Constantine Fitzgibbon, was prompted to ask Davies how well they knew each other. The novelist confirmed that the character was indeed based on Thomas, whom he had met four or five times. He had chosen the name Iolo because it sounded bardic (Iolo Morganwg had invented the ceremonies of the Gorsedd of Bards in the closing years of the eighteenth century), and Hancock was the name of a well-known South Wales firm of brewers.

Although Davies had been trying to shake off Wales as part of his personal identity, it remained an important part of his authorial identity, at least as far as his publisher and readers were concerned. Eva represents the Davies who, with the death of his parents, had lost the last connection he had with the Rhondda, and there is a certain wistfulness in his portrayal of her:

> She knew it so well, changed though the valley and the town at its mouth was. She felt she was there in search of a lost identity, of a self that had known happy security.

From now on, home and country would not be the primary sources of his inspiration.

Once again a novel of Davies's was favourably reviewed in the London press. John Davenport in *The Observer* called *The Perishable Quality* 'an excellent short novel, both moving and comic, never becoming farcical or sentimental. It has the delicious astringency of a good salad dressing.' This culinary touch was repeated by David Williams in *The Guardian*: 'His tale is as fresh and crisp as a lettuce plucked from the garden after a June shower... a satisfying piece of work from a mature and individual talent.' Davies's friend Fred Urquhart wrote in *Time and Tide* that the book was 'robust, rich and racy' and full of 'warmth, humour and commonsense'. Davies's reputation as a writer of short stories was also confirmed in 1956 with his inclusion in Gwyn Jones's anthology *Welsh Short Stories* which appeared in the *World's Classics* series published by Oxford University Press. Most of the contributors were represented by just one story but Rhys Davies, Caradoc Evans, Gwyn Jones, Alun Lewis, Dylan Thomas, Gwyn Thomas, and Kate Roberts all had two each.

It is difficult to locate Davies in any one artistic milieu. His connection with the ambience of Fitzrovia was by now tenuous and intermittent, as it had been with Bloomsbury. But he was friendly with the painter John Minton, who committed suicide in 1957, and his associates, the Scottish painters Robert MacBryde and Robert Colquhoun, generally known as 'the two Roberts'. All three artists were notorious hell-raisers, and so Davies gave them a wide berth socially though he admired their work and bought some of it. During the 1950s Louis Golding, another writer who had been part of the Lahr circle, opened a club frequented by homosexuals in Soho known as the Toucan Club. It was managed by two sisters called May and José Adair, who by coincidence lived in the same block of flats as Davies. He became a friend of theirs and his motives in visiting the club were social rather than alcoholic or sexual. Among the writers he knew at this time was the indigent and malodorous Paul Potts, a copy of whose book *Invitation to a Sacrament* (1973), bearing an inscription 'to a dear friend', was found among Davies's books at his death.

But the Soho scene of the 1950s never recovered from the deaths of several of its most colourful characters, notably Dylan Thomas, and a steep increase in the price of alcohol prevented many writers and artists from indulging themselves on a nightly basis as they had done before the war. In artistic terms, moreover, the Neo-Romanticism of the 1940s had been supplanted by the Movement, writers largely academic and concerned with precision rather than effusion, while Beckett and Pinter had introduced a new cerebralism to the London stage. If writers now made front-page news they were almost certainly Angry Young Men, whose concerns were perceived to be broadly left-wing and Redbrick rather than Oxbridge and patrician. From Europe a version of Existentialism was blowing through the coffee bars of Soho for which Davies had little taste.

None of this had any effect on him except to underscore the fact he was no longer in the literary avant-garde as he had been during the inter-war years. Fortunately for him, however, America was so far impervious to these trends and his work still found favour there. Most of his fan-mail, and there was a lot of it, came from across the Atlantic. One of his long-term correspondents, an American named Félix Martí-Ibáñez, was a distinguished psychologist who practised on classic Freudian principles and edited a glossy medical journal with the title *MD*, to which Davies sent his story 'River, Flow Gently'.[34] The American claimed friendship with W. Somerset Maugham but thought Davies the better writer.

The appeal of Davies's work to a Freudian is hardly surprising. Davies claimed to have no interest in abstract ideas – in this sense he cannot be called an intellectual – and is not recorded as ever having read Freud, though that is no proof he did not. In *Print of a Hare's Foot* he named him as 'a newly canonised redeemer of London in the 1920s'. It was hardly necessary for Davies to have read Freud, since he was part of current intellectual discourse and the intelligentsia of the inter-war years were influenced by him to an extent that now seems unimaginable. He may not have been influenced by Freud but his world-view was certainly Freudian. Both held a Classical rather than a Romantic view of humanity, believing human nature to be immutable and that only external circumstances change. It is a charge often levelled at Freud that, because he encountered only abnormal psychologies from which he drew his conclusions, they were somehow invalid. Similar charges have been laid at Davies's door by several commentators. One of these was Ron Heggie:

He was uncomfortable with 'normal' women and often I would be asked to be present when female visitors were coming. He could handle lesbians, drug-addicts and eccentrics but I don't think he liked or understood women. In his writing his women are either hard or fat or funny or blowsy. They are bitter spinsters or unfaithful wives. I can't think of any of his female characters for whom he showed any warmth or affection. He observed them but never seemed to 'feel' for them.

As we have seen, Davies was drawn, in both his personal and his fictional world, to the aberrant and the deviant. His great Welsh hero, Dr William Price of Llantrisant, can hardly be said to have been a 'normal' man. Anna Kavan, his closest friend of either sex, was not a 'normal' woman. What is so disturbing about Davies is that he places what might be described as psychological abnormalities in a 'normal' context. Thus Emma Bovary is reincarnated in Pontypridd, Orestes in war-time London, and Phaedra in Tonypandy. The near-contemporary with whom Davies had the closest parallels in this respect was perhaps Tennessee Williams. The present writer is aware that to describe someone as 'abnormal' carries a pejorative connotation that Davies certainly never intended. Oedipus and Elektra were 'abnormal' only to the extent that Freud named complexes after them, whereas Classical commentators do not dwell on their 'abnormality' any more than critics of King Lear, another fictional source for Davies, discuss the 'abnormality' of his daughters. Nor does Davies.

M. Wynn Thomas, who was the first to explore the nature of Davies's homosexuality at any length, found in him

a determining (and disturbing) underlying orientation. Davies strikes me, through his fiction, as being a deeply troubled man. To read these stories in bulk is

271

to wonder at their bleakness, which is if anything even more apparent in the comedy than in the pathos.[35]

The bleakness to which Wynn Thomas refers is, of course, the absence of love and its redemptive power, which was apparent both in Davies's life and work. Certainly his love life, if it can be called that, was divorced from his sexual life and in his fiction he gave primacy, not to love, but to the power-struggle between men and women in which the female is almost invariably triumphant. Wynn Thomas pointed out in his pioneering Rhys Davies Lecture of 1977 that the writer,

> while taking a 'liberated', anti-Puritan, post-Freudian and post-Lawrentian attitude towards sex, seems unable ever to conceive of it as coexisting with tenderness, or as contributing to an emotionally rich and complex human relationship.

To accept this view, however, is to attempt to impose broadly Christian ideals, in which *eros* and *agape* are as one, on a writer whose sensibility was essentially pre-Christian. There is not much love, as we understand it, in either classical literature or the Old Testament, nor in Freud for that matter. In Davies's mind, love was yet another construct, like social convention, superimposed on what he liked to call 'the Old Adam' – the primaeval urge for sex. In this he was wholly Freudian. It should come as no surprise to learn that his most ardent admirer in America was an orthodox Freudian and that his most enthusiastic readership in the United States should be among the Greenwich Village intelligentsia, where his admirers were legion.[36]

By 1959, or shortly thereafter, Davies's peripatetic existence had come to an end. Although he went abroad from time to time, mostly to France or Italy, he no longer changed address every few months and trips outside London were confined to the occasional jaunt to see Louise and Red Taylor at their country home. His friendships outside the capital lapsed and his letters ceased to complain about life in the metropolis. At last the hare had found its form.

Notes

1   *The Dark Daughters* (Heinemann, 1947; Doubleday, 1948; Swedish edn., *Folket i bilds förlag,* 1951); reprinted in an edn. of 30,000 copies by Readers Union. The novel's first title was *Petticoat House* but it was dropped before publication.

2   Gwyn Jones, 'Rhys Davies – his Last Book is his Best', in the *Western Mail* (11 May 1949). Not all reviews were as favourable, however. In *The Observer* (19 October 1947), Lionel Hale wrote: 'An uncommonly effective story by Mr Rhys Davies, *The Dark Daughters* does not bother to go very deep. It is happy enough with a Welsh chemist who makes his money out of brothels, with music hall soubrettes, with stultified daughters, and a little affair like lust and lunacy. Its Welsh origin naturally involves it in the idea of remorse (by Chapel out of Sin); and a good, gruesome time is had by all.'

3   Between 1991 and 1993 *The Darling Buds of May* was broadcast in a television series starring David Jason and Pam Ferris as Pa and Ma Larkin and Catherine Zeta-Jones as their nubile daughter Mariette.

4   *Books and Bookmen* (March 1979)

5 In 1942, 24 men were accused of committing acts of gross indecency in Abergavenny, 18 of whom received gaol sentences of between 10 months and 12 years; one defendant, aged 19, committed suicide before the trial. The case was reported in detail in the *News of the World* (8 November 1942).

6 In 1972, Red Taylor was given a major retrospective at Kettle's Yard in Cambridge, for the catalogue of which John Piper wrote an introduction.

7 Among the items Lewis Davies sold to the National Library of Wales in 1990 were about 400 letters RD sent to the Taylors between 1946 and 1972.

8 G.F. Adam, *Three Contemporary Anglo-Welsh Novelists: Jack Jones, Rhys Davies and Hilda Vaughan* (A. Francke A. G., 1948)

9 'The Dilemma of Catherine Fuchsias', in *Boy with a Trumpet* (1949); *Collected Stories* (ed. Meic Stephens, vol. 2, 1996)

10 RD received £800 for the story, at the time about the average annual wage for a manual worker; seven more of his stories appeared in the magazine between 1949 and 1966.

11 The interview was broadcast on the BBC's Welsh Home Service in January 1950 and published in the *New Welsh Review* (35, Winter 1996/97).

12 *Marianne* (Heinemann, 1951; Doubleday, 1952)

13 M. Wynn Thomas, '"Never Seek to Tell thy Love": Rhys Davies's Fiction', in *Decoding the Hare*

14 *Books of Today* (November 1951)

15 John Betjeman, in a review of *Marianne* from an unidentified London newspaper (n.d.), tipped into the author's own copy of his novel.

16 The radio talk was published in Patrick Hannan (ed.), *Wales on the Wireless* (1988).

17 'Conflict in Morfa' and 'The Bard', in *A Pig in a Poke* (1931) and 'Caleb's Ark' in *The Things Men Do* (1936), *Collected Stories* (ed. Meic Stephens, vol. 1, 1996); 'A

Dangerous Remedy' in *The Trip to London* (1946), *Collected Stories* (ed. Meic Stephens, vol. 2, 1996); 'A Human Condition', in *Boy with a trumpet* (1949), *Collected Stories* (ed. Meic Stephens, vol. 2, 1996). The BBC broadcast adaptations of the last two stories on the Third Programme (4 June and 10 July 1948) and the Welsh Home Service (1948), and in 'Woman's Hour' on the Light Programme (December 1949). The BBC discovered a new interest in the work of RD after his death: a Welsh version of 'The Contraption' was broadcast as *'Eistedd dros Dŵr'* (December 1987) and in English (July 1997) and 'Resurrection' (August 1992, October 1995); between 1992 and 1996 the following stories were broadcast: 'A Dangerous Remedy', 'Mrs Evans Number 6', 'The Dark World', 'Nightgown', 'The Public-House', and 'Gents Only'. A serialised adaptation in Welsh of *Nobody Answered the Bell* was broadcast on S4C in March 1987. It is a matter for regret that the BBC's archives are incomplete, so that other adaptations of RD's stories appear to have been lost. Grateful acknowledgement is made to the National Library of Wales for information about the above recordings.

18 'Gents Only', in *The Trip to London* (1946), *Collected Stories* (ed. Meic Stephens, vol. 2, 1996)

19 The film rights on *The Trip to London*, for example, were sold for £750 in 1965, just after RD had sold the rights on three other stories for the not inconsiderable sum of $2,500.

20 See Herman Schrijver, *Decoration for the Home* (1939)

21 Charles Burkhart, *Herman, Nancy and Ivy: Three Lives in Art* (Victor Gollancz, 1977)

22 In notes attached to Ron Heggie's letter to David Callard (January 1991)

23 Mrs Sarah Davies, the writer's mother, was persuaded to speak about him into a recording machine but the tape has been lost.

24 *The Painted King* (Heinemann, 1954, Doubleday, 1954)

25 The play *No Escape* is one of four included in *Ring Up the Curtain* (Heinemann, 1955).

26 *Honeysuckle Girl* (Heinemann, 1975)

27 *The Collected Stories of Rhys Davies* (Heinemann, 1955). Contents: 'The Dilemma of Catherine Fuchsias', 'Boy with a Trumpet', 'The Nature of Man', 'Canute', 'Fear', 'The Benefit Concert', 'The Contraption', 'Revelation', 'The Fashion Plate', 'Alice's Pint', 'Tomorrow', 'Resurrection', 'The Foolish One', 'Arfon', 'Abraham's Glory', 'Wrath', 'The Dark World', *The Trip to London*, 'The Last Struggle', 'Blodwen', 'The Public House', 'The Two Friends', 'Gents Only', 'Conflict in Morfa', 'Pleasures of the Table', 'A Man in Haste', 'Mourning for Ianto', 'River, Flow Gently', 'The Journey', 'The Bard', 'Death in the Family', 'Half-Holiday', 'The Farm', 'The Zinnias', 'The Wages of Love', 'Glimpses of the Moon', 'A Human Condition', 'Price of a Wedding Ring', 'Nightgown', 'Caleb's Ark', 'Over at Rainbow Bottom', 'The Pits are on the Top', 'A Dangerous Remedy'.

28 For example, 'What is There to Say?' in *Full Score* (ed. Fytton Armstrong, 1933), 'Half Holiday' in *The Adelphi* (May 1936), 'Deplorable Story' in *Wales* (3, 1937), 'The First Patient' in *Path and Pavement: Twenty New Tales of Britain* (ed. John Rowland (1937), 'Harvest Moon' in *Little Reviews Anthology* (ed. Denys Val Baker, 1946).

29 Review of Glyn Jones, *The Water Music*, in *The Welsh Review* (vol. 4, no.1, March 1945)

30 Writing to Fred Urquhart on 13 August 1955, RD asked, 'What is television but a trivial bauble invented by louts – or, rather, the worst kind of neurotics?'

31 The photographs taken by Julian Sheppard were commissioned by the Welsh Arts Council and are now housed in the National Library of Wales.

32 Tom Davies, the writer's father, left £3,306 at his death, which was shared between his two remaining sons and three daughters, with something extra bequeathed to Rhys.

33 *The Perishable Quality* (Heinemann, 1957)

34 'River, Flow Gently', in *MD* (12, December 1966), *The Trip to London* (1946), *Collected Stories* (ed. Meic Stephens, vol. 2, 1996)

35 M. Wynn Thomas, '"Never Seek to Tell thy Love": Rhys Davies's Fiction', in *Decoding the Hare*

36 It seems appropriate to quote here from a letter Philip Burton sent to RD in 1959: 'Had dinner with delightful Dorothy Parker on Friday. We talked of you.'

Rhys Davies 1955 photo Owen Thomas

Eight

No need for compromise

Houdini-like, Rhys Davies never failed to confound his critics and escape from the shackles imposed on him as a writer. The living death of confinement or stagnation as an artist, even the self-satisfied banality and philistinism of what Chekhov called *poshlost*, was his greatest fear. He shared this horror with Laevski in 'The Duel', with Berg in *War and Peace*, with Maupassant's Bel- Ami, and with Molly Bloom in *Ulysses*. It was as if every setback spurred him on to greater things that would put him beyond the reach of adverse criticism from those who would impose their own expectations on him. No unfavourable comment could deflect this plucky writer from his chosen course. In 1958 he produced a new volume, *The Darling of her Heart*, a collection of nine stories, seven of which were set in Wales, mostly the counties of Carmarthen and Cardigan.[1]

The Rhondda had now become a fading memory for him. It was the setting for only the cleverly plotted 'A Spot of Bother', in which Ormond, a young miner whose wife has left him, is photographed in compromising circumstances with a prostitute he has picked up on a night out in Cardiff (there were, for Davies, no whores in the Rhondda).[2] When a blackmailer calls at the house with the photographs, Ormond relies on the fact that his wife is short-sighted to pass them off as portrait shots. The blackmailer, losing his nerve, flees but is captured by the husband and his butties, and the snaps are retrieved. Ormond, on returning to the house, discovers his wife is not as nearsighted as he had thought and realizes she has played along with the deception. They quarrel, she strikes him with a stocking full of dried beans, and an amicable truce is reached:

> Later, tidily with hand-brush and pan, he swept all the beans from the floor. This was exceptional. In Bylau, men are not much addicted to domestic jobs, and Ormond in particular, always out with the boys, was not partial to them. There was a vague aspect of compliant reformation about his figure as he stooped to the task.

Once again the female triumphs over the meek-mannered male.

The collection gathered some favourable reviews in London. In *The Observer* Muriel Spark commented, 'It is seldom that a story collection of such variety is consistent in quality. Mr Davies's nine stories are excellent in nine different ways.' Naomi Lewis in *The New Statesman* wrote: 'Mr Rhys Davies has all the craft you could want: briskness, implication, surprise, and an artfully casual pace in which none of the detail is to be missed.' The reviewer in the *Times Literary Supplement* called Davies

> one of the best short story writers in Great Britain
> ... he is happiest when he gives his story everything
> he has, especially when he is working in the grim,
> the macabre, the sly or the uproarious... He has also
> a fully professional competence: stylistically and
> structurally he knows his job.

These were reviews to warm any writer's heart.

Two years later there was to be a further distancing from Wales in Davies's novel *Girl Waiting in the Shade*.[3] Although set partly in Shropshire and partly in the fictitious town of Henllys in Mid Wales, this was the first of his books to have mainly English characters. Having started life as a short story entitled 'The Walled City', it showed a tautening of style, as well as an undercurrent of what some readers thought puzzling, disturbing even. A great deal of the main character, Lottie Curlow, was derived from the emotional life of Anna Kavan. Kavan's mother had died in 1954 but the rancour she had felt at being an unwanted and neglected child still troubled her. In the novel the mother marries Lottie off to a man she despises, much as had happened to Kavan. The mother's second husband is, we are told in an oblique manner, homosexual, but partly from attraction and partly as revenge – at this point the textual obscurity about sexuality and motivation thickens – Lottie tries to seduce him. Many who knew Kavan thought she was in love with Hugh Tevis, her own stepfather, though this was never reciprocated. The significance of the theme is underscored elsewhere in the novel when we hear of actual father-daughter incest.[4]

The blurb for *Girl Waiting in the Shade* described the novel as 'a subtly composed study of character which will find Rhys Davies many new readers'. This was an optimistic prognosis. Davies had a publishing career of more than thirty years and a readership that had aged with him, and now he began losing readers who had no stomach for his new themes. The year of the *Lady Chatterley's Lover* trial might have seemed a propitious moment to publish a 'daring' novel, but the book was anything but Lawrentian in tone. The sense of perverse forces moving under a crystalline surface of language that hints at, but does not make its full meaning explicit, was characteristic as much of homosexual writing in the pre-Wolfenden years, as it was of Nabokov's depiction of paedophilia in *Lolita* (1958).[5]

Against the background of the *'Chatterley'* trial, in which a succession of witnesses took the stand to attest to the book's high moral tone (though Davies disliked it and thought it 'preachy'), Davies's novel stood little chance of popular success. It received hardly any reviews, sold poorly and the only foreign-language edition was published in Norway. But Davies regarded it highly, telling the journalist Graham Samuel in 1967, 'I still like it very much. It is my Cinderella, my orphan, my illegitimate child. It was unsuccessful in all respects, but I love it. And it is true to life. I insist upon that.' Even so, it was to be more than a decade before he would turn again to novel writing.

Between the publication of *The Darling of her Heart* and *Girl Waiting in the Shade* Davies resumed his association with Keidrych Rhys, whose magazine *Wales* had been revived for its third and final run in 1958.[6] Davies had seen little of Rhys during the magazine's first series between 1937 and 1939, and from 1943 to 1949 the editor had been either in the armed forces or living in Llanybri in Carmarthenshire. However, by the late 1950s he was in Hampstead, once more larger than life and spoiling for the many literary fights in which he revelled. The editor, described by Dylan Thomas as 'the best sort of crank', still thrived on controversy and was as fractious as ever. Davies, who had no taste for literary feuding, regarded him warily, describing Keidrych to the Taylors as 'a very odd man and unpredictable', adding, 'he has a great many hostile critics'. For his part, Keidrych Rhys had an abiding admiration for Davies, and was to be one of only two friends who turned up at his funeral. The novelist's *obiter dictum* in the second series, 'Amateurs are the curse of art in Wales', was taken up by the editor and adopted as his own. In February 1959 the magazine carried a laudatory article by David Rees entitled 'Rhys Davies: Professional Author', which took the unusual view that Davies's novels were of more importance than his short stories, but ended with the observation that 'perhaps… some of the aspects of the transition of Welsh society since the end of the Second World War has [sic] escaped him.' Rees, a native of Swansea, did not know Davies at the time but was introduced to him soon afterwards. They continued to meet occasionally in Keidrych Rhys's company and became better acquainted after Rees was appointed literary editor of *The Spectator* in 1963.[7]

The third series of *Wales*, struggling against rising production costs and lacking a new generation of literary talent, ceased publication in 1960. For all his sympathy, there was little Davies could do to help. Then, in February 1962, the magazine was declared bankrupt and the writer listed as a creditor, though he never claimed what was owed him. At this point he and Keidrych Rhys were still friends, the latter writing to Davies in March 1962:

> You are too modest. I've met a number of heavy European literary critics from Elias Canetti to Mario Praz and, bar Ernest Jones [the biographer of Sigmund Freud], you are the only other Welshman they have read!

Whether Davies was modest is a moot point; his self-confidence seemed at times to border on arrogance.

Despite the flattery Keidrych Rhys too was to suffer excommunication by Davies, in much the same way as so many other friends were cut off. According to Graham Samuel, the editor had visited Davies at Russell Court just before *Wales* was declared bankrupt. Davies had left the room for a moment to use the lavatory and come back to find Rhys stuffing his complete run of all three series of *Wales* into a bag. The editor made some excuse about needing to borrow them urgently and insisted on taking them all away, which Davies generously but naively allowed him to do; they were never returned. Keidrych Rhys dealt in secondhand books and Davies suspected they had been sold. For this reason he broke off his friendship with him until, many years later, they bumped into each other and things were patched up. Rhys, as an undischarged bankrupt, had been obliged to find another job, much against his inclinations, and out of sympathy and gratitude, Davies decided it was time to bury the hatchet.

With the demise of *Wales,* there was no other magazine of repute in Wales to which Davies could send his stories – he never contributed to *Dock Leaves* or its successor, *The Anglo-Welsh Review,* and *The Welsh Review* had ceased publication in 1948 – but in the early 1960s he hardly had need. His work had been well received in America and now he was about to achieve a breakthrough, contributing no fewer than five stories to *The New Yorker* over the next few years. Examples of his work had also been selected for the famous anthology *Tall Short Stories*, published by one of America's leading publishers, Simon and Schuster. He was even to be found in paperbacks produced for the mass market like *Moods of Love* (1960), where he kept company with D.H. Lawrence, Alberto Moravia, James Joyce, Emile Zola, Doris Lessing, Guy de Maupassant, and John Steinbeck; the only other Welsh contributor was Alun Lewis, with 'The Wanderers'.

In 1962 he took advantage of the growing market for twentieth-century literary manuscripts by selling some of his to the Humanities Research Center of the University of Texas in Austin and, in the year following, was paid £600 for another batch which went to the National Library of Wales. Both institutions would buy more in the years that followed. Also in 1963 he sold the film rights of three stories for the sum of $2,560. Given that his material needs were few and that he was by nature parsimonious, if not, in the opinion of some, downright tight-fisted, these were significant sums acquired for minimal effort.

It was in 1962, at the funeral of William Griffiths, one of the brothers who owned Griff's Welsh bookshop at

4 Cecil Court, off Tottenham Court Road, that Davies met the man with whom he was to have the last of his romantic friendships. Graham Samuel was Parliamentary Lobby Correspondent with the *Western Mail*, and he also reviewed plays and opera for the paper. He was young, good-looking, sociable and heterosexual, with aesthetic tastes chiming with Davies's own. For his part, Samuel came to regard the writer as a sort of father-figure, having had an unsatisfactory relationship with his own father. As their friendship deepened, he slowly grew aware of Davies's sexual orientation, but they were never lovers. The novelist never made a pass at him and seemed disinclined to discuss sexual matters with the younger man. Told that Davies had given the impression to others, including his own brother Lewis, that they were lovers, Samuel wearily replied, 'Yes, I can well believe he would do that.'

The two, accompanied by Samuel's girlfriend, would often go out together, to plays, concerts and exhibitions, though only rarely to the cinema – Davies was not by habit a film-goer. Samuel described Davies as 'a close one. He was by nature warm, kind, generous and with a rare gift of gratitude; qualities which he hid because he hated any show of emotion.' He found the older man 'hopelessly naive' about politics, calling him a socialist of the idealistic rather than the realistic kind, given to such statements as 'If people are homeless, why doesn't the Government just build more houses?' After a while, he too became aware of Davies's parsimony, recalling an incident on a bus when the writer had argued at length with the conductor over a twopenny fare. One topic Davies would not discuss with Samuel was D.H.

Lawrence. He was tired of being known as the man who once saw Lawrence plain and liked the fact that his young friend knew better than to mention the writer in his hearing.

The friendship betwen Davies and Graham Samuel would last for more than ten years, until the latter's return to Wales in the early 1970s. Like most in Davies's tightly compartmentalised life, their friendship was conducted on a strictly one-to-one basis. Davies saw Anna Kavan at least every few days, yet Samuel met her only once and he was taken to Herman Schrijver's flat on just one occasion. He met Kay Dick and Kathleen Farrell several times but many of the writer's other friends remained unknown to him. Most had no idea of the existence of Charlie Lahr, whom Davies still saw quite regularly and to whom he would always send signed copies of his books. None would have known about John Pope, Davies's fellow lodger from his early years in London, who was never mentioned. He revealed of himself only what he chose to show, and that was usually not much at all.

The 1960s were not a productive decade for Davies, but they were not unlucrative either. He even wrote articles for the periodical press in America, such as 'The God on the Oven Door', that appeared in *House and Garden* in October 1963. But the indifference with which *Girl Waiting in the Shade* had been received left him antipathetic to the novel form in general. His short stories, on the other hand, if diminished in number, still had a quality that attracted attention in America. In 1963, for example, he earned a total of $3,881 from *The New Yorker* alone and, three years later, signed a contract with the magazine that gave it first refusal on all the work he produced; he was even paid a retaining fee, regardless of output. His name was still kept before the public by his regular appearance in anthologies such as *English Short Stories of Today,* published by Oxford University Press, in the third series of which (1965) he is represented by 'Afternoon of a Faun' from *The Darling of her Heart.*[8] In addition, he occasionally read manuscripts for Heinemann. Though Davies was never a world-wide best-seller, his income as a writer was not insubstantial.

Now that Davies was permanently settled in Russell Court he became an inveterate hoarder, especially of book reviews by or about writers he knew, and of cuttings from newspapers and magazines, a great number of which were found after his death. He also clipped news items from *The News of the World*, particularly of court cases involving people discovered in weird and sometimes unspeakable circumstances, presumably either because he had a vicarious thrill from reading them or because he thought they might provide him with material for his stories, or perhaps both. The paper in those days had a circulation of four million, the world's largest, and thrived on scandal, its reporting unconstrained by press codes and pandering to the prurience of the Great British Public, a role it maintained until Rupert Murdoch's News International discontinued publication after the phone-hacking scandal of 2011. Hard though it is to understand now, many members of the British intelligentsia read it and writers, in particular, used it as Davies did.[9]

Davies's huge collection of clippings, a veritable lazaretto, included, for example, stories about matrimonial disputes, court cases involving rape, cannibalism and domestic violence, and the Christie murders at 10

Rillington Place, one of the most notorious addresses in the annals of British crime. He even went, with Raymond Marriott, on a macabre trip to see the place where the murders had taken place, writing to Louise and Red Taylor, 'What a street! The whole place was reeking of evil!' Among the more chaste items in his collection were a profile of Aneurin Bevan; a story about the opening of the Abbey Steelworks at Margam; a column by 'the Junior Member for Treorchy' about Welsh preachers of yesteryear; a report on a lecture by Saunders Lewis; an article about the musician Dr Joseph Parry; a review of a book about the Ladies of Llangollen; a feature about Tom Rees, the old town-crier of Tonypandy, whom he recalled bawling the news outside the Central Hotel in Blaenclydach; a story about the optional status of Welsh in the examinations of the Rhondda Education Committee; recipes ('How to get the best out of corned beef'); an article about the medieval poet Dafydd ap Gwilym; a report on the 1933 Census giving details of the English language in Wales; news stories about the progress of the war; and so on and so on in great profusion. The writer also seemed to be especially interested in an errant clergyman (such men were often featured in *the News of the World*) who had disappeared without trace, but not before adopting the alias of Davies, which must have tickled the writer. His archive also kept the editions of the *Western Mail* that reported the Aber-fan disaster of October 1966, and a colour supplement illustrating the investiture of the Prince of Wales in July 1969. The rest of the archive was made up of recipes and features about how to treat the minor ailments from which he suffered from time to time.

In the eyes of *The News of the World* those of Davies's sexual orientation were 'the men from the shadows'. It might be thought the writer would have welcomed the passing of the Sexual Offences Act of 1967, which enacted the recommendation of the Wolfenden Report, published a full decade earlier, that sexual acts in private between consenting males over the age of 21 should be decriminalised. If so, he passed no written comment on it, though a copy of the Report was found among his books after his death.

According to Francis King, the writer and homosexual who knew him well, Davies still went 'cottaging', which was not included within the terms of the Act. By now only an infrequent visitor to the homosexual haunts of Soho, Davies still depended on this activity for sexual gratification, seeming to enjoy the thrills that illegality lent it. He no longer went to pubs where Guardsmen congregated and, anyway, fewer could be found who were prepared to indulge in homosexual acts because soldiers were now better paid. Herman Schrijver once remarked to Davies that footballers had replaced Guardsmen as 'amateur tarts'; Davies's response had been, 'Oh, I'd never be able to afford a footballer! They must be terribly expensive.'

Francis King was of the opinion that, if his conversation was anything to go by, Davies was a man for whom sex remained a matter of abiding interest well into his sixth decade but that, towards the end of his life, a combination of waning sexual potency and an unwillingness to spend money had made a celibate of him. His brother Lewis told the present writer that although his brother had been promiscuous on first going to London and throughout the war years, he did not think him particularly highly-sexed. This conclusion seems to be borne out by the fact that a much-thumbed copy of George Moore's *Celibates* (1895) was found among his books. The writer was nevertheless fascinated by the new permissiveness of the 1960s, especially among the rebellious young, and would sometimes ask Anna Kavan to take him to hippy bars and parties where he could observe the Flower People at closer quarters.

In 1967, by now drawing a state pension, Davies saw a volume of short stories, *The Chosen One,* through the press for Heinemann in London and Dodd Mead in New York.[10] This was to be the last book of his stories to appear during his lifetime. Six of the seven stories collected had been previously published in American magazines, including *The New Yorker*. The eponymous story, which was reprinted in *Best Detective Stories of the Year*, an annual anthology published in America, recounts a moment of crisis in the relationship between Rufus, an inarticulate, simian young Welshman, and Audrey Vines, the rich, possessive, English harridan who lives at the big house, owns his cottage, spies on him as he bathes naked and goads him into killing her, knowing he will suffer the consequences while she achieves release. Kirsti Bohata in *Postcolonialism Revisited* points to the story's anthropological associations: Mrs Vines has lived among African savages and views her Welsh tenant in terms often employed to describe Africans and Afro-Americans:

To her eyes, the prognathous jaw, broad nose, and gypsy-black hair of this heavy-bodied but personable young man bore distinct atavistic elements. He

possessed, too, a primitive bloom, which often
lingered for years beyond adolescence with persons
of tardy mental development.

The story, which takes Davies's interest in the
domineering woman to its ultimate conclusion, was widely
praised, not least in *The Guardian* by William Trevor, then
making a name for himself as a master of the short story
form, and by Neville Braybrooke in *The Spectator*. It also
won the Edgar Award from the Mystery Writers of
America and was included in the roll of honour in that
august body's anthology of 1980. The M.W.A. (motto,
'Crime does not pay – enough') founded in 1945,
consisted at the time of about seven hundred professional
writers, publishers, editors, critics and scholars who
enjoyed writing and reading tales of detection, stories of
psychological suspense, police yarns, social commentaries
and nostalgic tales in which there is an element of crime
and punishment. The Edgar was an accolade like no other,
since it meant his story had been judged favourably by his
peers.[11] But Davies did not live long enough to see the
anthology in which his story appeared, although the bust
of Edgar Allan Poe that was part of the award stood on
his desk ever after and is now in the keeping of the Rhys
Davies Trust.

It was Neville Braybrooke who invited Davies to a
party at the house he shared with his wife June (the
novelist Isobel English), and there he met Brian Rooney,
their son-in-law, who was employed as production
manager at Faber and Faber. The firm's offices were close
to Russell Court and Rooney, who had warmed to Davies
on hearing he had been one of Jean Rhys's earliest

admirers, visited him in his flat on several occasions. Recalling the Welshman in an interview with David Callard, Rooney described Davies as:

> extremely fastidious and proper. Never without a tie, even in the hottest weather, and only once without a jacket – and on that day it was scorching. There was never any stinginess with the drink, and dainty canapés were always produced after about an hour or so.

Rooney could call to mind only one occasion when Davies had seemed to grow agitated:

> I do remember once saying something about the Bloomsbury Group and Rhys jumped in, not angry but exasperated. 'Oh I do get fed up with all this talk about the Bloomsbury Group. We weren't a "Group", we were friends who happened to live close to each other, and in those days we didn't spend our time in pubs, we went regularly to each other's houses for tea.'

Yet Davies often spoke about 'my old friends, the Woolfs', as if to suggest he had been on familiar terms with the Bloomsbury set. There is little or no evidence to suggest this claim was grounded in fact.[12] Again, in conversation with Graham Samuel, Davies expressed his annoyance with Alan Bennett's portrayal of Lady Ottoline Morrell in his satirical play *Forty Years On*. In fact, he had met her just once, in the company of Frieda Lawrence, and so his anger may have been feigned or an over-reaction.

Perhaps by now Davies had come to regret his spurning of Bloomsbury as well as his later disinclination to become one of Ivy Compton-Burnett's circle. A writer's reputation is not made on work alone but in the context of the wider literary world. Davies had not put himself about enough and had no talent or taste for self-publicity. But in later life he took to reading biographies, including Michael Holroyd's ground-breaking life of Lytton Strachey and Hilary Spurling's two-volume study of Ivy Compton-Burnett. Perhaps he wondered whether, in pursuing his solitary course, he had done the wrong thing. Brian Rooney's conclusion had been that Davies was

> basically a lonely man who realised his day had gone. It was only a few people of his generation, such as Kay Dick, who invited him out and I imagine he enjoyed hearing from me about the goings-on in Hampstead. In turn, I was fascinated by a man who had been close friends with D.H. Lawrence.

It is possible that Davies, as was his wont, found his new friend physically as well as intellectually attractive, yet he never revealed it. Rooney, who was 29 at the time and, in his own words, 'hardly naive', was astonished to learn years later that Davies was homosexual.

In 1968 the 'trusty and well beloved' Rhys Davies was admitted to the Civil Division of the Order of the British Empire in recognition of his services to literature, which meant he was a prolific and distinguished author, not that he had done anything much to further the careers of other writers. His only recorded comments make light of the award and, poignantly, he went alone to Buckingham Palace to receive it from the Queen Mother. To Louis Quinain on the 6th of November 1968 he wrote:

> Over two hours in the Palace, most of it spent walking about the vast ante-rooms and the place was not well heated. *No* refreshments. The investiture took place in the Throne Room. The Queen Mother pinned the insignia on my lapel, said how pleased she was to give it me on behalf of the Queen, we shook hands, and it was over in two minutes. Instructions on how to behave were given us in an ante-room. It was rather intimidating to have one's name bawled by an official as I stepped into the Throne Room.

He may not have been impressed by the Palace, but it is safe to assume he was secretly very proud of his gong for it was carefully kept in its case, with the flowery citation, until his dying day. Indeed, it may be, too, that like many another satirist, including Caradoc Evans, Davies was more conservative, and less able to resist the flummery on which the British class-system largely depends, than his radically-minded friends ever had reason to suspect.

A sort of summing-up (to borrow the title of Somerset Maugham's autobiography) seemed to be called for. But *Print of a Hare's Foot*, far from being a synopsis of his life and work in which he would give a full and frank account of himself, is a tissue of half-truths and evasions. The book he called 'an autobiographical beginning' or 'an informal autobiography' opens in Carmarthen with an evocation of Davies's family background. 'I hadn't been back for many years,' he wrote. That much was certainly true: his previous visit had been in 1938. The occasion this time was the Dynevor Arts Festival near Llandeilo, which a friend, Richard Jones, had a hand in organising. Jones's wife, Alma, had written perceptively about the novelist in the *Western Mail*:

> In person I met a man of quiet cordiality, with an out-looking attitude, as if seeking some kind of reassurance from the warmth of human contact. Only during the course of the evening did an occasional gimlet glance cause me to remember that here was a man of almost terrifying perception, whose penetration into the minds and motives of my sex, like that of the finest French and Russian writers, was something to be regarded as shocking, if not actually impermissible. [13]

Another friend, David Rees, met Davies in Carmarthen and they drove up the Cothi Valley together. By a slightly self-conscious Proustian device, the writer's past is evoked in *Print of a Hare's Foot* by the stimulus of a snatch of song heard through an open window and, in the market, the feel of Welsh flannel, always for him representative of everything that suppressed the instincts.

The book, elegantly written, went through five drafts before it was ready for publication. Barbara Prys-Williams, who read them all at the National Library of Wales while researching her book *Twentieth Century Autobiography* (2004), was of the opinion that Davies was 'a very guarded and manipulative autobiographer', the very epitome of 'the unreliable narrator'. The book, largely devoid of dates, names and places, is certainly not without interest but if Davies had told the truth, it would have been far more interesting.

For a start, and this throws the chronology into some confusion, the book covers only about the first thirty-five years of his life, does not begin at the beginning and breaks off abruptly at some unspecified point in the late 1930s. Davies's experience of the 1960s, when he was writing the book, explains to some extent the defeated tone of its last chapter in which he observes the baneful effect of unemployment as he arrives in his native place:

> In the spattered gloom of an autumn evening huddled groups of men in old raincoats and pulled-down caps looked long spent of arguments and jests. Most of them were too elderly to ever venture beyond the mountain ramparts. They stopped on the street corners... The pubs were quiet as the chapels. This was not the roaring Rhondda in which I had grown up. The battle of the pioneers was done: or at least had come to a nasty halt.

During the previous ten years more than seventy pits had been closed in South Wales, including the Cambrian in Blaenclydach, where an explosion had killed thirty-one miners in 1965. Davies was therefore recalling a community that by the time of writing had lost the original reason for its existence. There is, moreover, no mention of such details as his date of birth or his brothers and sisters, or indeed anything to indicate what his daily life was like. He sometimes goes to ridiculous lengths to preserve the impersonal tone of his narrative:

Calling on a Clydach Vale woman I had known, the headmistress of an infants' school, I found only her upper half visible above stacks and cartons of old clothes in her parlour.

This woman, who has been collecting clothes for the unemployed, and whom he calls Miss G, was, in fact, his own sister Gertie, headmistress at Ton Pentre. Another curious feature of the book, unusual in what purports to be an autobiography, is that it includes a whole chapter on Dr William Price.

Above all, he gives nothing away about his sexuality, which is central to an understanding of his personality and work. The necessity for remaining closeted, in life as in his writing, produced in Davies a range of subterfuges that allowed him to conceal or reveal, to articulate and yet to contain, just as much or as little as he wished on this score. This is one of the disappointing things about *Print of a Hare's Foot*: in a decade when sexual taboos were toppling, Davies cravenly insisted on writing in the codified manner that had been in vogue twenty or thirty years earlier. It was left to writers such as J.R. Ackerley to describe the sexual underworld with which Davies had been familiar since the 1920s, but which he shrank from depicting in a direct way. Just as many of the stories and novels take it as their principal theme without ever mentioning what Latin writers called *illum crimen horribile quod non nominandum est* ('the horrible crime that dares not speak its name'), there is only one explicit reference to homosexuality in *Print of a Hare's Foot*. His chapter on 'Caerphilly Jones, a Sprig of the Thirties' is extremely coy. Described by the writer as 'a simple boy, who could not even be called rough', this Caerphilly – so named by Davies, he tells us, because of his liking for cheese – was a most unlikely friend for an up-and-coming novelist of sophisticated tastes. The encounter with Jones, an ideal name for a man who has never been identified, was the nearest Davies came to admitting his homosexuality.

Moreover, Davies was writing at a time when he no longer had to be discreet about his proclivities, unless he wished to protect the sensibilities of his sisters, who were still alive and living in close proximity to each other in the town of Lewes in East Sussex. Whatever they may have suspected about their brother Viv, and they must surely have wondered about it, the matter of his sexuality was never raised in conversation. Although he never talked about her, they had heard Davies had a woman friend in London, and so their suspicions, if they had any, were allayed. He had never mentioned Louise Taylor to his sisters, but they had seen a Christmas card on the mantelpiece in Blaenclydach on which was written, 'To Rhys with love from Louise', and had, naturally enough, jumped to conclusions. Lewis Davies most definitely knew about his brother's sexual orientation because Rhys had introduced him to homosexual circles in London. Of all his sisters, Gertie, who was the pious one, would not have approved, though Gladys and Peggie were more broad-minded; but homosexuality was not something that was discussed in families like theirs in those days.

So Davies's discretion demanded that homosexual allusions in *Print of a Hare's Foot* had to be coded, with the consequence that many people and incidents were air-brushed from his account. When readers know the details of Davies's life they grow aware that every word has been carefully weighed for the effect it will have. The impression is given, in Barbara Prys-Williams's words, of a 'man lurking behind formidable defences'; for him, self-disclosure would have meant being perilously exposed.

Just as the content of *Print of a Hare's Foot* is strictly manipulated, the burnished elegance of its prose-style is another controlling device designed to keep its author's sexuality from the public gaze. Each of the sixteen chapters is written as if it were a short story, thus turning his life into a kind of fiction. A number of the excisions made because the author was not prepared to reveal too much of himself, even in a coded way, reduce many incidents to thin sketches. As Barbara Prys-Williams remarks, this is 'life as short story'. A final chapter that might have brought the narrative nearer the present was dropped just before publication, presumably for much the same reasons. Davies's principle seems to have been, 'Whatever you say, say nothing'.

The writer's horror of being trapped, pinned down, contained, or submitting to someone else's authority, may have had its origin in his having to undergo a surgical operation, for an unnamed reason, when he was about five years old. A fragment of one of the draft versions of *Print of a Hare's Foot* contains the following passage:

> I was laid on the kitchen table... I can still see the hovering of the mask of wadding, smell the chloroform... It was the sudden assault that branded me indelibly, this proof of the illusion of freedom and the will. This death... this prison. I struggled

against obliteration; was mercilessly held down by
the legs and arms.

This passage, together with its references to prisons and
manacling, was cut from the published version of the
book.

It was no wonder Cyril Connolly, whose weekly
reviews in *The Sunday Times* made him the eminent
literary critic of his day, after commending the writer's
graceful style and singling out the chapter about Lawrence
(which he had first published in his own magazine,
Horizon), wrote: 'Unfortunately, the material is thin. This
is not *Cider with Rosie* but a chronicle of a completely
uneventful life without strong ties and affections.' The
rest of the review (8 June 1969) was given over to
discussing Lawrence. In Wales, the book's publication
went largely unnoticed, except that Aneirin Talfan Davies
wrote an article about it in the *Western Mail*[14] in which
he expressed his dismay that such a distinguished writer
had never been given an honorary degree by the
University of Wales. The book also drew a tribute from
fellow-author Gwyn Thomas who, in a review published
in the same paper, wrote of growing up in the Rhondda:

Rhys was spared the ultimate wash of gall which,
for most of us, shared the bill with diluted *cawl*
[soup]. From the start his mood was of a wary
aloofness. Singing and politics, the great anodynes
of the valley, appalled him. He saw the valley-
dwellers very much as Maupassant saw the peasants
of his native Normandy: manic, sly, rather
dangerous and, in general terms, pungently

loathsome. He is certainly the hare of his title. One sees his foot-mark in the snow of his chilly experience, but the man himself, even in this act of self-revelation, is hard to come by. A great story-teller always finds it hard to shed the last sardonic veil of mystification and obliquity.[15]

Thomas, after envying Davies's experience with Vanna in the coke oven – 'Seeker after the odd as I seemed to have been, this never happened to me' – added:

A book to savour for its portrait of the South Welsh, for its brilliant insight into the world of D.H. Lawrence, Nina Hamnett and Ottoline Morrell, striking their little matches to startle the night-bound philistines.

It was to be nearly thirty years before critics began to examine more closely the footprint of the elusive hare. Barbara Prys-Williams asks a number of pertinent questions arising from her reading of the five drafts of *Print of a Hare's Foot*. [16] Why did Davies have such scant regard for the literal truth? Why did he find it necessary to cover his tracks by fragmenting, omitting and editing what he had actually written in earlier drafts? Why did he need to be so manipulative in what he was prepared to tell the reader? Why was there such dissociation from feeling and such shallow depiction of human emotions in the book? Why were emotions depicted as farce? Why did he describe voyeurism so often? Why did he seem so afraid of entrapment? Why the obsession with the macabre rituals of death and why did he find it necessary to subvert death so often? The answers to all these questions, according to Prys-Williams, was that Davies was, in the clinical sense of the term, a narcissist.

Here is not the place to go very far into the causes of narcissism, even if the present writer were qualified to do so, and so this account may strike the specialist as hopelessly inadequate in its description of the condition. But the psychoanalytic insights of Prys-Williams, who draws on wide reading of the medical literature available, offer illumination of several features of Davies that the reader may find useful for a better understanding of this complex man. First of all, in summary, she records that Christopher Lasch, in his most famous book, *The Culture of Narcissism* (1979), showed that narcissists lack a capacity to mourn for others, particularly their parents. Their terror of emotional dependence and what can appear to be an exploitative attitude to other people result in superficial and deeply unsatisfying relationships. They tend to be sexually promiscuous rather than repressed and to seek 'instantaneous intimacy'. They often have unsatisfied oral cravings, for example, for food or cigarettes. They are prey to a profound sense of inner emptiness and are terrified of old age and death. From what is known about the salient features of Davies's life, it seems reasonable to conclude that he was, on this analysis, a narcissist of a particularly detached kind. However, in a letter to the present writer Lewis Davies flatly rejected this view of his brother:

> Rhys, as I have often said, had my mother's personality and she, of all people, could not be accused of narcissism, having brought up six

children and controlled her husband who, but for her, would undoubtedly have become bankrupt. No, Prys-Williams is quite wrong. Much of the rest of the article is what I can only describe as pernickety pedantry. I suppose all this stems from Rhys's work having been taken up by the Welsh establishment and is the inevitable price to be paid. He certainly never had such adverse publicity during his lifetime.[17]

Lewis Davies's rejection of the view that his brother was a narcissist is quite understandable, of course, but perhaps he was not in a position to judge and this was only his highly subjective opinion.

By 1970 Davies was within a few years of his death. In 1971 he was awarded the Welsh Arts Council's Prize of £750 but felt unable to attend a reception in Cardiff at which he was due to receive it. Nothing could be said or done to persuade him to make the journey.[18] The award was the first Davies had received in Wales and, in a letter to the present writer, who was the Arts Council's Literature Director at the time, he expressed his gratitude. What he did not say was that he was still recovering his nervous composure after the shock of Anna Kavan's death two years previously and hardly ever left London.[19]

Kavan, a lonely woman, aloof with strangers, found it possible to relax only among a few intimate friends, of whom Davies was one. According to Jennifer Sturm, Kavan's most recent biographer, their friendship had sprung from a common interest in writing but had grown much more personal and, in Anna's case, fulfilled a need for human communication. Davies was a non-threatening presence in her life and would not make sexual demands of her, while she provided intelligent female company in which he could be comfortable for the same reason. She had made at least two suicide attempts, the first in 1943 and the second in 1964, shortly after the death of Dr Karl Theodor Bluth, her Indian psychiatrist and devoted mentor, who had supplied her with the heroin to which she was addicted. Bluth, in the opinion of Judith Sturm, had been 'the most important person in Kavan's life, sustaining her heroin habit and supporting her through the vagaries of her emotional and mental state', although the suspicion lurks that this was not done for entirely altruistic reasons. A search for another doctor who would provide her with the drug proved very difficult and, because she was shunned by the National Health Service as an incurable addict, she tended to stockpile her heroin.

Both Davies and Raymond Marriott, the latter living in Kavan's house but in a flat downstairs, were aware of her vulnerable state and wish to kill herself. At her second suicide attempt, unable to raise her on the telephone, they broke into her flat and had her rushed to hospital where her life was saved. But their prompt action did not endear them to her.

I was desperate not to go on living. In front of those who were left, I put on an act and concealed my intention. But, accidentally, or thinking one of my so-called friends [she meant Davies] really was well-disposed towards me, I must have given some indication of what I meant to do. So these people frustrated me, forced me to live my impossible life and go on suffering. I can't say how profoundly I resent their interference. I write this to prevent any misunderstanding.[21]

Even so, her will, in which Davies and Marriott were named as legatees, remained unchanged. As part of her therapy, they persuaded her to begin work on a series of autobiographical short stories. She also had ready the manuscript of a new novel, then called *The Cold World*, which she began sending to publishers. But her despair was now affecting the balance of her mind. In 1966 she overdosed for a third time and, in panic, rang Davies to tell him what she had done. Again she was saved after having her stomach pumped. Her behaviour became even more wilful thereafter, and yet she was never excommunicated by Davies, as others had been, no matter how numerous and extreme her trangressions.

Davies cared for her almost on a daily basis, even going to the trouble of familiarising himself with the range of illegal substances that were now available. In his introduction to her novel *Julia and the Bazooka*, he described Kavan thus:

> In the world of reality her social conduct was apt to become erratic, passing too swiftly from the most delicate perception of a guest's mood to hurling a roast fowl across the table at him, then retiring to her bazooka [her name for her syringe] and shortly afterwards be discovered on her bed reading a novel and eating chocolates out of a box.[22]

It is some measure of Davies's patience that he did not record that the target for this outburst was, in fact, himself.

The novel *The Cold World*, after many revisons,
appeared as *Ice* in 1967 and, thanks largely to its
nomination by Brian Aldiss as the best book of science
fiction in its year, became a cult success. This came as a
surprise to Kavan, who claimed not to be aware she was
writing sci-fi. In a copy of the book now in the present
writer's possession which she gave to Davies she wrote:
'Not meant to be science fiction. And there are
unauthorized alterations, please remember. Love from
Anna'. Despite the accolade, Kavan did not live to enjoy
the recognition she had always craved. On the evening of
the 4th of December 1968, the evening before she was
due to attend a party where the guest of honour was to
have been the novelist Anaïs Nin, one of her keenest
admirers but whom she had never met, she died of a heart
attack. Again summoned by Davies and Marriott, who
suspected something was amiss, the police broke into her
flat, where the Scotland Yard Drug Squad found her body,
'enough heroin to kill the whole street', forty varieties of
lipstick and a huge wardrobe full of clothes.[23] A full
syringe was found in her hand, which suggested she had
not injected herself.[24] Davies was one of a handful of
people who were present at Kavan's funeral.

The Welsh writer Glyn Jones, who had known Davies
since the 1940s, encountered him by chance in a London
street about a month after Kavan's death and found him
still troubled by it. Graham Samuel also remembered, in
a letter to David Callard, the watershed effect her death
had on Davies. The same cannot be said of any of his male
companions, a number of whom had died since 1945, and
if Davies could be said to have loved anyone, it seems, it
must have been Anna Kavan.

Her death, however, led to the excommunication of his oldest continuous friend, Raymond Marriott, whom he had known since the mid-1930s. Kavan had died with her finances in disarray. She had been largely dependent on an allowance from her wealthy stepfather and had never declared the rent she received from Marriott to the Inland Revenue. Sorting out her financial affairs was the sort of practical task at which Davies had proved himself hopelessly inept once before, at the time of his parents' deaths: he was not even capable of keeping an account of his own tax affairs. Herman Schrijver, who possessed considerable financial acumen and had experience in settling estates, offered to help but his offer was turned down.[25]

Relations between Davies and Marriott, soured by Davies's refusal to lend him money, now quickly deteriorated, with Marriott referring to his friend as Mr Scrooge. All they could agree on was the destruction of several of Anna Kavan's paintings, in particular a number of grossly sadistic images of executions and suicides hanging from their own entrails, that they thought would have damaged her reputation. Several of the more tolerable paintings were given to Brian Aldiss; a few landscapes and the Chinese lion, hugely fanged and ruffed, that for Kavan had represented her demons, were kept by Davies and have survived. The crux of the falling out between Davies and Marriott was the fate of her literary remains. She had left a fair number of short stories, as well as the manuscripts of novels and memoirs. Davies felt these were his domain and he was anxious to keep Kavan's memory before the public, while Marriott also wanted a hand in the process. Her estate, when it was finally settled in 1969, brought Davies and Marriott about £4,000 each and a half-share in the royalties on her books. The money in Davies's case was welcome but it came at the cost of yet another friendship.[26]

Undertaking the role of editor for Kavan's publisher Peter Owen, Davies extracted enough stories to make three books, namely *Julia and the Bazooka* (1970), *Let Me Alone* (1974) and *My Soul in China* (1975), for all of which he wrote introductions. These books, and others by Kavan, were translated into several foreign languages and are still selling well. It is partly for this reason Kavan has kept her cult status, though she has never been given her full meed of praise in England.[27]

In 1971 Davies published his novel *Nobody Answered the Bell*, a claustrophobic story of passion between Kenny and Rose, a lesbian and a woman secretly drawn to men, in which murder, with the inevitability of the Greek tragedies Davies had admired since his youth, is the outcome.[28] Set in an unnamed seaside town easily identifiable as Brighton, it is brief, taut, and utterly perverse, and continues the fictional exploration, begun with *Girl Waiting in the Shade*, of aberrant forms of human passion and experience. It takes Davies's preoccupation with the struggle for sexual and social dominance to its ultimate expression in murder. Rose kills her stepmother and she and Kenny hide the body in the attic. Kenny then dresses in the stepmother's clothes in a bid to deceive the neighbours but their relationship is spoiled by the corpse rotting in the attic and rapidly degenerates into mendacity, deception and surveillance of each other. This last, surveillance, was one of Davies's phobias; he saw evidence of it everywhere as a threat to his own closeted sexual identity. By the end of this Gothic imbroglio, Rose has strangled Kenny and, while trying to hide her body in a cupboard, she too expires.

The novel was well received on both sides of the Atlantic, though by 1971 lesbianism was not a theme to scandalise the literary world, and sales were modest. Francis King gave the book a favourable review in *The Sunday Telegraph* and admired it so much he dramatised it. He thought the characters of Kenny and Rose were based on Kay Dick and Kathleen Farrell. Certainly Dick suspected Farrell of heterosexual tendencies, most notably displayed in the presence of Frank Tuohy, a homosexual writer, an attraction that King told Davies was 'as likely as my boxer having it off with my pekinese'. If the novel was indeed based on Dick and Farrell, as seems likely, Dick did not recognise herself in the book: she wrote to Davies to say she found the novel 'very good, but very frightening'.

The theme of addiction is carried into Davies's last novel, *Honeysuckle Girl* (1975).[29] Whatever he may have felt about Anna Kavan's writing, Davies was not prepared to write anything critical of her in the introductions he contributed to her three posthumous books. In *Let Me Alone* he quoted a passage about the heroine that might easily have applied to himself:

She wanted to go through life alone, in her own independent, detached fashion... The idea of being bound up with another person in such a relationship as marriage was hateful to her... reading a Life of Luther, from the midst of the printed page, there suddenly sprang out at her these words: 'Here I stand; I can no other', a great enlightenment came to her, a sudden illumination... How easy and simple to face life from the single basis of her own undeniable individuality. She was what she was: herself. No need for compromise or apology or modification or defence.[30]

Davies had experienced no such epiphany but a revelation of this order must have held great appeal for him. Asked by her agent whether he would write Kavan's biography, Davies told him that, even after many years of seeing her almost daily, he did not know enough about her; she, he thought, would have said the same about him. For both of them the act of writing a biography of the other would have been tantamount to an invasion of privacy and a form of personal betrayal. However, the suggestion, together with the task of writing introductions to her books, led Davies to *Honeysuckle Girl*, a novel examining the life of a middle-class heroin addict and the collapse of her marriage.

The main character is Karen, a talented artist who paints pictures that give no hint of the deep-rooted problems stemming from her loveless childhood. Her husband is not at first aware of her addiction and, on discovering it, is a helpless bystander unable to prevent her tragedy. The solace and hallucinations of drug use are vividly depicted, but without the sensationalism that the subject so often excites. Unusually, Karen reaches out into a world of beauty and pleasure, and in the final paragraph is lying on the bank of a river looking down at her own face reflected in the silvered water, just as the narcissistic Anna Kavan had been in the habit of staring at herself in a mirror. Auberon Waugh, in a review of the novel, wrote: 'If I had any say in the matter Mr Davies would win the *Prix Femina* for the next five years on the strength of this book alone.'

After *Honeysuckle Girl*, the last of his books to be published during the author's lifetime, Davies entered that period, familiar to writers whose writing careers span several decades, of having outlived much of his original readership and failed to attract a new generation of readers. His themes were topical enough – there were shelves of books about lesbianism and drug abuse in the bookshops of the 1970s – but his innate detachment from his material worked against him.

Davies was gradually surrendering most of his connections with the literary world. Most of his old friends were dead, excommunicated, or living outside London. Fred Urquhart was in Scotland but kept up a regular correspondence with Davies, sending him affectionately-inscribed copies of all his books. Davies was still friendly with the Taylors, but their country house was now in Belcham, near Sudbury in Suffolk. Visits to them and his sisters in Lewes were about the only trips he took outside the capital. Now in the last few years remaining to him, he 'cast a cold eye on life, on death' in his usual detached manner.

Red Taylor, who was many years younger than his wife, predeceased her in 1975, after which Louise went into rapid decline. Some three months after her husband's death, she made a will naming Davies and Bill Naughton as her co-legatees, then entered a nursing home. There, found to be suffering from Alzheimer's disease, she was the subject of a court order naming Davies as her 'receiver'. When she died in July 1977 her estate was valued at £134,276. Again Davies was faced with the practical chore at which he was so incompetent, complicated by the fact that part of the estate consisted of property to be sold and valuable antiques to be auctioned. There was another difficulty: Davies did not have much regard for Bill Naughton, and the feeling was mutual. Naughton had never liked Davies, thinking him mean-spirited in that he could have done more for struggling writers like himself. Davies therefore corresponded mainly with Naughton's efficient German wife, Erna, and eventually received half Louise Taylor's estate, amounting to £65,000.

Even before that, he was hardly destitute. A note among his papers shows his income in 1975 to have been well over £6,000. He was still earning modest fees for stories selected by anthologists like Denys Val Baker, who included him in *Stories of Country Life* (1975), *Stories of the Night* (1976) and *My Favourite Story* (1977), alongside writers such as V.S. Pritchett, Daphne du Maurier, Dennis Wheatley, John Steinbeck, Henry Williamson, and George Mackay Brown. His last holiday, a trip to Venice in 1975, was brought to an abrupt end when he caught influenza and had to return to London early. In 1978 he sold another batch of manuscripts to Texas, as well as a waistcoat that had once belonged to Gertrude Stein for which he was paid £100. An examination of his Barclays Bank giro credits for 1976 to 1978 reveals he was regularly paying substantial amounts into his account, including dividends from three building societies, royalties from the agents Curtis Brown and David Higham, as well as quite generous gifts from his sisters.

Unfortunately, this money had come too late. He contemplated a world tour that would have taken in a visit to Philip Burton in Florida, yet did nothing about it. His health was beginning to give serious cause for concern. The long years of a sedentary lifestyle, a punishing work-schedule and addiction to nicotine were taking their toll. He began to suffer panic attacks when out walking and would have to be brought home by strangers. After collapsing in the street some way from Russell Square, he was loth to venture very far. In his last few years he spent summer afternoons sitting on a bench where he would watch the world go by, noting people's clothes and gestures, a camera to the last.

On the advice of his sister Gladys, who had been a nurse at St Mary Abbott's Hospital in London, he also began taking Diazepam and Mogadon, tranquilisers used to treat anxiety and insomnia. Both were then readily available prescription drugs and their addictive properties had not yet been confirmed, though it was known both reacted badly when taken with alcohol. Davies took Mogadon for so long that, in the opinion of his brother Lewis, he became mildly habituated. Eventually the stress he was suffering manifested itself in facial shingles, an unpleasant and debilitating condition that kept him indoors and from writing. As if that were not enough, the persistent throbbing of a large refrigerator in a nearby hotel caused him to threaten legal action, after which, to his great relief, the nuisance stopped.

By this time Davies's friendship with Graham Samuel had run into difficulty, owing to the latter's increasing dependence on alcohol. The affection felt by Samuel for Davies was apparent enough in the article he published about the writer in the *Western Mail* (4 April 1967). But by 1972 the journalist's problem had become so severe he had to be taken into a Hampstead clinic. He escaped almost immediately through a window but suffered an attack of *delirium tremens* before he could get away, after which he was held under sedation. Davies visited him while he recovered and then Samuel moved back to his home town of Burry Port in South Wales. On his mother's death he inherited a large house and invited Davies to share it with him, but the writer declined. Their friendship did not survive for much longer and eventually petered out.

Further troubles followed almost at once. Davies's sister Gladys suffered a nervous breakdown brought on, or so Lewis Davies thought, by her domineering sister, Gertie. Eventually Gladys left her nursing job and went to live in Lewes with Peggie Williams, her married sister, who was a domestic science teacher at nearby Ringmer; Davies wrote to the Taylors that he was very depressed by all this. A final blow was that his novel, eventually published after his death as *Ram with Red Horns*, was turned down by Heinemann.[31]

Rhys Davies now had only a little while to live. He had been a heavy smoker since the age of 14 and was suffering severe bronchial attacks. During the interview he gave Delyth Davies of BBC Wales in 1977 the tape picked up the sound of his wheezing chest. His attempts to cut down on cigarettes had been only partially successful. Early in 1978 he was taken into University College Hospital and then moved to St Pancras Hospital where lung cancer was diagnosed, and there he died, with no one else present at his bedside, on the 21st of August 1978. The cause of his death was given as bronchopneumonia and carcinoma of bronchus, and he was described on the death certificate as a novelist.

A brief notice of Rhys Davies's death appeared in the *Western Mail* [32] and in an obituary in *The Times*, published anonymously but in fact written by Kay Dick, he was described as

> a sweet-souled man of immense courtesy and loyalty, beloved by many friends, extraordinarily modest about his achievements... a gentle man, full of compassion, an artist in every fibre of his being, whose work must survive the trends of fashion. [33]

His funeral was held at Golders Green Crematorium. The only people present were his brother Lewis, his three sisters, Gertie, Gladys and Peggie, his friend Raymond Marriott, and Keidrych Rhys and his wife Eva. After a short secular ceremony, in which there was 'no pomp and no oratory', and without further a-do, the small group went their separate ways; the writer's ashes were later scattered in the rose garden. [34]

Notes

1   *The Darling of her Heart and other stories* (Heinemann, 1958); Hungarian edn., *A mama kedvence* (Európa, 1959). The book's reviewer in *The Times* (24 July 1958) wrote: 'His work is packed full of incident. His subjects seem to come bubbling up to him out of some natural spring. He finds without effort material which he shapes so neatly to his purpose that he usually manages to give an impression of complete spontaneity.' Douglas Phillips in the *Western Mail* wrote: 'In his handling of the Welsh scene, Rhys

Davies has transcended documentary and satire. His people are three-dimensional; they have their own life; they are not merely projections or caricatures of stock types. Again, his prose has sloughed off the less valuable Anglo-Welsh eccentricities of style. It is still a Welshman's prose, but there is no straining after effect... In his ability to transmute the raw material of life into significant form and miraculous capacity to make every sentence shimmer with a multiplicity of references, Rhys Davies is worthy to rank among the masters.'

2   'A Spot of Bother', in *The Darling of her Heart* (1958), *Collected Stories* (ed. Meic Stephens, vol. 2, 1996)

3   *Girl Waiting in the Shade* (Heinemann, 1960)

4   The suspicion that Anna Kavan was in love with Tevis can easily be dismissed, just as rumours of her lesbian tendencies have been exaggerated, as Jennifer Sturm showed in *Anna Kavan's New Zealand: a Pacific interlude in a turbulent life* (A Vintage Book, Random House, 2009). Sturm describes the two years Kavan spent in New Zealand with Ian Hamilton, but her book is a reliable account of her life in general; see also the thesis by Victoria Walker.

5   Self-deprecating as ever, RD referred to his novel on the fly-leaf of the copy he presented to Philip Burton as 'such a sad little book'.

6   Few regard the third series of *Wales* as its most distinguished. It had no emergent stars like Dylan Thomas, Vernon Watkins and Idris Davies, who had been in the first series, or Alun Lewis, who had been in the second.

7   It was David Rees who wrote the first monograph on RD in the *Writers of Wales* series (University of Wales Press, 1975), though the writer made no comment on it and it was, anyway, only the briefest introduction to his work and, of course, avoids discussion of his sexuality.

8   'Afternoon of a Faun', in *Collected Stories* (ed. Meic Stephens, vol. 2, 1996)

9   According to his biographer, Michael Parnell, the prose-writer Gwyn Thomas was another who used the paper in this way. The paper's advertising slogan was 'All Human Life is There'.

10   *The Chosen One and other stories* (Heinemann, 1967). Contents: 'The Chosen One', 'The Little Heiress', 'I Will Keep her Company', 'The Old Adam', 'Betty Leyshon's Marathon', 'The Shriving of Gwenny Treharne', 'Love Kept Waiting'.

11   The only other Welsh writer to win the Edgar was Elwyn Jones, best-known for writing the television series *Z Cars*, who won it for his book *The Last Two to Hang* (1966).

12   While there were no membership cards for this legendary nexus, RD is not mentioned in any of the books about the Bloomsbury Group that have been consulted for the purposes of the present work.

13   Alma Jones, 'A universally human writer', in the *Western Mail* (2 December 1961)

14   Aneirin Talfan Davies in the *Western Mail* (28 June 1969)

15   Gwyn Thomas in the *Western Mail* (7 June 1969)

16   Barbara Prys-Williams: 'Rhys Davies as Autobiographer: Hare or Houdini?' in *Decoding the Hare* and in *Twentieth Century Autobiography* (University of Wales Press, 2004)

17   Lewis Davies in a letter to Meic Stephens (16 May 1998). The article by Barbara Prys-Williams had first appeared in *Welsh Writing in English* (4, 1998).

18   The Welsh-language writer T.H. Parry-Williams, then aged 84, was similarly honoured and came to receive his Prize.

19   According to his brother Lewis, he was also suffering from agoraphobia.

20   Anna Kavan lived alone at 19 Hillsleigh Road, off Holland Park Avenue; the house is no longer there.

21   This passage is believed to come from an unpublished story which David Callard must have seen in the McFarlin Library at the University of Tulsa, Oklahoma. It is quoted

in his book *The Case of Anna Kavan* (1992) as if it were taken from a letter or journal, but no source is given.

22   Anna Kavan, *Julia and the Bazooka* (Peter Owen, 1970)

23   Jennifer Sturm dismisses the detail of the forty varieties of lipstick and a wardrobe full of clothes, both recorded by David Callard and Jeremy Reed, pointing out it would not be said of a man that he had forty kinds of aftershave and a hundred ties. In a spirited defence of the author in *Anna Kavan's New Zealand*, she writes: 'So she threw a chicken; she had forty lipsticks; she smelt vaguely of heroin after 8pm – as interesting as these snippets might be, they should not define the woman.' There is, she argues, more to Kavan than her heroin addiction, just as the present writer would argue that there is more to RD than his homosexuality.

24   Jeremy Reed, *A Stranger on Earth: the Life and Work of Anna Kavan* (Peter Owen, 2006)

25   Schrijver was among those who thought RD mean. When he died in 1971, leaving about half a million pounds to his Italian housekeeper, the writer was put out to learn he was to receive only £100.

26   RD's share of Kavan's estate passed, on his death, to his brother Lewis and, in 2011, to the Rhys Davies Trust, which now owns half her literary estate.

27   Anna Kavan had made it into *Who's Who* in 1946. There is a brief entry on her in Margaret Drabble's *Oxford Companion to English Literature* (6th edn., 2000) but she was dropped by Dinah Birch for the 7th edn. of 2009; she is also included in *The Bloomsbury Guide to English Literature* (2nd edn., ed. Marion Wynne-Davies, 1995)

28   *Nobody Answered the Bell* (Heinemann, 1971; Dodd, Mead, 1971). The novel was serialized in Welsh by Teliesyn for S4C in 1987.

29   *Honeysuckle Girl* (Heinemann, 1975). Victoria Walker, in her doctoral thesis (Queen Mary, London, 2012), has

319

pointed out that certain elements of this novel found their way into the biographies of Kavan by David Callard and Jeremy Reed. In her view, RD's account is in some respects 'limited and tendentious' but nevertheless the best first-hand account of Kavan's life that is available.

30 Anna Kavan, *Let Me Alone* (Peter Owen, 1974)

31 *Ram with Red Horns* (Seren, 1996); the original title was *Cariad* (Welsh for 'love') but this was dropped before publication.

32 *Western Mail* (24 August 1978)

33 *The Times* (24 August 1978)

34 RD died intestate and letters of administration were granted to his brother Lewis, who in due course received the net value of his estate amounting to £80,572.

Nine

Postscript

Gwyn Jones, one of my Professors at Aberystwyth, once remarked that everything an author writes may be taken down and used in evidence against him. Rhys Davies was brought before his peers many times during his lifetime, with eminent men of letters like H.E. Bates, Cyril Connolly and John Betjeman taking the stand to speak for and against him and critics such as R.L. Mégroz, G.F. Adam and David Rees coming forward to attest to the qualities and blemishes in his work. None of this had much effect on the writer, who carried on writing what he wanted to write and in his own way, his own man to the very last.

It is fairly certain he would not have relished the thought of someone, even an admirer like me, writing a biography of him, given the obsessive lengths to which he habitually went in defence of his privacy. But it has been in the nature of literary criticism, in Wales as elsewhere, that the living are loth to let go of their dead writers' lives and are anxious to find out as much as possible about them in order to throw light on their work. In the case of Rhys Davies, this process has inevitably revealed facets of his personality he did so much to conceal, not the least among which was his homosexuality. It began when M. Wynn Thomas, Professor of English at the University of Wales, Swansea, and Director of the Centre for Research into the English Literature and Language of Wales, delivered the Rhys Davies Lecture[1] of 1997, in the presence and to the satisfaction of the writer's brother Lewis. It was thus we were brought to a fuller understanding of the fiction, if not yet of the life.

Using Queer Theory and other aspects of Masculine Studies, Wynn Thomas uncovered previously unexamined levels of implication in Davies's writing. His enquiry into why the best of Davies's stories seemed to him so disturbing while discussion of his work failed to register, let alone address, such a reaction, had begun when he reviewed *Fire Green as Grass*, a symposium of studies dealing with 'the creative impulse' in Welsh writing in English during the twentieth century, in the magazine *The New Welsh Review*:

One reason why there is such a pronounced anti-intellectual bias in Welsh cultural life is undoubtedly because it continues to be significantly informed by the 'democratic' ideal of an undifferentiated *gwerin* (common folk) and is therefore predisposed to tolerate ideas only of a consensual kind couched in language that is readily accessible... As a quintessential misfit, Rhys Davies has tended to get short shrift from the acolytes of the collective... It has long seemed obvious to me that Davies's fiction would benefit immensely by being approached from the direction of gay studies – this would provide us with a language for understanding his dark fascination with voyeurism, his delight in the aesthetic, his ambiguous feelings about the macho male, his attraction to the nexus of sex and power, and his coolly elegant mastery of the dandyism of style. Criticism of Anglo-Welsh literature has been so heavily dominated by historical and socio-political discourse that large areas, or dimensions, of the literature remain unexplored for want of the language to dis-cover it... The best compliment I can pay this valuable book is to say that here, at least, we have *adult* criticism – criticism that does not shrink from a full and frank engagement with literature, and that does not exhibit a kind of *pudeur* when it comes to dealing with intellectual matters. The result is a text that is both worth reading and that significantly enhances our reading of other texts – those Anglo-Welsh poems and short stories that are, at their best, so much more demandingly adult in their modes of being than we Welsh critics are, in general, intellectually prepared or terminologically equipped to recognise.[2]

At the time Wynn Thomas was writing his review the only example of Davies's work still available in print was *The Best of Rhys Davies* (1979), a personal selection of twelve short stories made towards the end of his life and published posthumously.[3] It was to be seventeen years before there appeared, in 1996 and 1998, under my editorship, the three volumes of Davies's *Collected Stories*, with an introduction touching on the salient features of his life. They were followed by a novel, *Ram with Red Horns* (1996), the title suggested by Fred Urquhart, with an introduction by Philippa Davies; a reprint of *Print of a Hare's Foot* (1998), introduced by Simon Baker; *A Human Condition* (2001), a selection of seven stories; *Nightgown* (2003), another seven stories, in the *Corgi Series*; and a reprint of *A Withered Root* (2007), in the *Library of Wales*, with an introduction by Lewis Davies (not the writer's brother but the publisher who runs the Parthian imprint).[4] [5] [6] Suddenly, Rhys Davies was available again and demanding critical attention.

But the milestone in Rhys Davies studies was undoubtedly the 1997 lecture by Wynn Thomas. Never before had there been such a full and frank discussion of Davies's sexuality. We at last were given to understand that his life and work were of a piece and that, in particular, his homosexual proclivities were an integral and dominant part of almost everything he did and wrote. This view was confirmed when a number of our best critics came together to produce the essays in *Rhys Davies: Decoding the Hare* in 2001.[7] They employed a range of contemporary critical discourses in discussion of Davies's work, but one constant was the assumption that sexual orientation and gender identity were deeply ingrained in his fiction. The book was properly regarded not only as the first substantial attempt to assess Rhys Davies in the round but also as a landmark in the field of Welsh writing in English. If the essays sometimes contradicted each other in their readings of Davies's work, so much the better: their disagreement was meant to make for lively discussion of a writer who seems to suggest that the world, and human experience of it, are capable of various interpretations and defy a final analysis: the hare may be decoded but ultimately he cannot be snared. Since then, Huw Edwin Osborne has written a detailed and critically enlightening monograph in the *Writers of Wales* series, which is primarily a study of how Davies's homosexuality underpins just about all his fiction.[8]

What I have tried to do in the present book has been, without duplicating too much of what has been written since the author's death in 1978, to produce a Life of Rhys Davies by indicating who and what he was, where he came from, the world he lived in, what other people said and wrote about him, what he said about himself, and what the points of contact between all these may have been, thus providing a framework for a better understanding of the complexities and apparent contradictions inherent in his character and work. I have tried to avoid critical theory, which Davies himself distrusted, to employ hypothesis only where no other explanation seems possible, and to stick to the facts most of the time. Above all, I have tried to give him the serious attention and dignity he deserves as a writer and to make no moral judgements about a way of life that is, after all, outside my own experience.

At the same time, I am acutely aware the writer had no wish to be defined or identified by mere facts, and that is why he often evaded or refashioned them when writing about himself. Yet he yearned to be considered a serious writer, and this wish I have tried to fulfil, albeit posthumously. I have not reduced his work to the single issue of his sexuality or seen evidence of it in each and every detail of his stories and novels. Concealment may well have been all as far as Davies was concerned and so I have respected his wish to avoid revealing too much of himself to an uncomprehending or unsympathetic world. Rather, I have preferred to consider him as a talented writer and one whose devotion to his craft, often in difficult circumstances, was exemplary. Davies, for me, teaches the lessons of craftsmanship, and demonstrates a ruthless concern with human motive and behaviour, which no writer of any age or nationality can do without. He is also to be admired for keeping his nose to the grindstone or, to change the metaphor, for sticking to his last.

In his Welsh context, from which he cannot properly be extricated since he was very much of his time and place, Davies holds a pre-eminent position as the most determined and inventive of those writers who have written about industrial South Wales. Many of the themes in the work of our younger writers have been explored, or at least adumbrated, by him. He wrote earlier and at greater length about the society thrown up by the coal industry, into which he had been born, than any other major Welsh writer, and, without the advantages of education beyond his fourteenth year, tried to think, sometimes in contradictory ways, about the origins and nature of the Welsh industrial experience. In his critique of what he perceived to be the joylessness of Welsh Nonconformity – obsessive, exaggerated, inconsistent and relentless though it was, and delivered for reasons to do with his own outsider status – he was to blaze a trail that others followed. His perspective was never less than challenging and innovative in the way it was expressed. Stephen Knight has called him 'the first major writer in English from South Wales':

Others would write more directly and more politically, and he was never to have real imitators in Wales, but he broke the silence about the Welsh industrial world and almost certainly made it easier for the other industrial writers of the 1930s to make their own voices heard.[9]

The fact that Davies began writing at a moment when London publishers decided what the market wanted from Welsh writers, and knew what would sell, had its consequences for what is sometimes called the first flowering of Welsh writing in English, and for Rhys Davies in particular. Life in Wales seemed to the metropolis, in the long afterburn of Caradoc Evans and the runaway success of *How Green Was My Valley*, to be full of a local colour – venal peasants, rustic sex, radical politics and lyrical miners – that was eminently marketable in England. In an essay on Brenda Chamberlain, Anthony Conran has described the writers who first took their work to London as:

a bravely cosmopolitan, rather exotic generation, the first Welsh-born writers to take advantage of the English market. Not since the Welsh buccaneers and soldiers of fortune of Tudor times had Welshness seemed so colourful and exportable a commodity... Most of them had something of the mountebank about them, perhaps not in their personal relation to their art, but in the dynamics of the group as a whole: a glitter of phrase, a perhaps too eager gift of the gab, a sense that bards and mountains and colliers were hot news, to be rushed into print before anyone else got there first.[10]

Caradoc Evans and Rhys Davies were the first Welsh writers to take advantage of publication in London and their work had to pay the price for having been taken up by publishers who knew next to nothing about Wales. It was to be a generation or more before novelists like Emyr Humphreys, Ron Berry and Alun Richards would show how misleading the caricature had been and before an indigenous publishing industry would begin to bring out the work of Welsh writers in English that bore a greater semblance to the actual condition of the Welsh people.

Even so, there is a remarkable consistency of quality in Rhys Davies's mature work that puts it in the first rank of twentieth-century short fiction. His novels, too, though perhaps not to everyone's taste, and not always reflecting Welsh life as it has been lived these last hundred years, repay close attention. The themes of alienation and the absurdity of human existence, and the ambivalence of the pathos and irony found in his work, make him a modernist writer of the first water. An enemy of abstraction he may very well be, and he certainly defies any attempt to pin him down to a clearly-defined philosophy. Yet despite his reliance, in his early work, on melodrama and some pretty unlikely coincidences, and the occasional longueurs in his later books, he still manages to beguile us. At his best he has an eye for significant detail, an instinct for moments of high drama, an ear for dialogue and the telling phrase, for lively speech, and, more than anything, a delight in human nature in all its lovely and unlovely variety. In short, by practising the story-teller's craft to such excellent effect, he wrote books that have a timeless and universal quality and that will, I feel confident, ensure their lasting appeal.

The grocer's boy from Blaenclydach will continue to entertain, and disturb, us for some while yet.

Notes

1   The lecture was delivered at the University of Glamorgan on 24 April 1997.

2   Review of *Fire Green as Grass* (ed. Belinda Humfrey, 1995) in *The New Welsh Review* (29, Summer 1995)

3   *The Best of Rhys Davies* (David & Charles, 1979). Contents: 'The Chosen One', 'The Old Adam', 'Fear', 'I Will Keep Her Company', 'A Visit to Eggeswick Castle', 'Nightgown', 'Gents Only', 'A Human Condition', 'Boy with a Trumpet', 'All Through the Night', 'Canute', 'The Dilemma of Catherine Fuchsias'. Reviewing the book in *The Anglo-Welsh Review* (66, 1980), John Stuart Williams wrote: 'One of the problems of national or regional patronage is that certain writers are over-praised, presumably because they can claim an easy identification with national or regional group identity, and others undervalued, shuffled off into corners, given an equivocal acceptance at best. The most obvious example of this in Wales is Caradoc Evans, who told us what we didn't want to hear. It has always seemed to me that he was so secure in his Welshness that he assumed a similar maturity on the part of his readers. If we cannot be sardonic about ourselves, what weak selves do we live with? Nostalgia is not enough. Sentimentality is a cosy trap. Spurious political commitment is even worse. Evans kicked against the easy way to national acceptance. In his cooler manner, Rhys Davies does the same. Perhaps that is why, in Wales, we have not given him the attention he deserves.' The beginning of what might now be called Rhys Davies Studies may be properly dated from this review.

4   *A Human Condition* (Parthian, 2001). Contents: 'The Dilemma of Catherine Fuchsias', 'The Sisters', 'The Song

of Songs', 'The Darling of her Heart', 'I Will Keep Her Company', 'The Fashion Plate', 'A Human Condition'.

5   *Nightgown and other stories* (Carreg Gwalch, 2003). Contents: 'Nightgown', 'The Dark World', 'The Last Struggle', 'The Public House', 'Canute', 'Fear'.

6   *The Withered Root* in the *Library of Wales* series (Parthian, 2007)

7   *Rhys Davies: Decoding the Hare*. The contributors were Dai Smith, Michael J. Dixon, Stephen Knight, Tony Brown, Daniel Williams, Barbara Prys-Williams, D.A. Callard, J. Lawrence Mitchell, Linden Peach, Jeff Wallace, James A. Davies, Katie Gramich, Jane Aaron, Kirsti Bohata, Simon Baker, Joanna Furber, and M. Wynn Thomas. I am grateful to them all for their insights into RD's work and to the book's publisher, the University of Wales Press, for permission to quote from some of their essays.

8   Huw Edwin Osborne, *Rhys Davies* in the *Writers of Wales* series (University of Wales Press, 2009)

9   Stephen Knight, *A Hundred Years of Fiction* (University of Wales Press, 2004)

10 Anthony Conran, in *The Anglo-Welsh Review* (46, Spring 1972) and *The Cost of Strangeness* (Gomer, 1982).

Acknowledgements

I am grateful, first of all, to the Rhys Davies Trust for commissioning me to write this biography, and to its Chairman, Dai Smith, and his two co-trustees, Sam Adams and Peter Finch, with whom I have the pleasure and responsibility of working as the Trust's Secretary. All three read the work in draft form and made a number of helpful suggestions, as did Tony Brown, the independent reader, though I hasten to add that for any errors of fact or judgement still remaining I alone should be held responsible.

Next, I should like to put on record my warm appreciation of the work carried out by the late David Callard during the 1990s while he was enquiring into the life of Rhys Davies with a view to writing a biographical sketch of him. Unfortunately, the draft he produced, with the financial assistance of the Trust and the Welsh Arts Council, was left unfinished at his death in 2003. I am grateful to his brother, Christopher Callard, and sister-in-law, Sheryl Callard, for generously giving me permission to use the material David collected, including the transcripts of interviews he carried out with people who knew the writer and a number of letters he received from people acquainted with him. This groundwork has proved invaluable, especially since so many of those interviewed have since died.

I have also had the advantage of reading two unpublished dissertations: Jean Pol Le Lay's 'Rhys Davies as an Anglo-Welsh Story-teller' (University of Brest, 1969) and Sarah Leigh Mabbett's 'A Portrait of Rhys Davies', based on a selection of 113 letters to his friends Raymond Marriott, Louis and Greta Quinain, and Redvers and Louise Taylor, which she submitted for the degree of M.A. at the University of Wales College of Swansea in 1996. I have, moreover, read the doctoral thesis of Victoria Walker (Queen Mary College, London, 2012), 'The Fiction of Anna Kavan (1901-1968)', and discussed with her the relationship between Kavan and Davies.

The quotations from Rhys Davies's letters and from letters addressed to him by his correspondents, are from the collections held at the National Library of Wales, the McFarlin Library at Tulsa, Oklahoma, the Harry Ransom Humanities Research Center at Austin, Texas, and the Sterling Library at the University of London. The publisher has made every reasonable effort to contact copyright-holders and apologises for any oversight that may have occurred.

My debt to the critics who contributed to the symposium I edited for the University of Wales Press in 2001, *Rhys Davies: Decoding the Hare: critical essays to mark the centenary of the writer's birth*, will be evident to those who have read that book; I thank the contributors and the Press for permission to quote from the essays. In addition, I acknowledge the late David Rees and Huw Edwin Osborne, authors of monographs on Rhys Davies in the *Writers of Wales* series, which I co-edit, that were published by the University of Wales Press in 1975 and 2009 respectively.

For valuable insights into the life and work of Anna Kavan and her close but largely undocumented relationship with Rhys Davies I am indebted to David Callard's *The Strange Case of Anna Kavan* (Peter Owen, 1992), Jeremy Reed's *A Stranger on Earth* (Peter Owen, 2006) and Jennifer Sturm's *Anna Kavan's New Zealand* (Random House, 2009). My debt to other authors and publications is evident from the works cited in the text and the footnotes.

A number of other individuals gave me practical assistance while I was writing this book. They include the following: Colin Affleck, Brian Aldiss, Sarah Bebb (*née* Mabbett), Edward Burns, Iwan ap Dafydd, Bob Davenport, Delyth Davies, Eileen Davies, Keith Fletcher, Catherine Gerbrands, Cheryl Gunselman, the late Owen Vernon Jones, Rose Knox-Peebles, Oonagh Lahr, Sheila Leslie *née* Lahr, Hywel W. Matthews, Leigh Morgan, Stephen Ongpin, Patrick Parrinder, Pat Powell, Peter Quinain, Michael Schmidt, Tony Shaw, Roger Simmons, Huw and Sara Stephens, David Sutton, Victoria Walker, Margaret Watson (*née* Quinain), Abigail Williams, and Tessa Williams.

I should also like to thank the staffs of the National Library of Wales, Whitchurch Public Library, and the Manuscripts Department of the British Library.

Of all the people who helped me to a better understanding of Rhys Davies, I am most indebted to his brother, the late Arthur Lewis Davies, who over a period of some twenty-one years wrote and spoke to me frankly and at length about him, usually on a weekly basis, and provided me with documents and information I could not otherwise have come by. Lewis died in December 2011 and, although he lived to the grand old age of 98, I regret it was not quite long enough to see this biography published in the centenary of his birth. It was Lewis's remarkable generosity and genial personality, our last living link with the Davieses of Royal Stores, Blaenclydach, that enabled me to establish the Rhys Davies Trust in 1990.

The Trust, whose logo is a leaping hare, is a registered charity devoted to keeping the writer's work in public view and to encouraging the writing and study of all other aspects of Welsh writing in English. It was set up after Lewis Davies approached me, on the recommendation of Philip Davies of the National Library of Wales, and invited me to visit him at his home in Lewes, East Sussex. He not only immediately gave the Trust a substantial sum of money but, on his death, left it the remainder of his estate, including copyright on his brother's work and a half-share of the rights in the work of Anna Kavan. As a result, the Rhys Davies Trust is one of the best-endowed private literary charities in Britain today.

The Trust has already sponsored a number of projects, including reprints of some of Rhys Davies's books, a biennial short story competition now administered by Literature Wales, a series of plaques commemorating some of our most important English-language writers, and so on. Now that we have much greater funds at our disposal, the Trust will sponsor more ambitious literary projects within the terms of its charitable status. I wish to put on record that without Lewis Davies, none of this would have been possible, and for that reason I dedicate this book to his memory.

Meic Stephens
Whitchurch
Cardiff
June 2013

THE RHYS DAVIES TRUST

RD at Anna Kavan's flat in the 1960s

Bibliography

a check-list of works by and about Rhys Davies

A Novels

The Withered Root (London: Robert Holden, 1927; New York : Holt, 1928; Cardigan, Parthian, 2007)

Rings on her Fingers (London: Harold Shaylor, 1930; New York: Harcourt Brace, 1930; Bath: Chivers, 1969, Portway Reprints)

Count your Blessings (London: Putnam, 1932; New York: Covici Friede, 1933)

The Red Hills (London: Putnam, 1932; New York: Covici Friede, 1933; Leipzig: Tauchnitz, 1934; Bath: Chivers, 1970, Portway Reprints)

Two Loves I Have (London: Cape, 1933; as Owen Pitman)

Honey and Bread (London: Putnam, 1935; Bath: Chivers, 1970, Portway Reprints)

A Time to Laugh (London: Heinemann, 1937; New York: Stackpole, 1938; cheap edn., 1938)

Jubilee Blues (London: Heinemann, 1938; Bath, Chivers, 1969, Portway Reprints)

337

Under the Rose (London: Heinemann, 1940); adapted for the stage as *No Escape* (see below)

To-morrow to Fresh Woods (London: Heinemann, 1941)

The Black Venus (London: Heinemann, 1944; New York: Howell, Soskin, 1946; Readers' Union, 1948; Pan Books, 1950; Bath: Chivers, 1966, Portway Reprints; Copenhagen: Povl Branners Forlag, 1947; Stockholm: Fritzes Bokförlags Aktiebolag, 1948; Helsingfors: Söderström, 1948)

The Dark Daughters (London: Heinemann, 1947; New York: Doubleday, 1948; Readers' Union, 1948; Stockholm: Folket i bilds förlag, 1951)

Marianne (London: Heinemann, 1951; New York, Doubleday, 1952; London: Heinemann, Popular Library, 1952)

The Painted King (London: Heinemann, 1954; cheap edn., 1965; New York, Doubleday, 1954)

The Perishable Quality (London: Heinemann, 1957; cheap edn., 1959)

Girl Waiting in the Shade (London: Heinemann, 1960; Oslo: Green, 1969)

Nobody Answered the Bell (London: Heinemann, 1971; New York: Dodd, Mead, 1971)

Honeysuckle Girl (London: Heinemann, 1975)

Ram with Red Horns (Bridgend: Seren, 1996)

B Stories and novellas

The Song of Songs and Other Stories (London: E. Archer, 1927)

Aaron (London: E. Archer, 1927)

A Bed of Feathers (London: The Mandrake Press, 1929)

Tale (London: E. Lahr; New York: Black Hawk Press, 1935)

The Stars, the World and the Women (London: William Jackson, 1930)

A Pig in a Poke (London: Joiner & Steele, 1931)

Arfon (London: W. and G. Foyle, 1931)

A Woman (London: Capell at the Bronze Snail Press, 1931)

Daisy Matthews and Three Other Tales (Waltham St Lawrence: Golden Cockerel Press, 1932)

Love Provoked (London: Putnam, 1933)

One of Norah's Early Days (London: Grayson & Grayson, 1935)

The Things Men Do (London: Heinemann, 1936)

The Skull (Chepstow: Tintern Press, 1936)

A Finger in Every Pie (London: Heinemann, 1942)

Selected Stories (London and Dublin: Maurice Fridburg, 1945)

The Trip to London (London: Heinemann, 1946; New York: Howell, Soskin, 1946; Bath: Chivers, 1966, Portway Reprint)

Boy with a Trumpet (London: Heinemann, 1949; New York, Doubleday, 1951; Munich: Nymphenburger Verlagshandlung, 1960)

The Collected Stories of Rhys Davies (London: Heinemann, 1955)

The Darling of her Heart (London: Heinemann, 1958; Budapest: Európa, 1959)

The Chosen One (London: Heinemann, 1967; New York: Dodd, Mead, 1969)

The Best of Rhys Davies (Newton Abbott and London: David & Charles, 1979)

Rhys Davies: Collected Stories (Llandysul, vols. 1 and 2, 1996, vol 3, 1988)

A Human Condition (Cardigan: Parthian, 2001)

Nightgown (Llanrwst: Carreg Gwalch, 2003)

C Miscellaneous

The Woman among Women (London: E. Lahr, Blue Moon poem for Christmas 1931)

My Wales (London: Jarrolds, 1937; New York: Funk &Wagnalls, 1938)

Y Ferch o Gefn Ydfa (Liverpool: Brython, 1938); Welsh trans. of the unpublished play, *The Maid of Cefn Ydfa*

Sea Urchin (London: Duckworth, 1940; Reykjavik: Bókfellsutgáfan, 1943)

The Story of Wales (London: Collins, 1943; New York: Howell Soskin, 1946)

No Escape (London: Evans Brothers, 1955); also in *Ring Up the Curtain* (London: Heinemann, 1955)

Print of a Hare's Foot (London: Heinemann, 1969; Bridgend: Seren, 1998)

D Criticism

R. L. Mégroz, *Rhys Davies: a critical sketch* (London: W. & G. Foyle, 1932)

G. F. Adam, *Three Contemporary Anglo-Welsh Novelists: Jack Jones, Rhys Davies and Hilda Vaughan* (Bern: A. Francke AG., n.d.)

David Rees, *Rhys Davies* in the *Writers of Wales* series (Cardiff: University of Wales Press, 1975)

Meic Stephens (ed.), *Rhys Davies: Decoding the Hare; critical essays to mark the centenary of the writer's birth* (Cardiff: University of Wales Press, 2001)

Huw Edwin Osborne, *Rhys Davies* in the *Writers of Wales* series (Cardiff: University of Wales Press, 2009)

Index of Persons

Index of Publications

*the works of Rhys Davies are shown
in bold type*

WWW.THELIBRARYOFWALES.COM

PARTHIAN

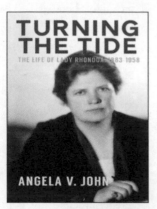

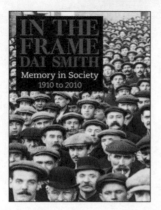

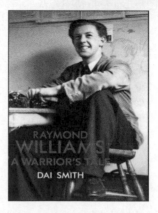

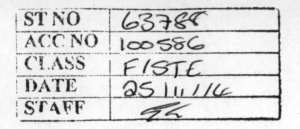